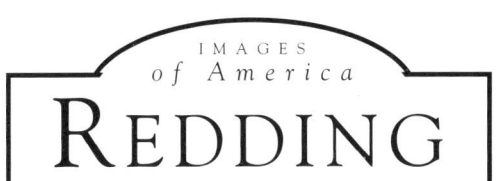

IMAGES
of America

REDDING

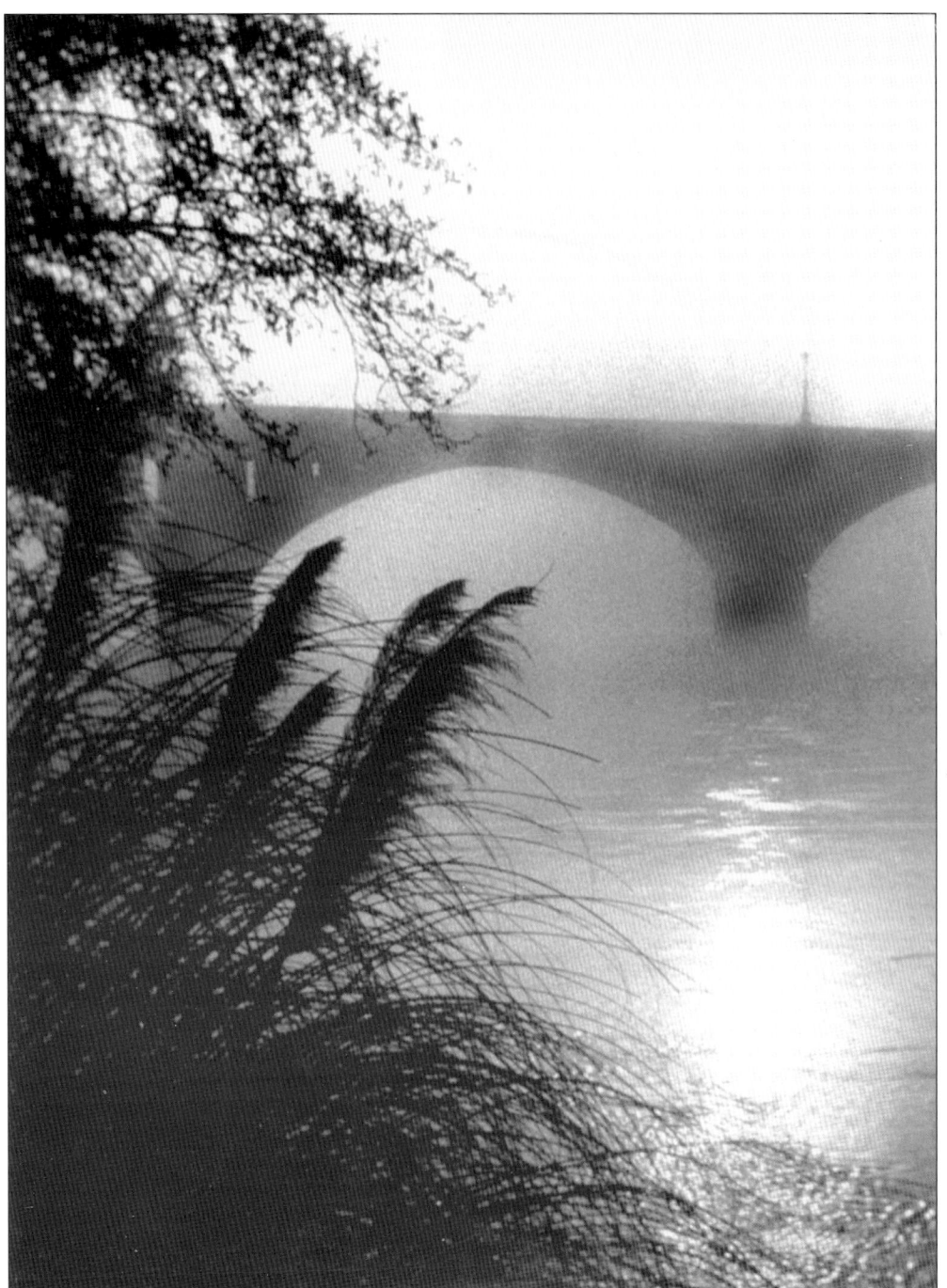

The Diestelhorst Bridge was built in 1915 and named for Gotlieb Diestelhorst. The bridge replaced Reid's Ferry, which had been in operation since 1860. The new bridge was called "Reid's Ferry Bridge" for a short time. Whatever the name, it was the first reinforced concrete bridge and the first automobile bridge built across the Sacramento River in Northern California. Today the bridge has been reduced to one lane of automobile traffic and is a link in the Sacramento River Trail.

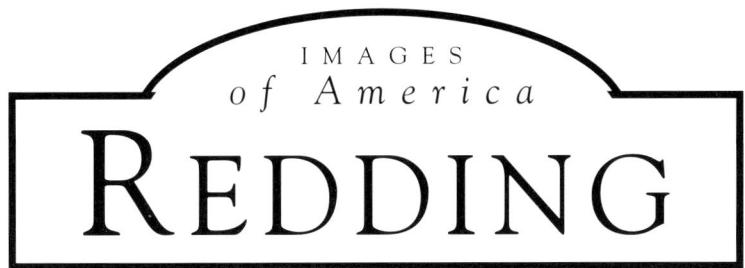

Shasta Historical Society
with Al Rocca

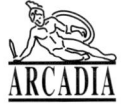

Copyright © 2004 by Shasta Historical Society
ISBN 0-7385-2934-6

Published by Arcadia Publishing
Charleston SC, Chicago IL, Portsmouth NH, San Francisco CA

Printed in Great Britain

Library of Congress Catalog Card Number: 2004109619

For all general information contact Arcadia Publishing at:
Telephone 843-853-2070
Fax 843-853-0044
E-mail sales@arcadiapublishing.com
For customer service and orders:
Toll-Free 1-888-313-2665

Visit us on the internet at http://www.arcadiapublishing.com

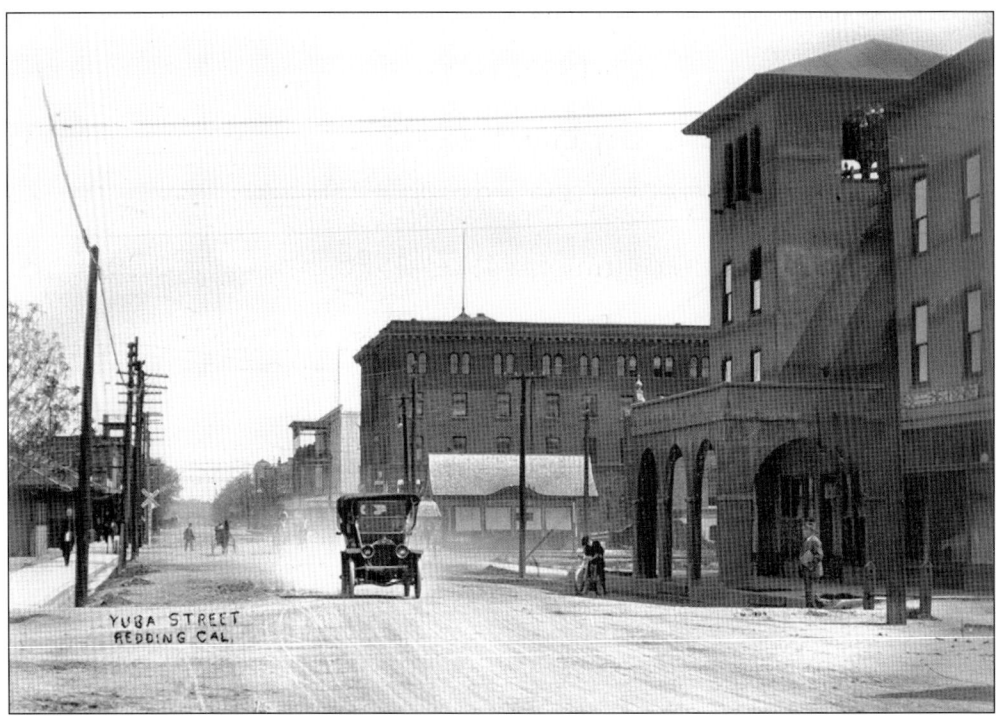

Yuba Street *c.* 1900 was typical of Redding's unpaved streets—muddy in the winter and dusty in the summer. The Redding Hotel, the Reddng Chamber of Commerce, and the Lorenz Hotel are pictured on the right.

CONTENTS

Acknowledgments		6
Introduction		7
1.	The Railroad Town: 1877–1900	9
2.	Homes and Everyday Life: 1900–1930	35
3.	Business and Work: 1900–1930	69
4.	Sports and Entertainment: 1900–1920	89
5.	Depression, Shasta Dam, and the Post-War Boom	109

ACKNOWLEDGMENTS

When the City of Redding was founded in 1872, the art of photography was well advanced. In 1930, the founders of the Shasta Historical Society had the foresight to gather the pioneers' stories, artifacts, documents, and photographs. Thanks to them we are able to present a glimpse of Redding's earliest days.

The society is also grateful to present-day volunteers for routinely giving the society one day each week to work on history projects of importance to them. For this new book on the town of Redding, the following helped with the research, proofreading, and photo enhancement: Coral Caldwell, Pat Ferreira, Marie Carr-Fitzgerald, Evelyn Hoppes, Lola Louthan, Susana Luzier, Bonnie Proebstel, Jeremy Tuggle, and Larry Watters. I would like to offer a special thanks to Betty McKean for her knowledge of the library and her many hours of research.

Professor Al Rocca was kind enough to share his own excitement for the history of Redding and Shasta County in the text he has written in the foreword and chapter headings.

The society would like to thank Arcadia Publishing for the opportunity to share its photographs and stories with the local people who were raised in Redding as well as with the great number of new arrivals who come in search of the area's natural resources, much like the earlier adventurers in their quest for gold.

—Diane Kathleen
Shasta Historical Society Office Manager

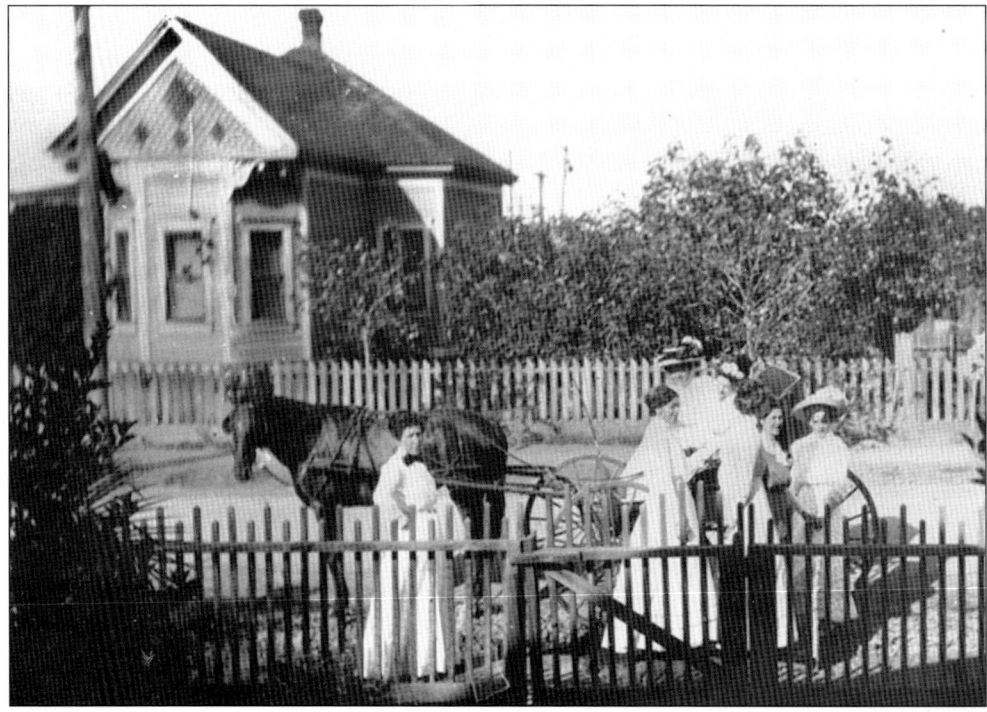

Agnes Mullar and Nell Bidwell are among the group of women in front of the Bystle home at 1218 West Street, c. 1909.

INTRODUCTION
By Al Rocca

Geographic location is the single most important factor for the creation and success of the town of Redding in the late 1800s. Today geographic location continues to play the deciding factor in the city's substantial growth. Early city officials and storeowners noted how their town was located "perfectly between Sacramento and Portland" and at the head of California's great Central Valley. Any physical map of Northern California will reveal that Redding is also centrally located between the western and eastern boundary lines of the state. Mountains sprawl majestically to the north, east, and west, reminding visitors that Redding truly is the "gateway from the valley to the mountains." Add to this the fact that the mighty Sacramento River flows through the city, providing more than ample water supplies and recreational opportunities.

In 1872, when Southern Pacific Railroad officials decided to push a spur rail line north of Sacramento, they chose to stop at a place where the Sacramento River takes a sharp turn west and where its riverbed narrows and the terrain becomes steep. The area where railroad engineers chose to place their turnaround roundhouse was known to settlers as "Poverty Flats." To the surprise and chagrin of residents in the nearby mining town of Shasta, railroad officials decided to lay out a new town at the terminus of the railroad instead of bringing the tracks a few miles west to Shasta. The new town would be named Redding after a prominent Sacramento politician who was then serving as General Land Agent for the railroad company. Slowly the town grew and so did tensions between it and the town of Shasta. A political tug of war began in the 1880s for the right to be the county seat. The struggle ended in 1888 when Redding dethroned Shasta after bitter legal battles and two local elections. From that date on, Shasta declined significantly, while Redding grew steadily.

By the turn of the century, Redding was clearly on the path to becoming the "Hub of the North State." The train was continually bringing in new visitors, who eventually turned into new residents. Local entrepreneurs like James McCormick realized the geographic importance of Redding's location and from the early days of the settlement, took every advantage to stock up on supplies to sell to residents scattered among the many nearby mountain communities. During this time the automobile made its appearance in the state, but with only dirt roads that turned into a morass of mud in the winter months and solid rubber tires on the "gasoline powered contraptions," Redding saw few automobiles at first. However, location again played a role in Redding's historical development when State Highway 99 came through the area in the 1920s. Now, with newly paved roads and affordable and more comfortable automobiles, travelers heading north and south passed through on a regular basis.

Redding's growth in the first decade of the 20th century is closely tied to the growing worldwide demand for copper. Large copper deposits had been discovered earlier in and around the mountainous portions of the county and were exploited, but now demand increased and with it the demand for more goods and services from Redding. Business boomed as wagonloads of supplies headed for mining towns such as Kennett, Coram, Ingot, Mammoth, and Keswick. Hundreds of jobseekers poured into Redding looking for work at the copper smelters. To help house these new arrivals, many of them Italian immigrants, new brick and wood multi-storied hotels were constructed. Demand for copper increased with Europe's and, later, America's involvement in World War I.

The mini-economic copper boom began a rapid decline immediately following the Great War. Copper smelters shut down and hundreds of working families left the area. While most of the country prospered in the subsequent "Roaring Twenties" Redding slid into an economic recession. Local residents tightened their belts and waited for business to improve. On the upswing side of life, the availability of credit allowed numerous Reddingites to purchase automobiles. Along with the increasing number of cars and trucks came the need for all-weather roads. During the 1920s much of the downtown Redding streets were paved for the first time. By the end of the decade, Highway 99 was widened and straightened, and this helped to increase drive-through business. Additionally, heavy durable goods could now be sent quickly and safely from Sacramento and the Bay Area to Redding.

When the Great Depression began on October 29, 1929, Redding had already seen hard economic times for most of the previous decade, and residents bravely waited for the federal government under President Franklin Roosevelt to deliver on his "New Deal." Roosevelt had been briefed by local Judge Francis Carr about the efforts of state, regional, and local businessmen and politicians to get the federal government to build a large concrete dam somewhere in the county. By 1932 the United States Bureau of Reclamation had already drawn up preliminary plans for a massive gravity-arch dam that would rank as the second largest in the nation. In 1938 Congress finally appropriated the money and Bureau of Reclamation officials announced that work on the dam would begin. With unemployment still prevalent throughout the country, the news of this new multi-year construction project brought in a new flood of anxious jobseekers. During the summer of 1938, with major excavation work starting, first hundreds then thousands of desperate job hopefuls descended on Redding and the areas north of town. In Redding, worried townspeople became nervous as local lodging and food relief programs were strained to the breaking point.

Over 4,000 new settlers arrived between 1938 and 1941, and new boomtowns sprang up in areas north of Redding and adjacent to the Shasta Dam Federal Reservation. Redding area businesses boomed as dam workers and their families spent much of their earnings on goods and services there. In addition, all of this federal money encouraged investment in the new boomtowns and in the expansion of Redding facilities. New hotels, stores, and automobile garages were built and new homes spread south and west, expanding the city limits.

When the United States entered World War II, however, the previous prosperity gave way to new hardships, including rationing of gasoline, food, and numerous other consumer items. Redding did its part for the war effort and a goodly number of its young people served in combat and in a variety of support roles. With the conclusion of hostilities in September 1945, a new post-war economic boom boosted the morale of returning veterans. Much of the new prosperity was based on lumber, and dozens of lumber mills were opened or expanded. Because a new product called plywood appeared to have a solid future—particularly in the construction of new homes—a large plywood plant was built in Anderson. With the war over and the assembly of domestic automobiles a reality, along with abundant fuel supplies, men and women living in Redding discovered that they could commute miles to work and still live in the "big town."

Meanwhile, newly formed Shasta Lake, with its unlimited opportunity for houseboat and powerboat recreation, increased state and national awareness of the area and drew thousands of tourists during the summer months. Another important milestone in Redding's history was the construction of Interstate 5 and the resulting need for rooming and supplies for the large numbers of tourists and businesspeople passing through. Because the new freeway actually bypassed the downtown area by some two miles, a new, more convenient strip of hotels, gas stations, and restaurants arose just east of the freeway, along Hilltop Drive. As the years progressed, more and more of the "business" of downtown Redding moved to the Hilltop area, enticed by increased Interstate 5 traffic and the construction of the Mount Shasta Mall in the 1970s.

Redding has realized tremendous growth since 1970, doubling its population from 40,000 in just 30 years. The town is currently poised to transform itself from a mid-sized economic center supplying the needs of Shasta County into the major regional economic and cultural hub of Northern California. Much of this current growth and prosperity is due, in large part, to its geographic location, the same advantage that helped create the town in 1872.

One

THE RAILROAD TOWN
1877–1900

Not much is known about the area we now call the City of Redding before the railroad appeared in 1872. Of course, local Native Americans, especially the Wintu, had inhabited the Sacramento River bottomlands for hundreds of years. These brave, self-reliant people numbered perhaps several thousand by the time Pierson Barton Reading, the first white settler in Shasta County, arrived and built his home in the Ball's Ferry area.

During the summer months most Wintus wore little clothing and spent much of their time making beautifully woven baskets and gathering and preparing food. Life must have been difficult in the winter months. Just trying to stay dry proved impossible, and cold, damp nights—night after night—contributed to sickness. Yet, through the years, the Wintu prospered.

In 1826 Jedidiah Strong Smith, a tough, bearded mountain man walked through the southern portion of Shasta County as part of his famous Western trailblazing trek. Soon other whites, including Peter Skene Ogden and Alexander McLeod, arrived to check out economic opportunities. One of these adventurers, Pierson Barton Reading, visited the area in the early 1840s and, smitten with its beauty and ranching possibilities, petitioned the Mexican government for a land grant, which he succeeded in obtaining in 1844. Reading's grant, the Rancho Buena Ventura, extended south from the "turn in the river" (where the City of Redding now stands) 15 miles along the Sacramento River. Reading built a small adobe in the Ball's Ferry area and tried to live peacefully with the Wintus. When gold was discovered in the Sacramento area in 1848, Reading rounded up some of the local natives and convinced them to help him look for gold along Clear Creek. Reading did find gold, and within a very short time gold-hungry whites poured into the area.

Gold miners quickly learned that small creeks, not major rivers, held the nuggets and "dust" they so eagerly sought. While many of these nameless individuals camped above the "turn in the river" (to get their bearings on the geography of the area), they did not stay long. Instead, hundreds, then thousands of them spread out between 1849 and 1852, heading for mountain creeks both west and east. To support this far northern gold rush, a town sprang up west of the "turn in the river." The town was named Shasta, a common name used by whites for the local tribes. Sensing big profits from the new gold boom, freshly arrived entrepreneurs nailed rough-hewn boards into stores, restaurants, and livery stables. One of the new migrants, an educated and intelligent young man named Benjamin Shurtleff who made friends easily and was recognized for his leadership, was elected the first mayor. While few gold miners in the Redding area struck the "bonanza," the hope of doing so remained so that by 1856 the tiny town's population had risen to over 2,500 persons. By this time, Shasta was known as the "Queen City," providing goods and services to a large geographic region in all four directions, and producing a highly acclaimed local newspaper, the *Shasta Courier*.

Local Shasta businessmen began to worry as, year by year, less and less gold was being assayed or traded in the would-be boomtown. The 1860s saw gold miners leave newly formed Shasta County and business activity take a major downturn. By 1867 the town was in trouble. The population had dwindled to 800 hardy souls, who hoped for something to kindle a new economic surge. There had been hope that a new railroad, connecting the Bay Area to Portland, might be constructed and that the route would go through the town of Shasta. In 1872 the Southern Pacific Railroad did decide to build its tracks north, with government permission. Initial excitement by Shasta residents waned when it was discovered that the railroad would not come to town, but instead would terminate, teasingly close, at a location some three miles to the east and on the river. The location was on the bluffs above the "turn in the river" in an area nicknamed Poverty Flats. The derivation of that name is not clear, but certainly had to do with the level terrain and the unfulfilled gold-finding hopes of previous occupants.

Southern Pacific officials in Sacramento advised their railroad engineers to build a roundhouse at the "turn in the river" and to lay out a "suitable" town plan that would provide support for railroad personnel and "profitable opportunities" for local residents. The engineers did as instructed, drawing a map complete with street names and naming the new town Redding for Benjamin Bernard Redding, who was then serving as general land agent for the Southern Pacific Railroad. In effect, the engineers had named the new town for "their own big boss." Local residents wondered if "Redding" was "Reading" and for a number of years confusion reigned with both names being used interchangeably—even in local newspaper advertisements. Whatever the name, it did not take long to see that the new railroad town held the best possibility for future development, so one by one Shasta merchants and residents moved there. One of the first to arrive and set up a home and business in Redding was Chauncy Carroll Bush, whose mercantile store anchored the new business zone developing along Market Street.

Bush and his entrepreneurial counterparts lauded the business opportunities of Redding, encouraging others to get involved. Hotels were erected to house newly arrived visitors and settlers. The Depot Hotel was among the first to turn a good profit. Located right across from the main railroad depot, the two-storied hotel boasted "large windows" and the "best food in Redding." The *Reading Independent* newspaper, run by W.L. Carter, began providing news and advertisements in 1875. A look at an 1878 issue reveals early pioneers of the town and their advertised businesses. Dr. Elliot D. Curtis, a homeopathic physician with an office on Market Street, claimed he would "answer all calls at all times of the day or night." J.N. Bell, another physician, had his office in the "Reading Hotel." James McCormick advertised that he was "Justice of the Peace and Notary Public" who also provided "conveyances of deeds and mortgages" from his office in the new post office. Meanwhile, John Madison cut men's hair from his new shop on the "fringes of Reading" on Tehama Street. After a haircut Madison offered to draw you a bath—hot or cold. On the corner of Butte and Market Streets stood Joseph Greenwood's fashionable Boot & Shoe Maker Shop. The Reading Hotel was a gathering place for early town residents. In addition to its fine eatery the hotel noted that it was the general stage office for all stages heading for Oregon, and that "all intermediate points and all points in Trinity, Siskiyou, Modoc, and Shasta Counties leave this house daily."

As Redding grew, a bitter dispute erupted over the location of a permanent county seat. A disputed ballot count in the special county election of 1882 left residents in both Shasta and Redding angrier than ever toward each other. Another election in 1886 clearly revealed that Redding would be the new county seat. With the official changeover of power the following year, Shasta residents left in droves. Redding built an impressive new courthouse, and new homes and businesses spread outward along Placer and California Streets. Despite a new respectability that appeared in town along with the transfer of political control, Redding residents from time to time reverted to "frontier law and order." The most celebrated breach of respectability came in July 1892 when a local mob dragged Charles and John Ruggles, arrested for stagecoach robbery and murder, from the Redding jail and hanged them both from a pair of trees. But acts of vigilante violence were rare and, for the most part, Redding residents looked to the upcoming 20th century with enthusiasm and optimism.

The town of Redding was named for Benjamin Bernard Redding, the land agent for the Central Pacific Railroad from 1864 until his death in 1882. Redding donated a bell to the Presbyterian church in 1881, and it was tolled in his honor throughout his funeral services.

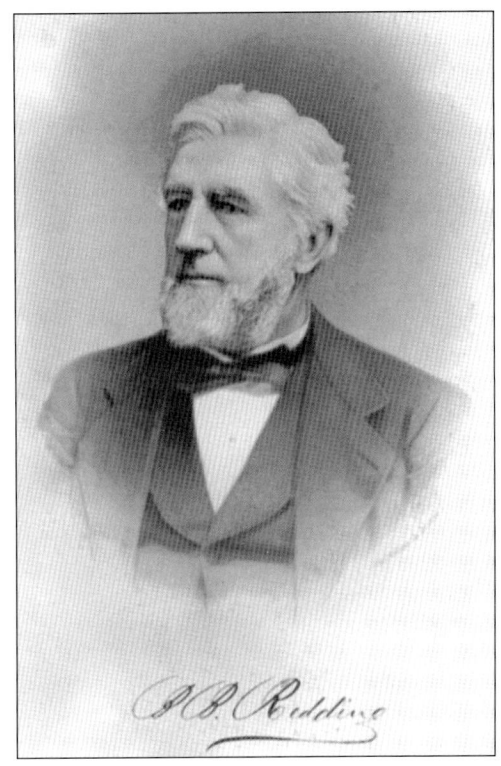

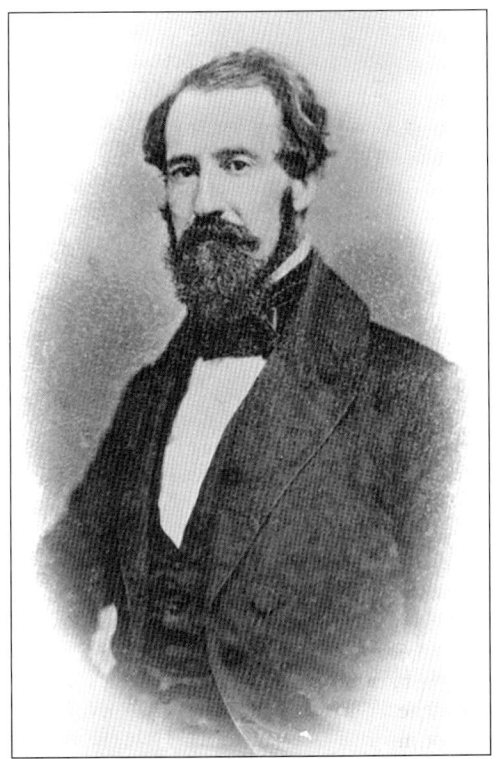

"Father of Shasta County," Maj. Pierson B. Reading was born in 1816 and worked for John Sutter as a clerk and trapper. In 1848 Reading discovered gold in Shasta County on Clear Creek, which was the second major gold discovery in the state. In 1874 local residents preferred to honor the first settler by spelling the town of Redding as Reading. But even after a bill passed to change the name to Reading, the railroad and U.S. Post Office refused to recognize the change and another bill had to be passed to change the name back to Redding. Major Reading died in 1868.

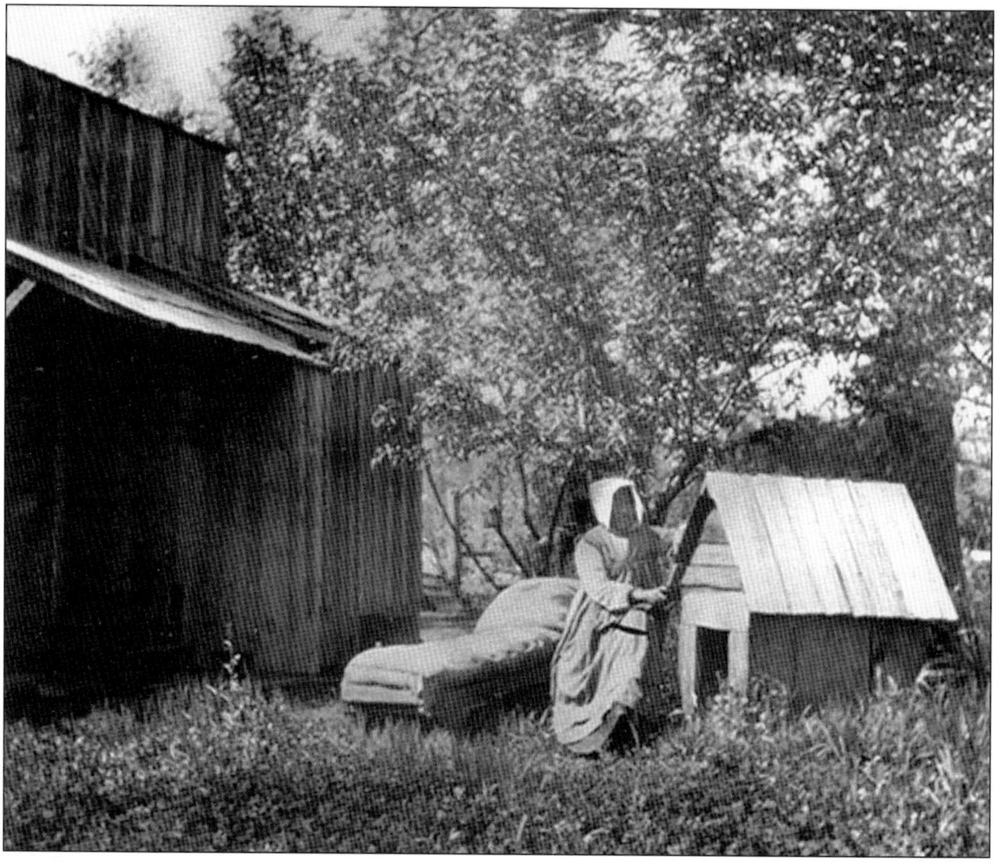

This photo shows "Old Kate" on the Indian Rancheria at the foot of Butte Street in Redding, c. 1900. Old Kate was the laundress for Mrs. J.F. Scamman. Native American women were often enlisted to perform chores for the settlers.

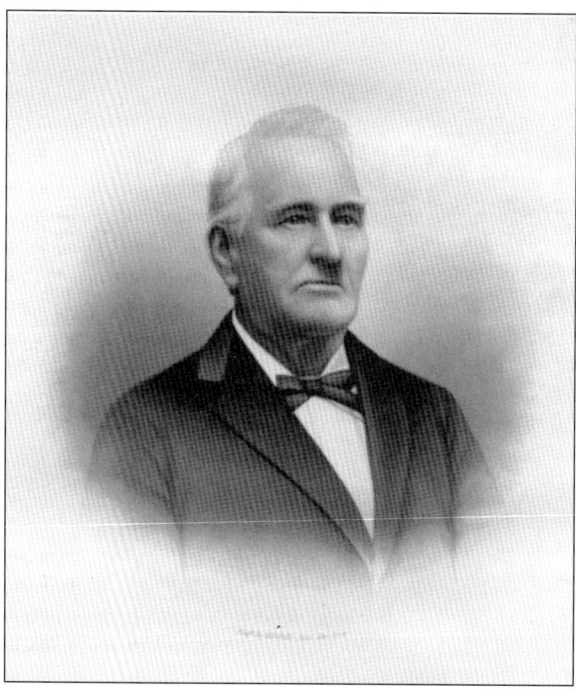

William Magee came to Shasta County in 1850, and he surveyed Pierson B. Reading's rancho in 1853. Magee was appointed United States deputy surveyor and elected county surveyor in 1854. Magee made the first complete map of Shasta County in 1862.

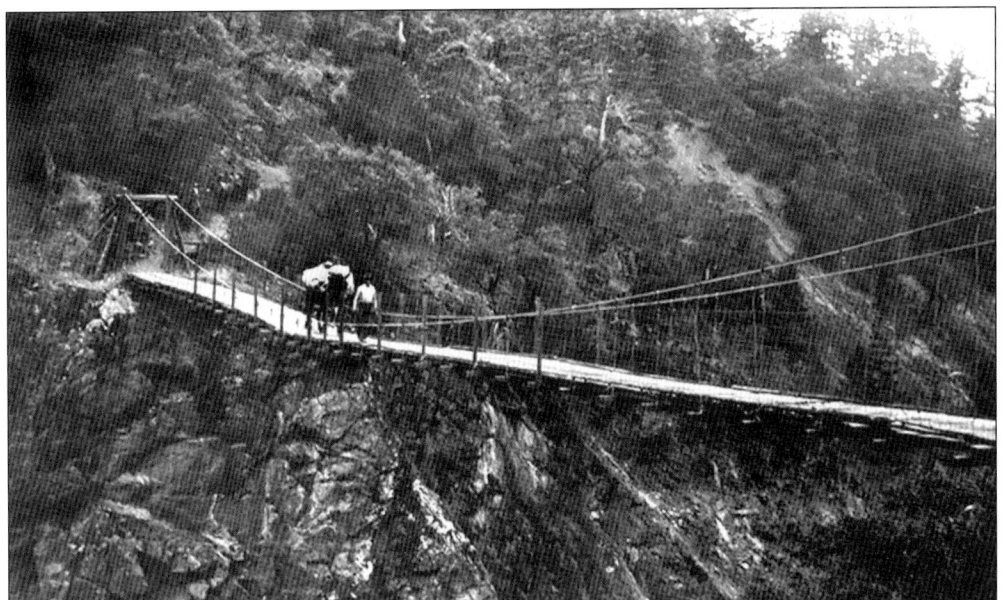

Before roads serviced Shasta County, donkeys and mules carried supplies to outlying mining camps. The Sacramento River was crossed by ferries and footbridges, such as the Keswick footbridge shown here.

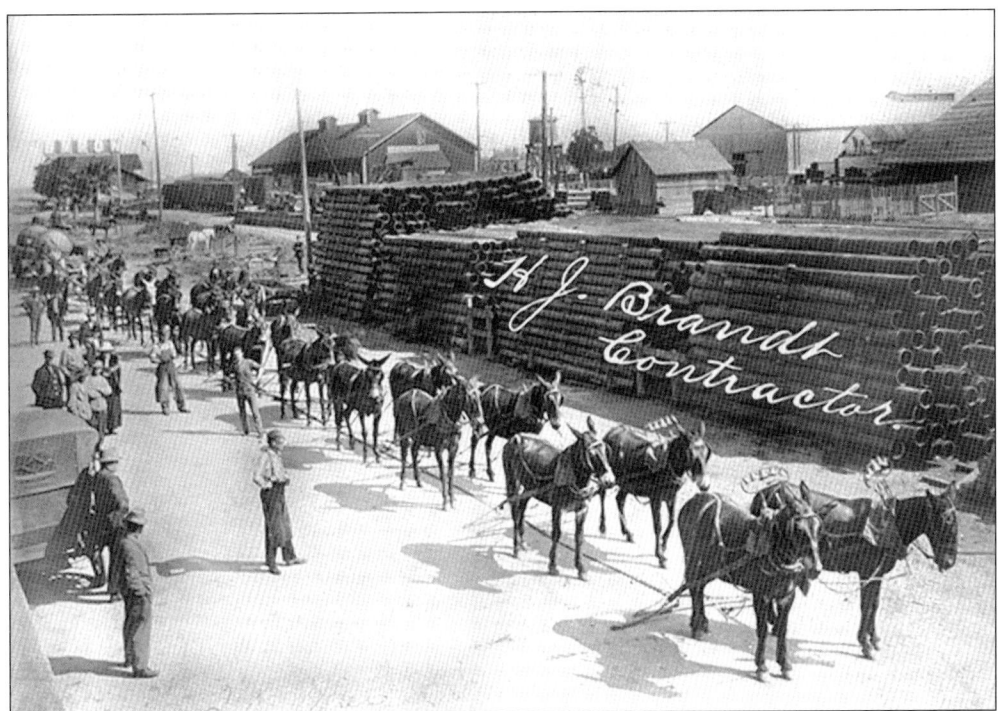

Plagued by snow in the mountains and floods along the Sacramento River and its tributaries, faithful animals such as H.J. Brandt Contractor's 22-mule-team, shown here c. 1920, carried supplies. In 1854 more than 2,000 pack mules were employed in Shasta County to carry loads weighing up to 200 pounds each.

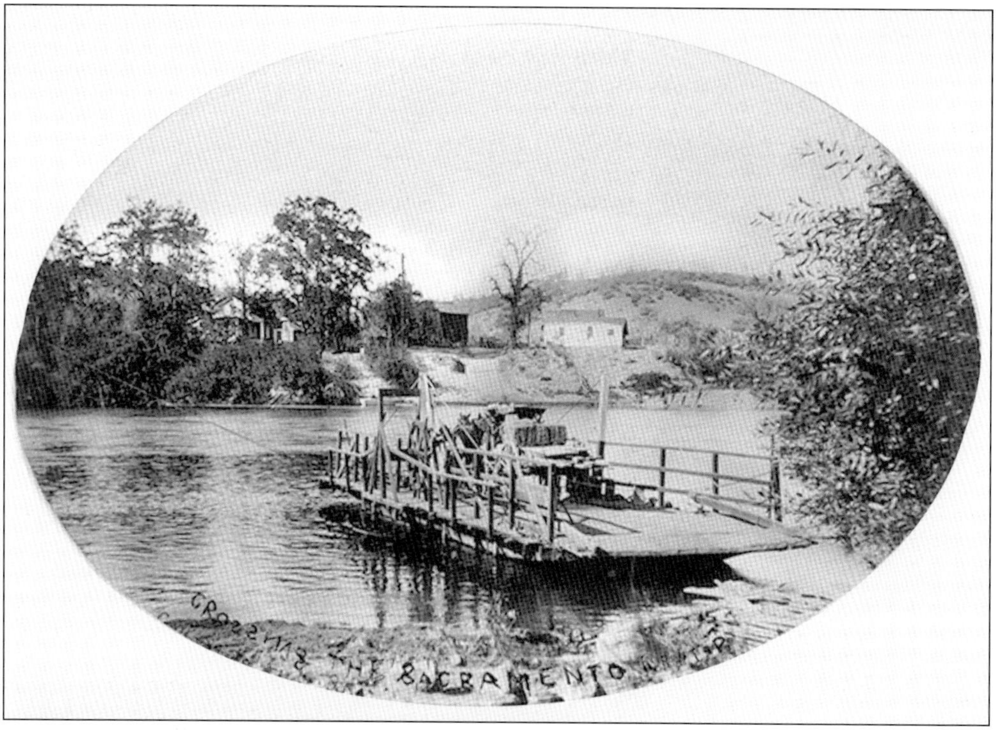

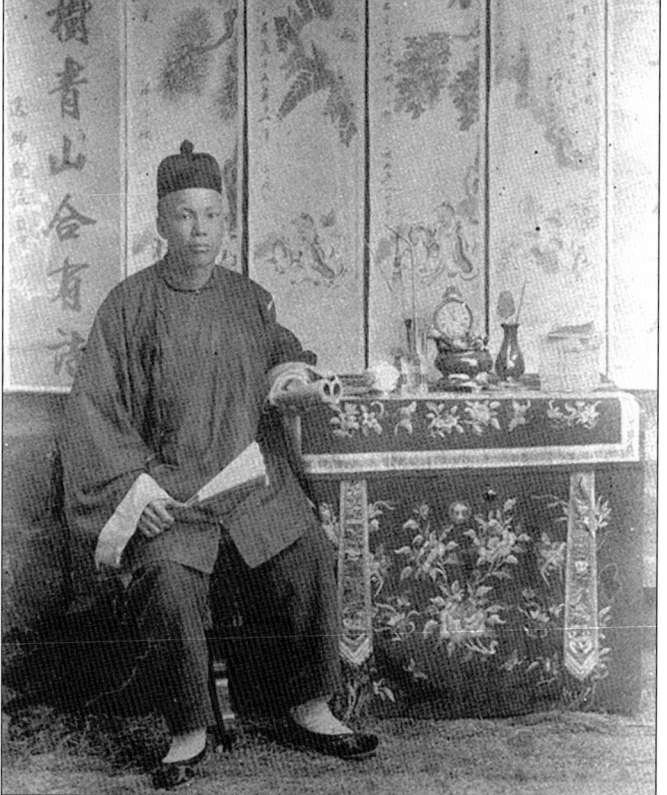

Reid's Ferry operated from 1854 until the Diestelhorst Bridge put it out of business in 1915.

The Chinese in Shasta County were concentrated in the gold camps before they were hired to work on the railroad. In Redding, the Chinese lived on Shasta Street. Serious racial problems developed and in 1886 the Chinese were expelled from the county.

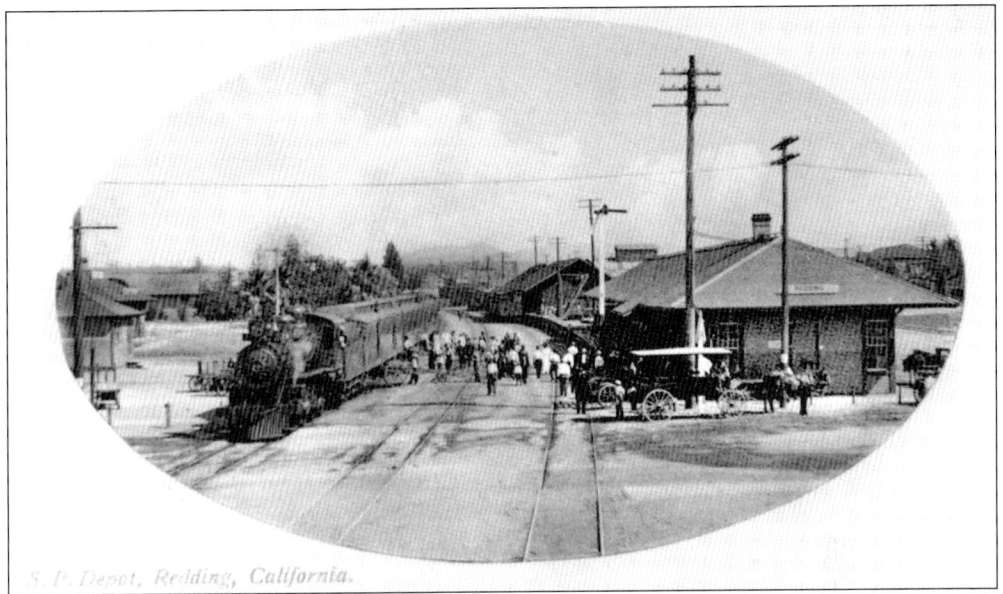

S. P. Depot, Redding, California.

In 1885 the Central Pacific Railroad built a freight depot on the west side of the tracks adjacent to the unpaved Yuba Street. Later it became the Southern Pacific Freight Office before being dismantled in 1994 and stored for future restoration.

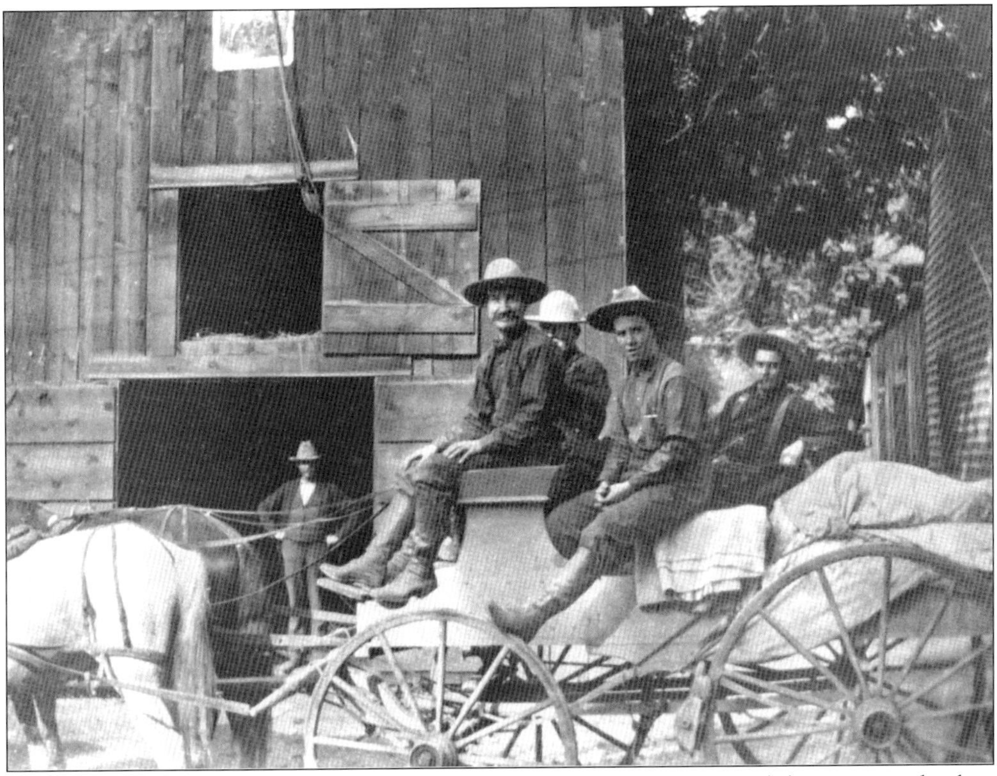

C.C. Bush, seated on the far left, drives a wagon loaded with hunters and their gear in this late 1880s photo. His driving enthusiasm and business and civic leadership earned him the title of "Father of Redding."

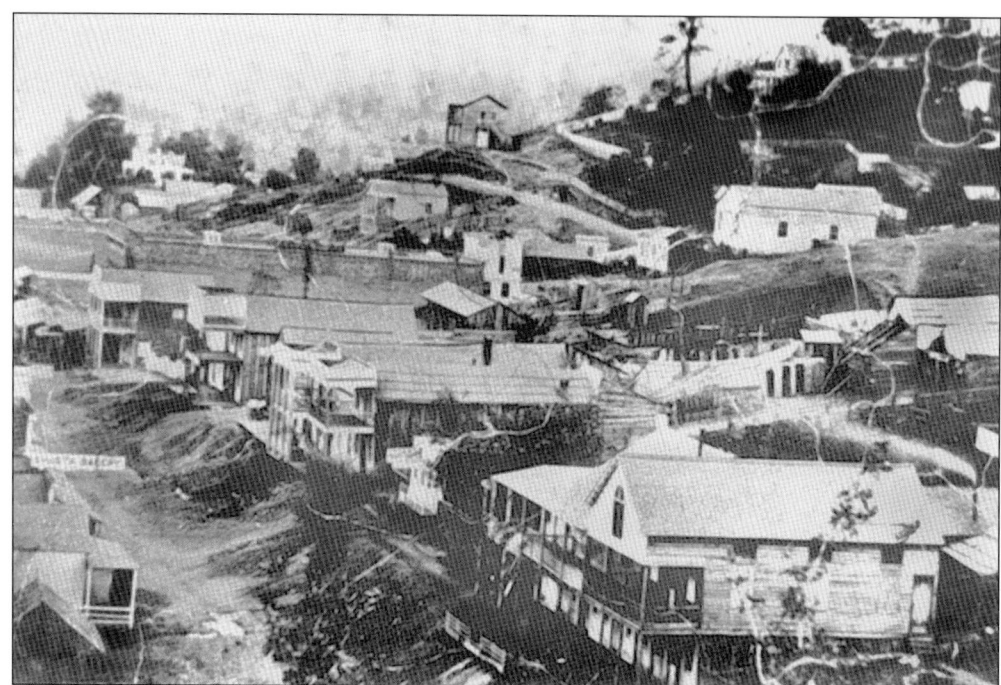

This photo shows the town of Shasta in 1856. The town was first settled in 1848 and served as the county seat until *c.* 1888. In 1872 the railroad bypassed the town of Shasta for the town of Redding, sending Shasta into decline.

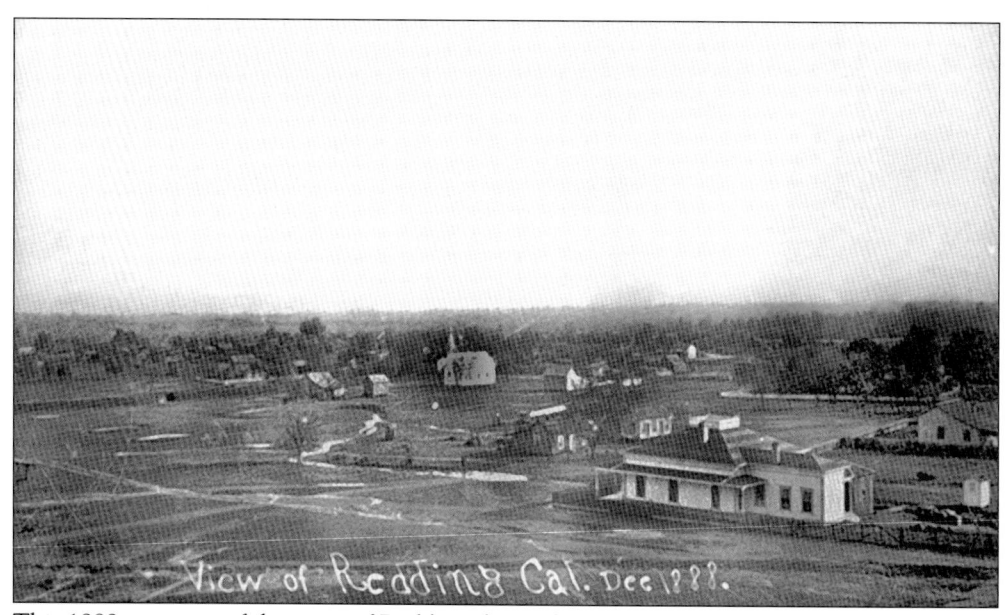

This 1888 overview of the town of Redding shows the Catholic church in the center. In 1872 work began laying out the one-half-mile-square town. Within a month, 100 lots had been sold and 23 buildings were under construction.

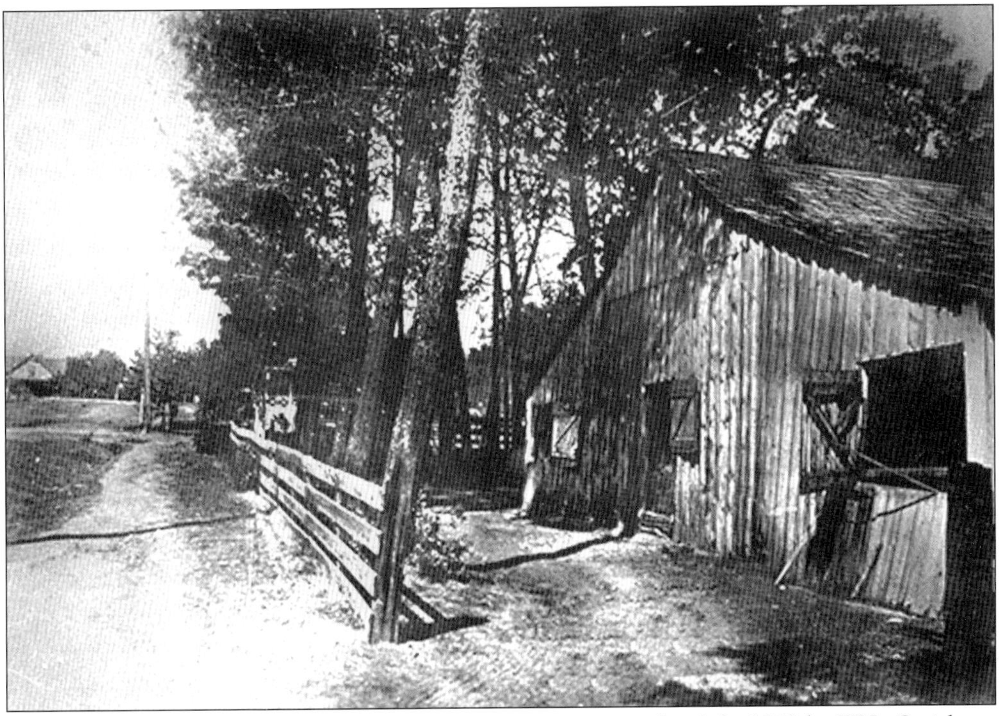

This barn, used for the Overland Stage Company, was erected in July 1872 by W.L. Smith on the corner of Court and Butte Streets. The barn was 100 feet long and built at a cost of $500.

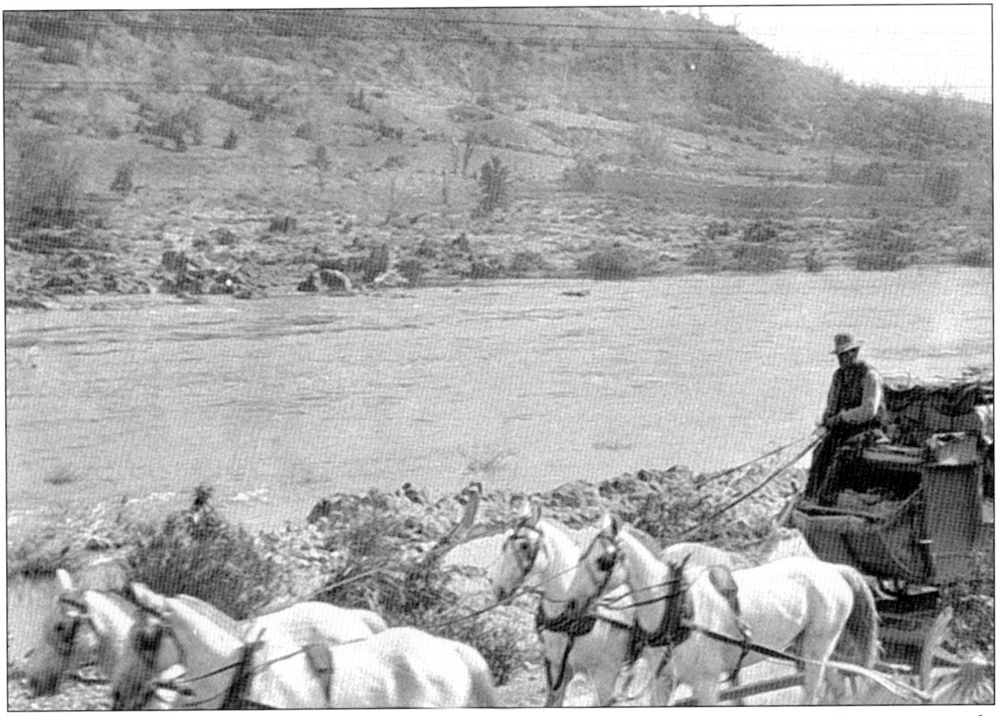

Stage drivers, like the one shown in this photo driving along the Sacramento River, not only took pride in their horses and coaches, they took great pride in their whips.

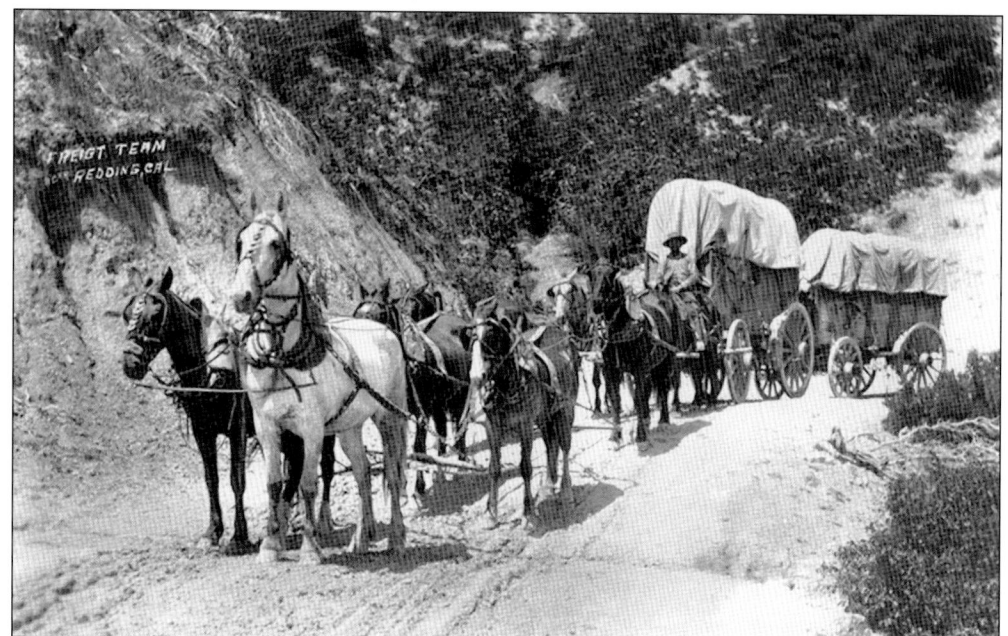

Freight teams like this one, c. 1906, brought supplies to the growing communities of Shasta County. A freight team usually consisted of two sturdy wagons drawn by six or eight horses. The driver rode on the left wheel horse and, with one line, managed each horse so that it would do its share of the pulling.

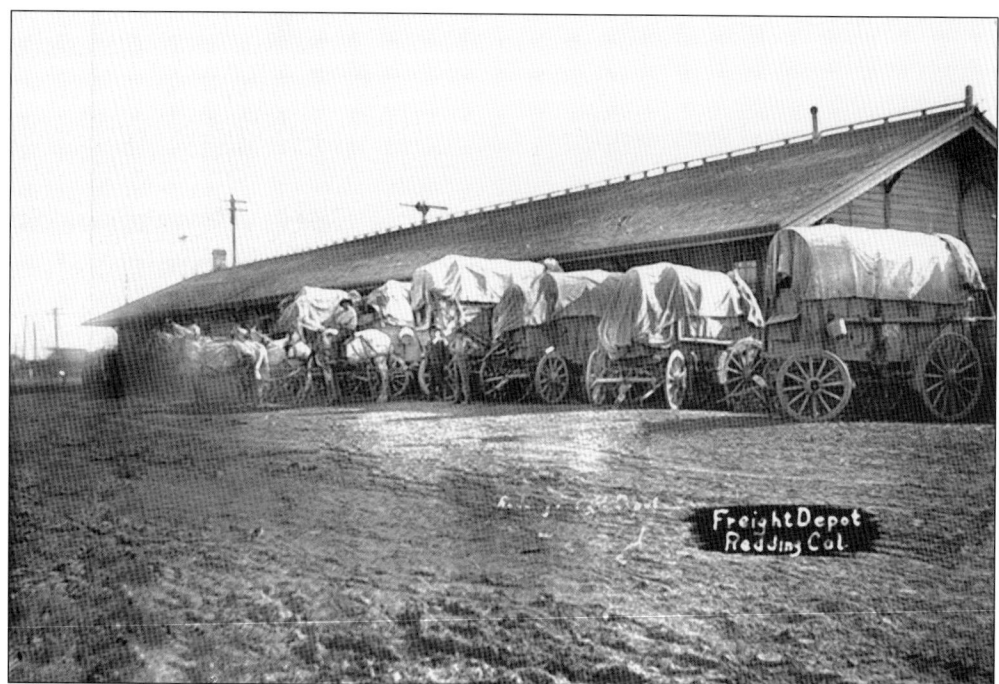

Covered freight wagons are shown here at the freight depot on the east side of Redding in 1908. Whenever possible these freighters loaded their wagons with grain and other produce and hauled it to Redding, which for many years was the nearest shipping point for the railroad.

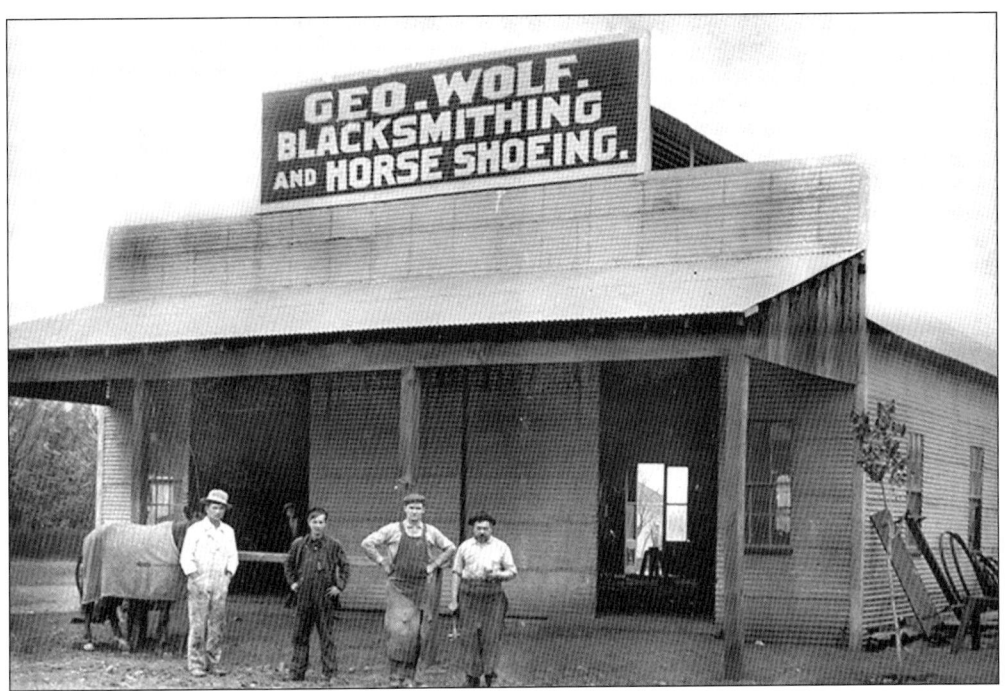

George Wolf Blacksmithing and Horse Shoeing shop on Oregon Street not only shod horses, but the blacksmith also repaired and mended everything made of iron.

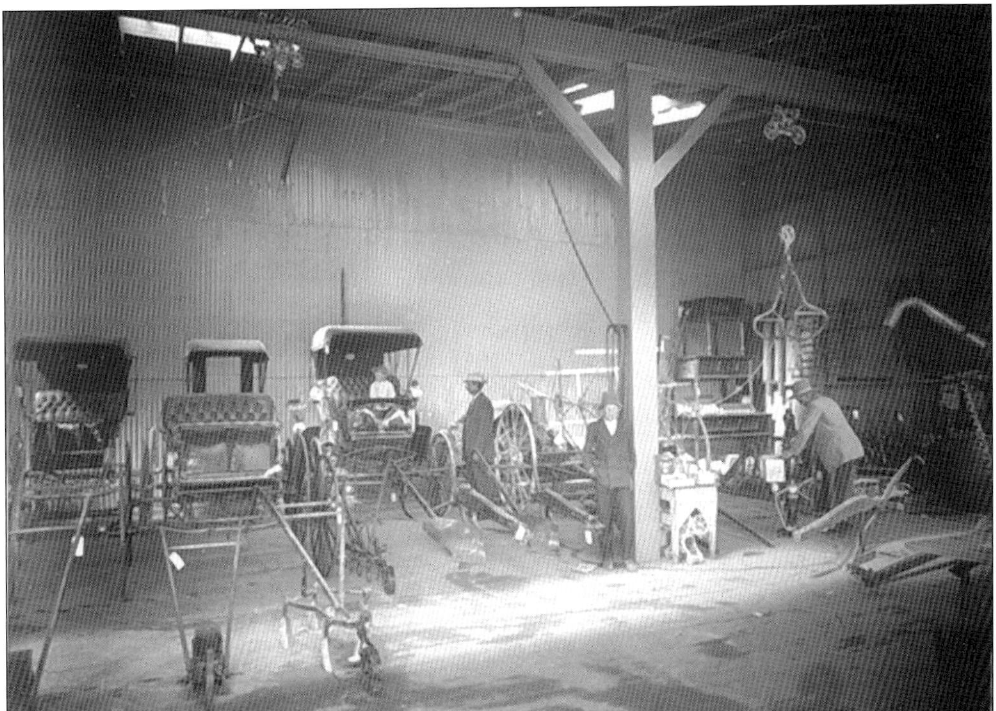

Buggies and farm equipment, each with a tag, indicate that this may be a repair shop for the McCormick-Saeltzer store.

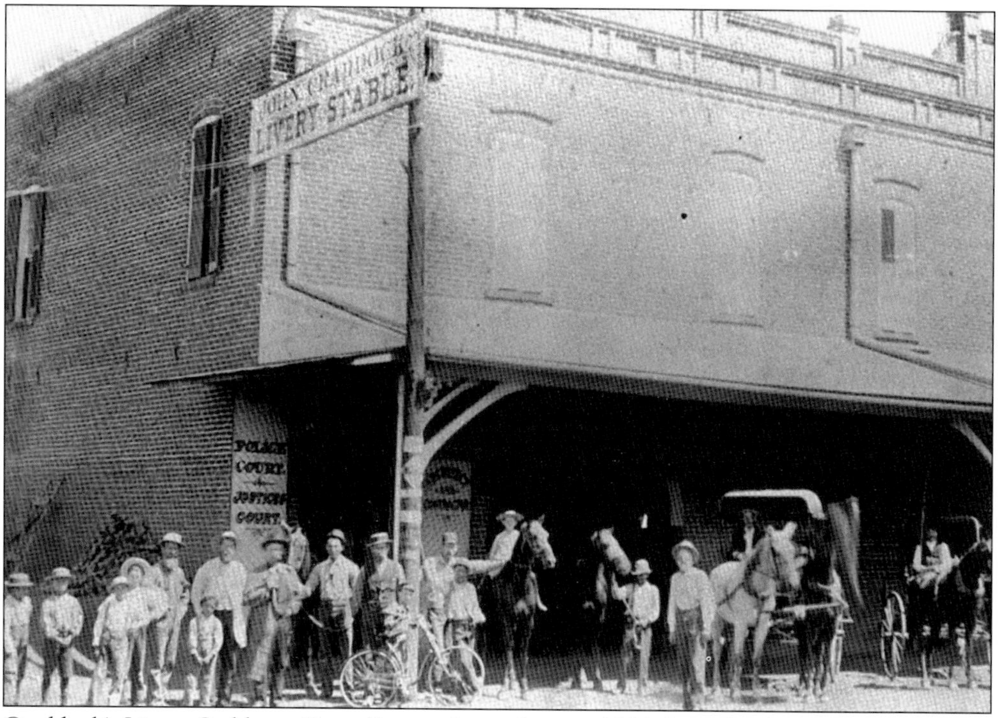

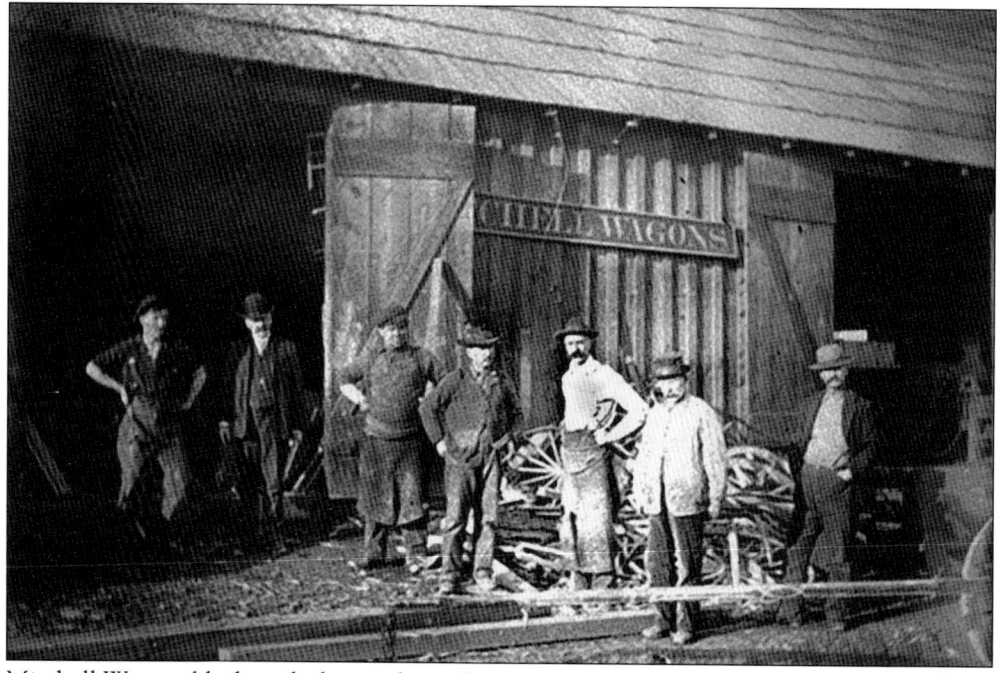

Craddock's Livery Stable on Butte Street, shown here c. 1880, hosted gala events on its upper floor, such as Jennie Bailey as "Little Buttercup" in a performance of *Pinafore*. She played to a packed house.

Mitchell Wagons blacksmith shop is shown here in 1915. The transition from horse and buggy to automobile closed an era of the blacksmith's trade.

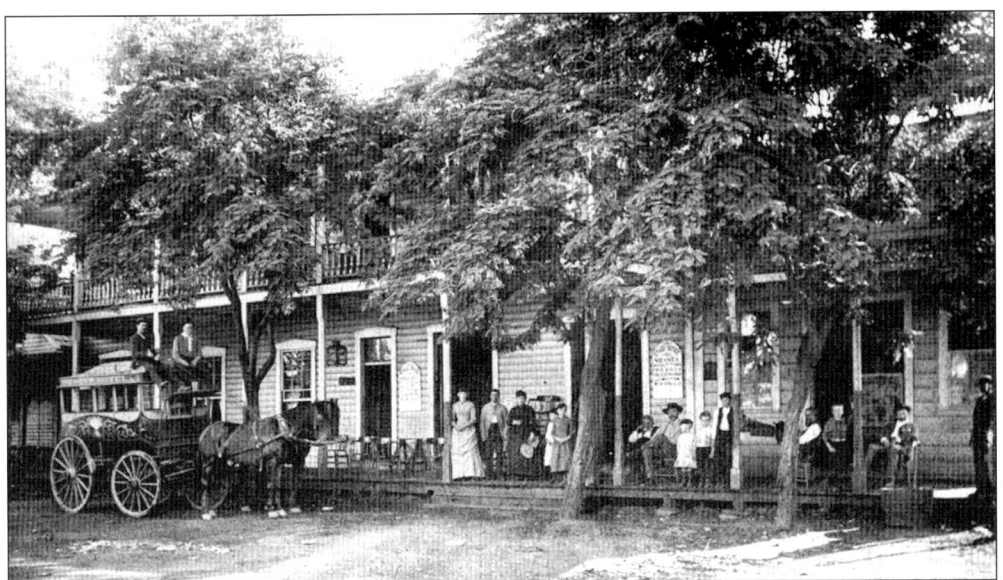

Stump Ranch Hotel, shown here in 1887, was located on the corner of Market and Butte Streets. Frank Thompson, a stagecoach driver, came from Shasta to Redding in 1872 and purchased a town lot at the first sale. The original hotel built there was a canvas draped over tree stumps.

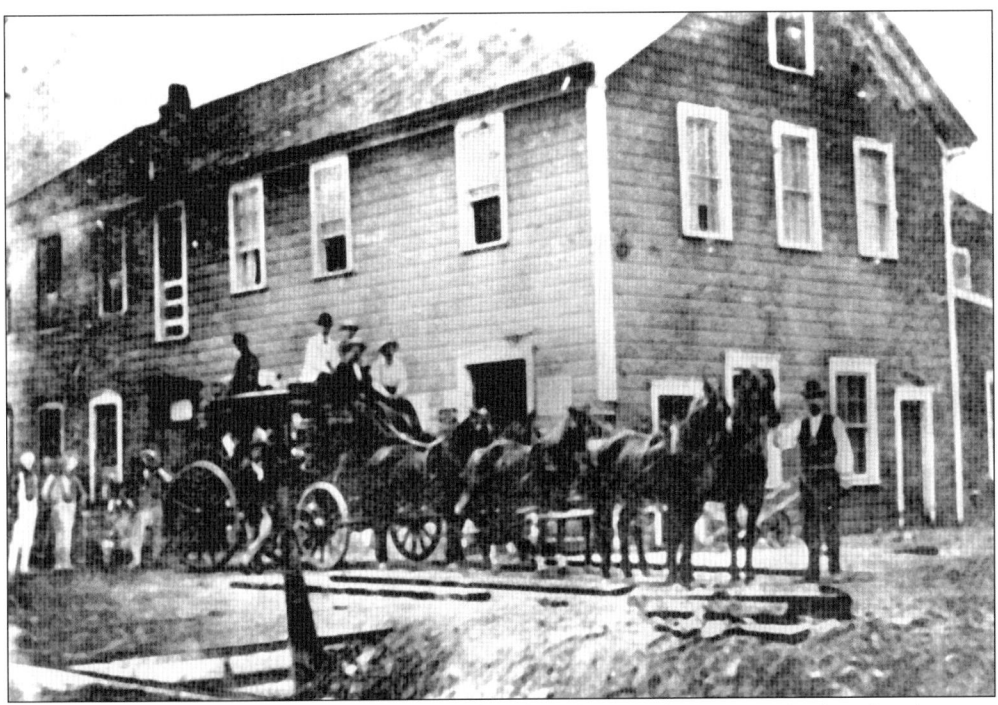

The first Depot Hotel, located west of the railroad tracks, was three stories high with a frontage of 200 feet and boasted 80 rooms for the accommodation of tourists and businessmen. John E. Reynolds is the driver of the Wells Fargo stage in front of the hotel, c. 1872.

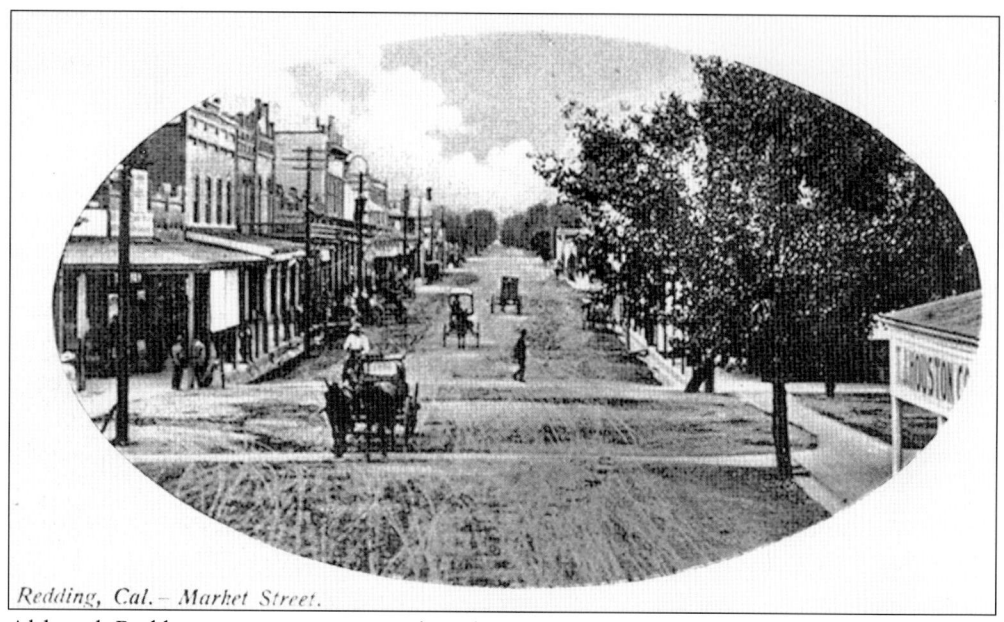

Although Redding streets were unpaved, as shown in this c. 1890 photo of Market Street, they were lined with trees planted by the Women's Improvement Club.

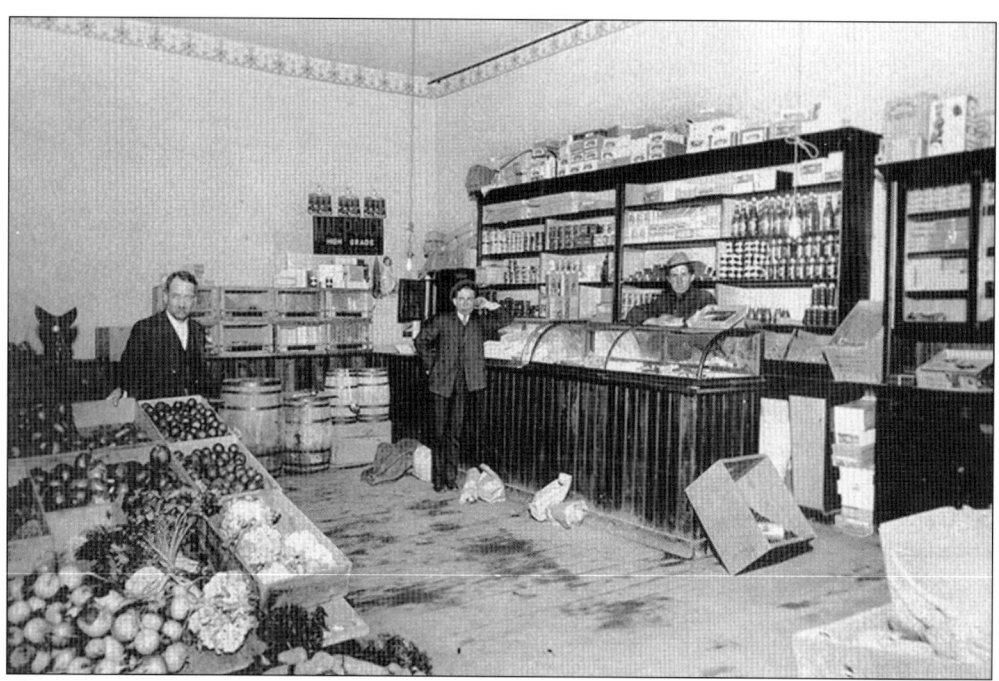

This c. 1900 interior of Orndorff and Son Fruit & Produce shows Fred Orndorff behind the counter. Jasper Ordorff is wearing the suit.

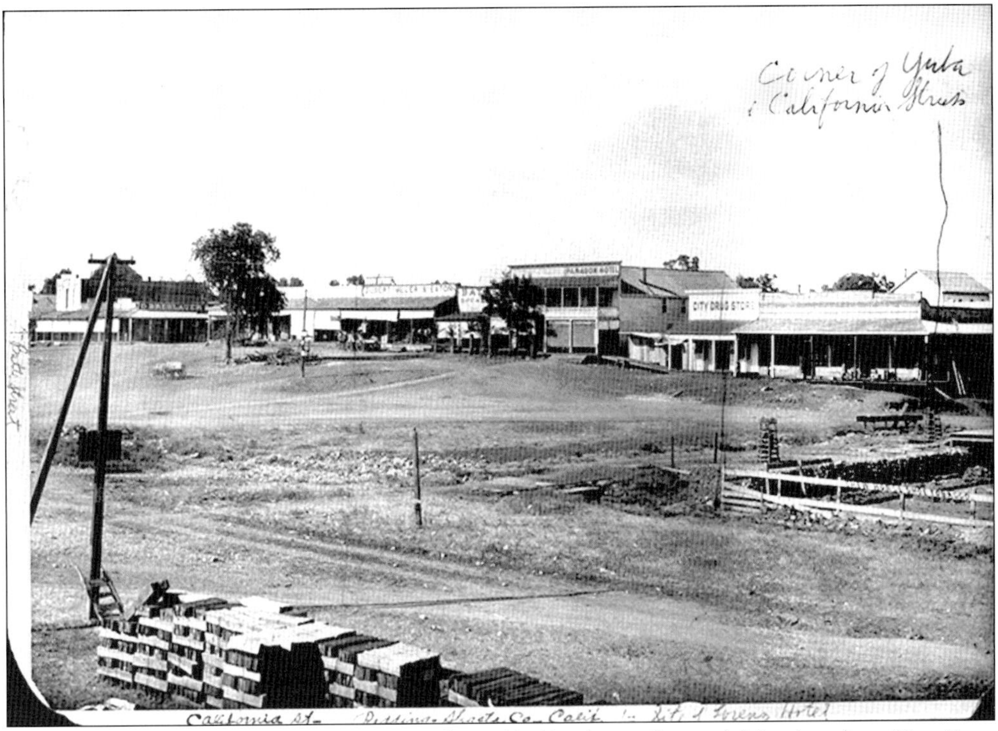

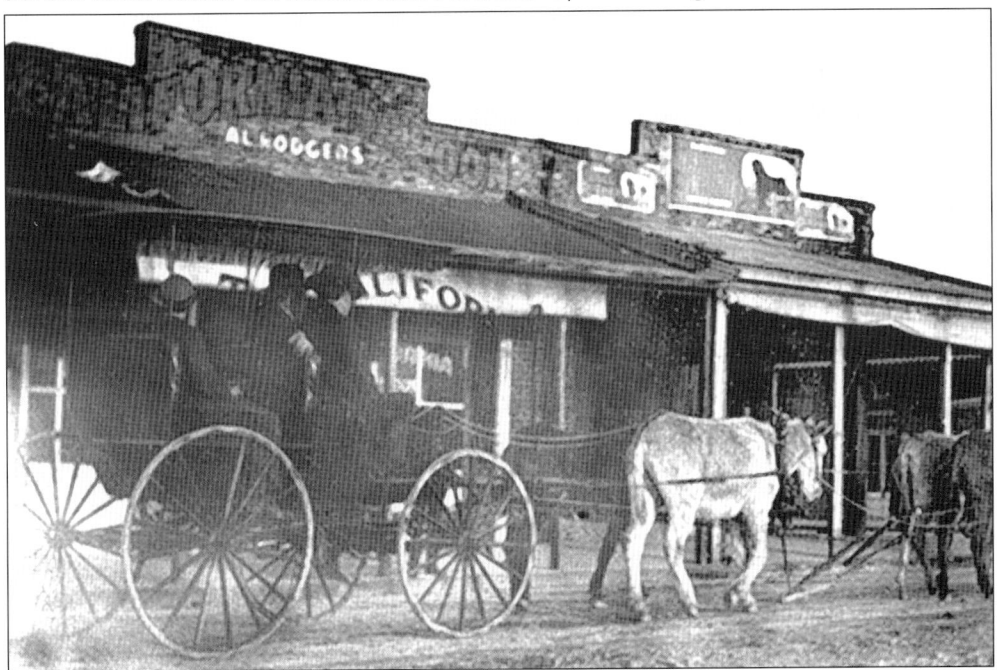

This c. 1890 photo of California Street shows D. Breslauer General Merchandise, City Drug Store, Paragon Hotel, Gilbert Miller & Eaton Drug Store, and the Bush Building visible behind the tree in the center. The Lorenz Hotel was underway in the foreground.

Rogers' California Saloon on California Street offered customers liquor, cigars, billiards, food, and companionship.

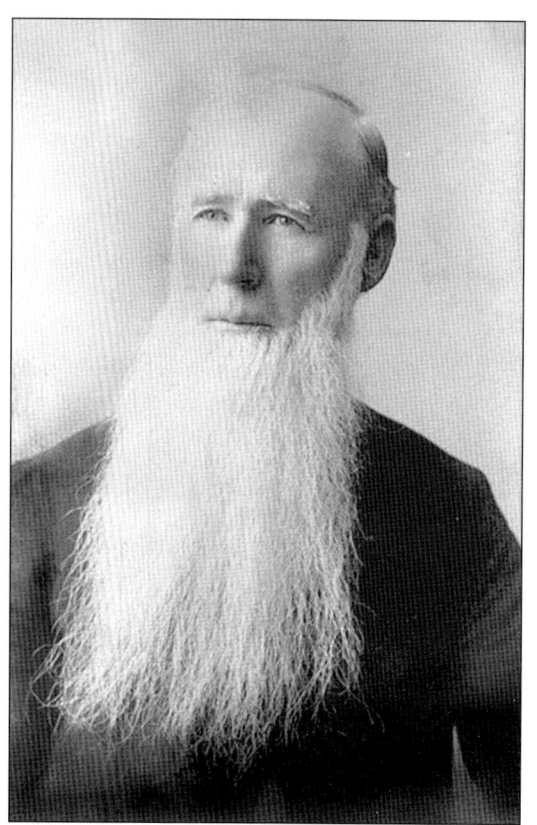

Judge Aaron Bell of Redding was nicknamed "Billy Goat Bell." One of his notable cases was ruling on the removal of the county seat from Shasta. Judge Bell gave his decision to award the seat to Redding to a packed courthouse. Great excitement prevailed, and anvils were fired by citizens of Redding in celebration.

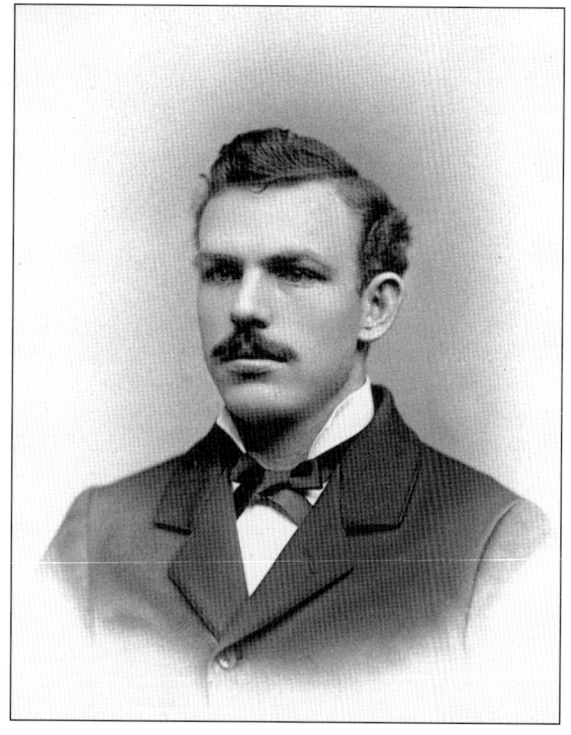

Judge Albert Ross Sr., born in Millville in 1861, was educated in public schools in Shasta County and graduated from Napa College in 1882. Elected Shasta County clerk in 1886, he served two terms, then two terms as sheriff of Shasta County, during which he was killed in the Redding jail by an insane prisoner in January 1919.

Chauncey Carroll Bush is shown here with his wife, Ida Schroeder Bush. Bush was the first merchant to come to Redding. He served as the city's first mayor, was a county judge, and was also the first fire chief and first postmaster.

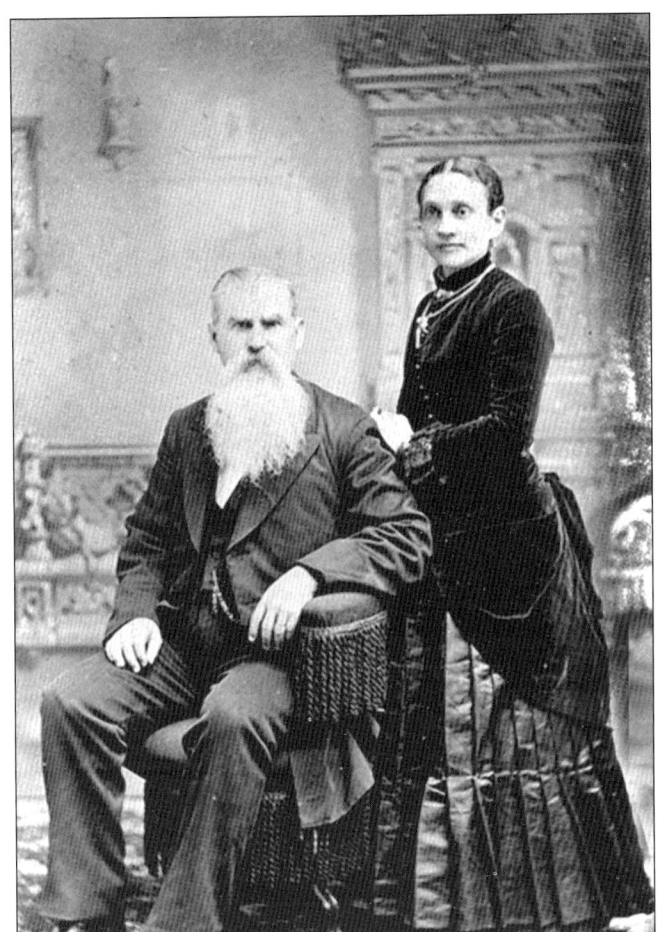

This etching is of Judge C.C. Bush's house, the first built in Redding, which stood on the northwest corner of Sacramento and Market Streets. The Redding Hotel now stands in its place.

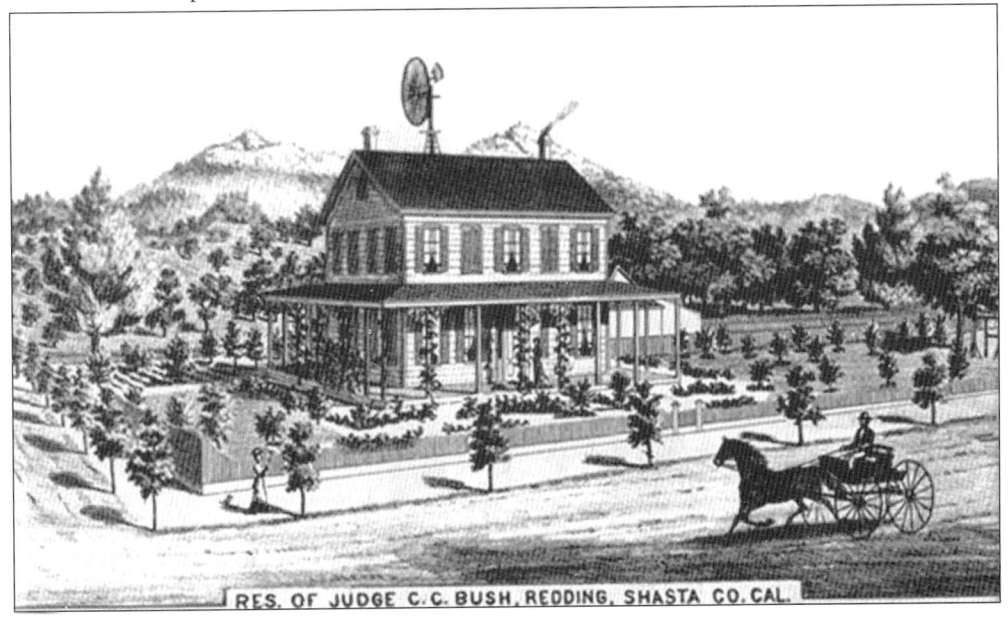

RES. OF JUDGE C.C. BUSH, REDDING, SHASTA CO. CAL.

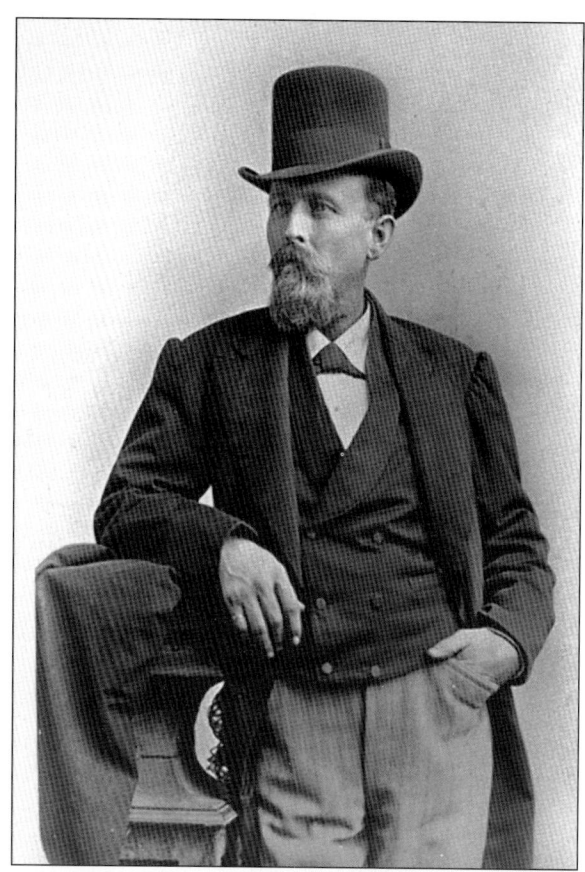

James McCormick, born in Pennsylvania in 1831, came to Redding in 1873. He was a member of the first Redding Board of Trustees, founded the Bank of Northern California, and became Redding postmaster in 1880. He built one of the first residences on Oregon Street, which at the time was the only house in Redding to contain servant's quarters.

McCormick-Saeltzer employees pose outside the "Big Store" on Market Street in 1903. In 1877 the first McCormick-Saeltzer store opened on the corner of Butte and California Streets, then moved to larger quarters on the corner of Yuba and Market Streets in 1888. The store was destroyed by a spectacular fire in 1938.

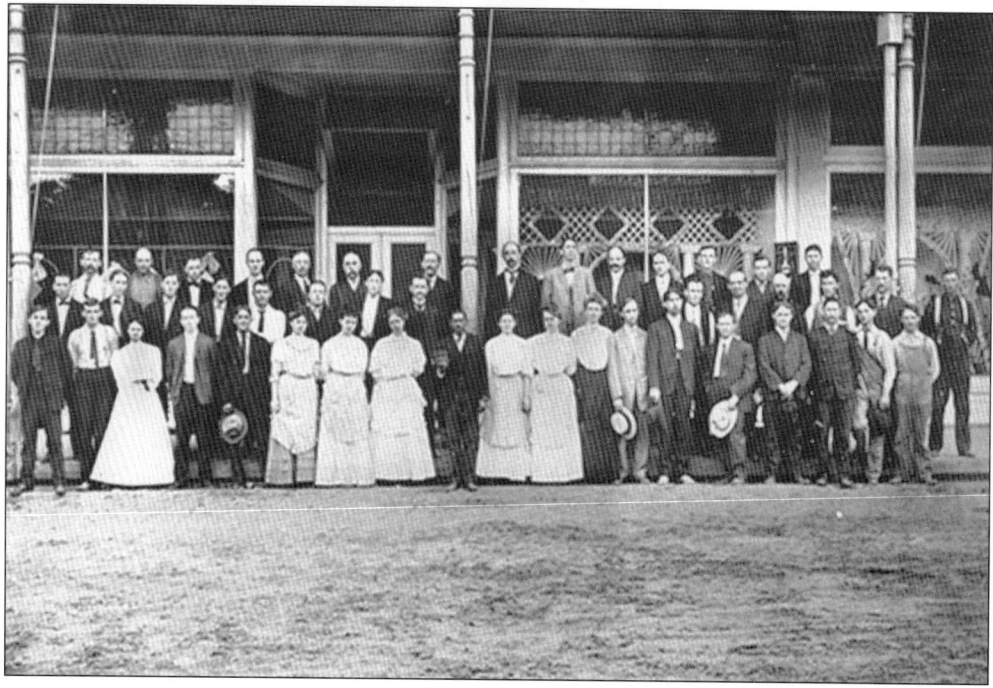

Mark and Leah Lavinia Firth are shown here with baby Clara Alice in 1890. As a young man in 1885, Mark came to Shasta County from England with his future brother-in-law, Edgar Firth, and started the Firth Brothers Store. Mark was active in the business and the Odd Fellow Lodge, and also became a director of a local bank.

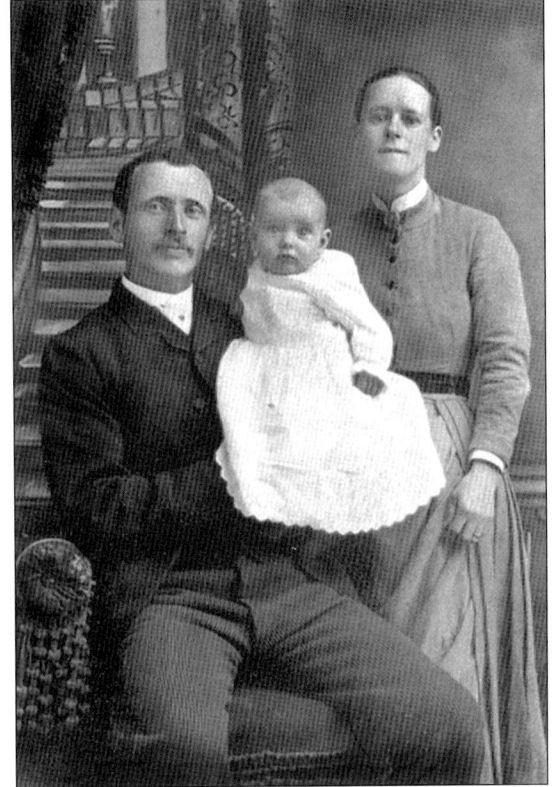

In the early 1890s, Mark and Edgar Firth operated a dry-goods store on the corner of Market and Butte Streets, shown here c. 1920. "Firth Brothers" served Redding's early residents for many years until it closed in 1940. The building, now located in the downtown mall, is still in use today.

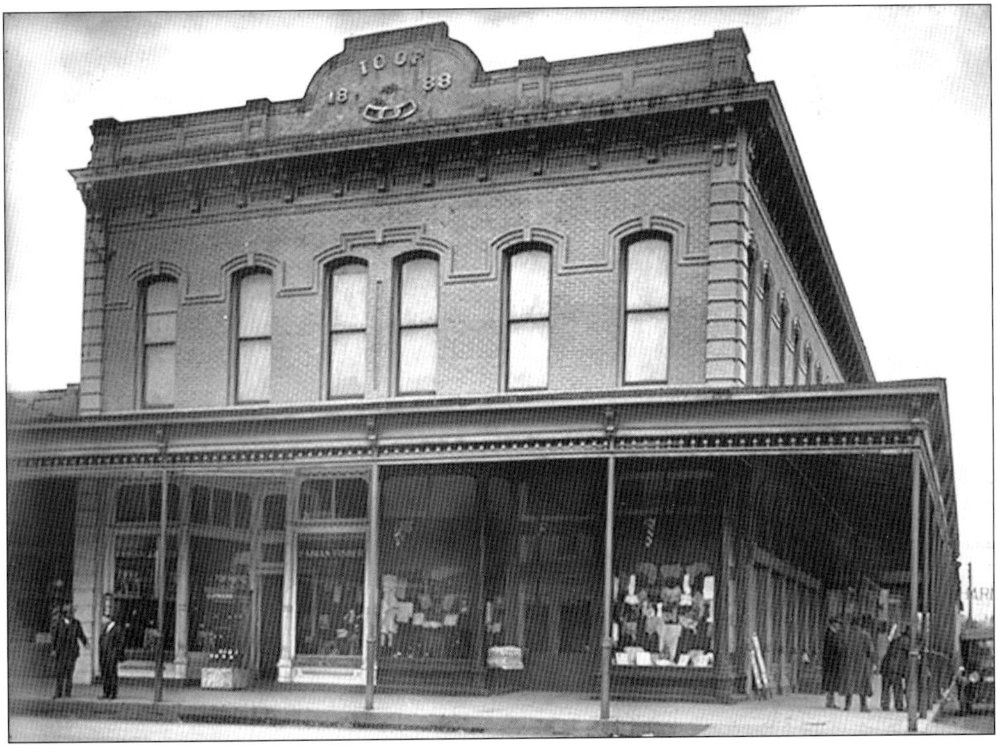

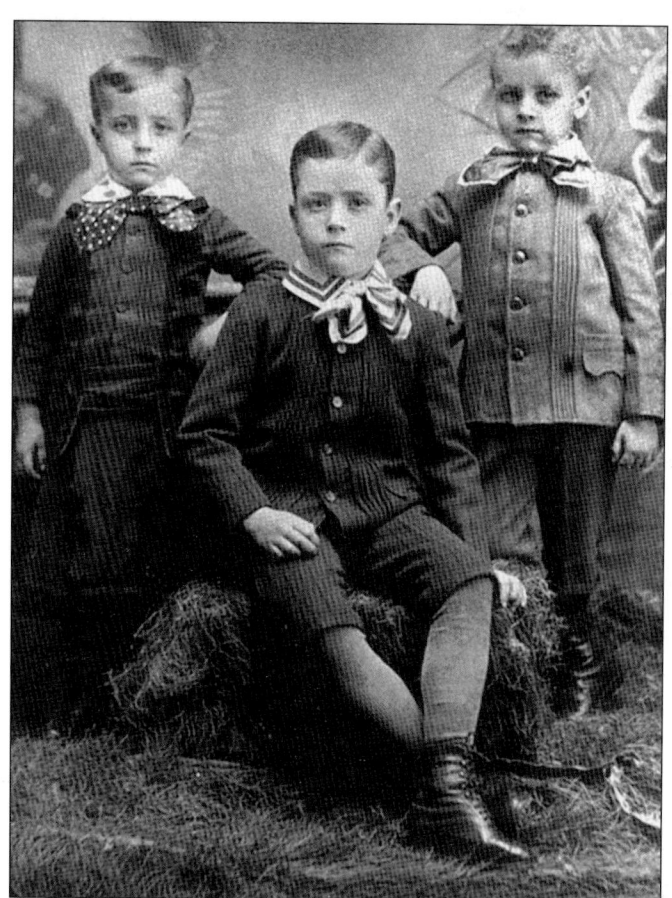

Harry, William, and Charles Thompson were three of the nine children born to Francis and Caroline Dickinson Thompson. Their father, Francis, owned the first eight-mule team in Northern California. He was also a stagecoach driver, worked for the railroad, and started the Tremont Hotel.

Thompsons' Clothes for Men was founded in 1926 by Harry and Jack Thompson on Market Street. Harry had previously worked in the McCormick-Saeltzer store. The store passed down to Harry's sons, Russell and Dudley Thompson, and was eventually moved to the Dickinson home, the oldest house in Redding. Today it is run by Dudley's sons, Scott and Jay Thompson.

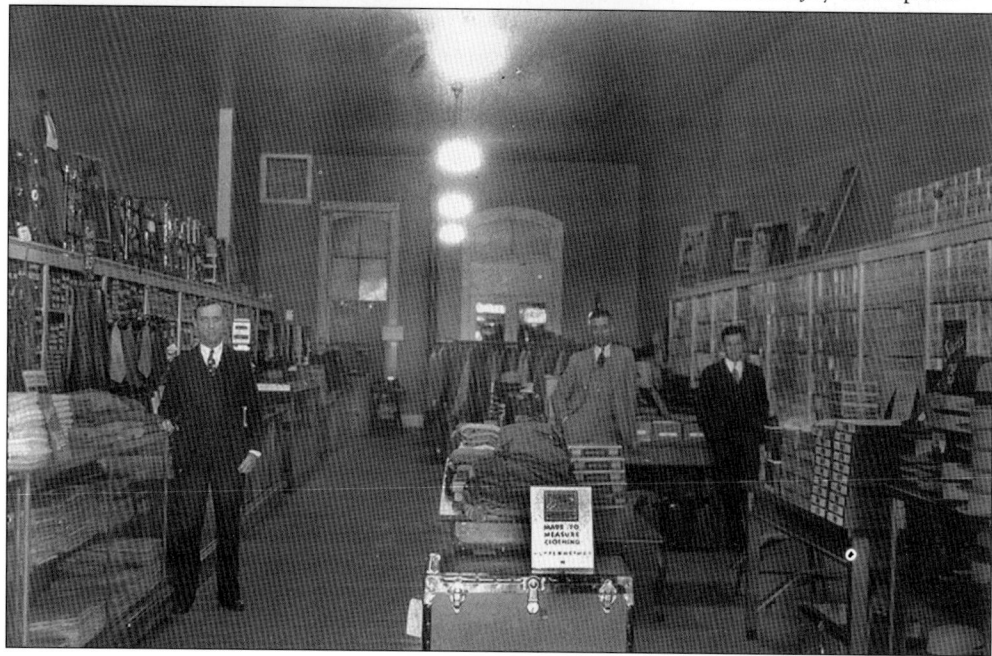

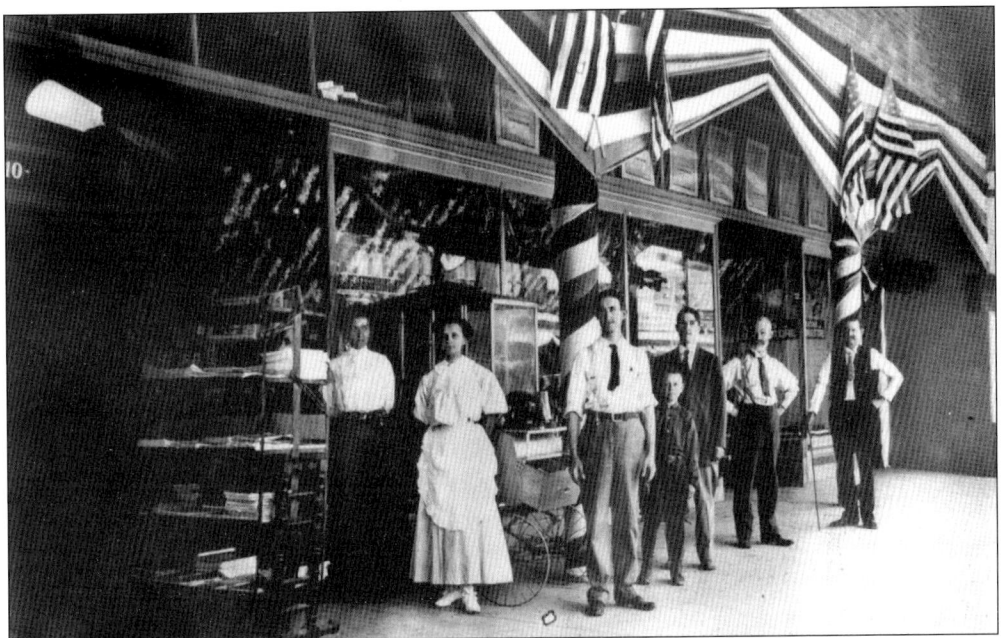

Posing in front of Eaton's Drug Store on Market Street, from left to right, are unidentified, May Peterson, Bryon Eaton, unidentified, Clifford Eaton, James Parley Eaton, and Steve Kelly. The store, which was built in 1903, sold drugs and also had an extensive toy department and a confectionery that was a popular gathering spot in the early 1900s. The building was demolished in 1972 to make way for the downtown mall.

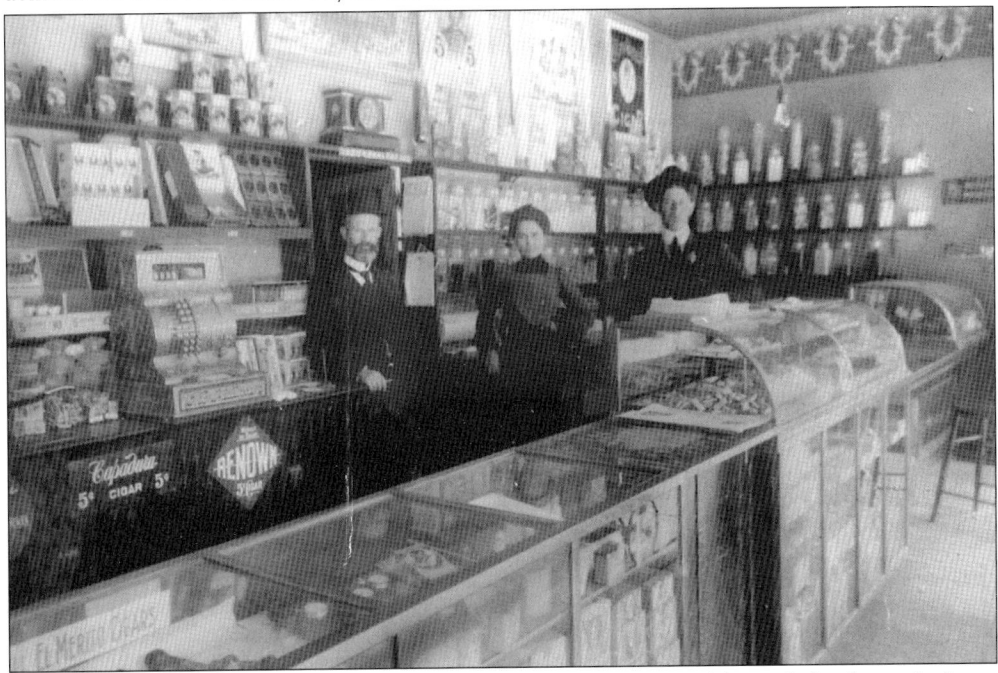

The first Eaton's Drug Store was located on California Street and housed the first telephone switchboard, c. 1881. Shown here, from left to right, are James Eaton, Charlotte Eaton, and an unidentified man.

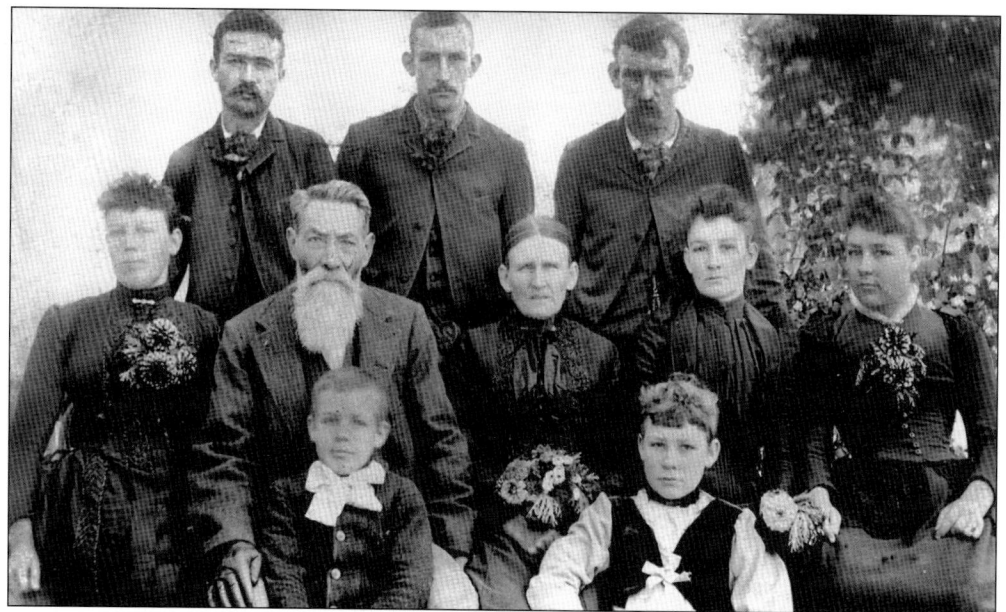

The Lorenz family owned and operated the once famous Red Hill Placer Mine at Junction City, Trinity County. Thousands of dollars in gold was taken from this mine and Mrs. Susan Lorenz, wanting to invest the money in a business that all the family could profit from, bought a block of marshy ground on California Street. It was here that she built her four-story brick hotel. This photo shows the Lorenz family in the late 1880s. (Courtesy of Richard Lorenz.)

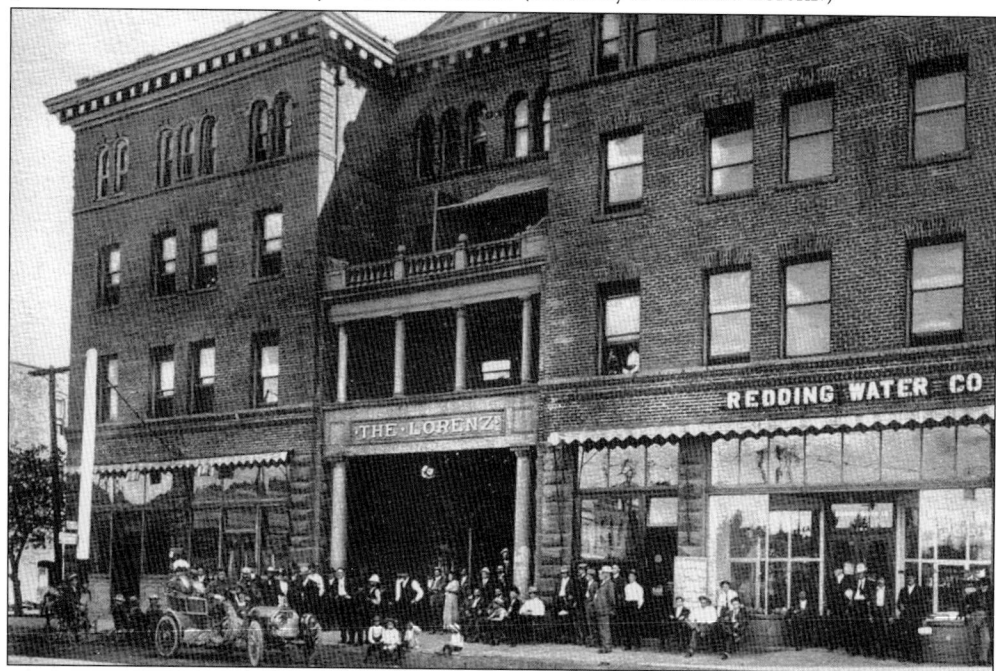

The Lorenz Hotel is shown here in the early 1900s with the Redding Water Company on the right. The hotel is the third oldest brick building remaining in Redding, with bricks manufactured at the Holt and Gregg Company Brick Manufacturing Plant. (Courtesy of Richard Lorenz.)

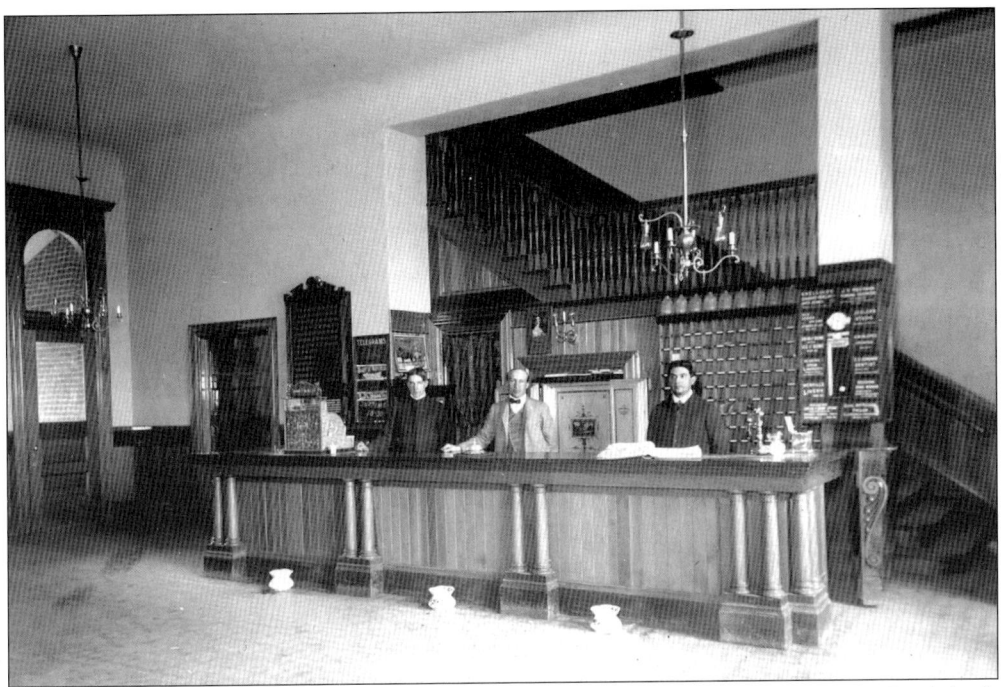

This is the lobby of the Lorenz Hotel as it appeared in the early 1900s. The Depot Hotel, built when Redding was the end of the railroad, had become outmoded. The Depot Hotel manager, Mr. Gillespie, and his clerk came to work at the Lorenz Hotel bringing with them several pieces of beautiful lobby furniture. (Courtesy of Richard Lorenz.)

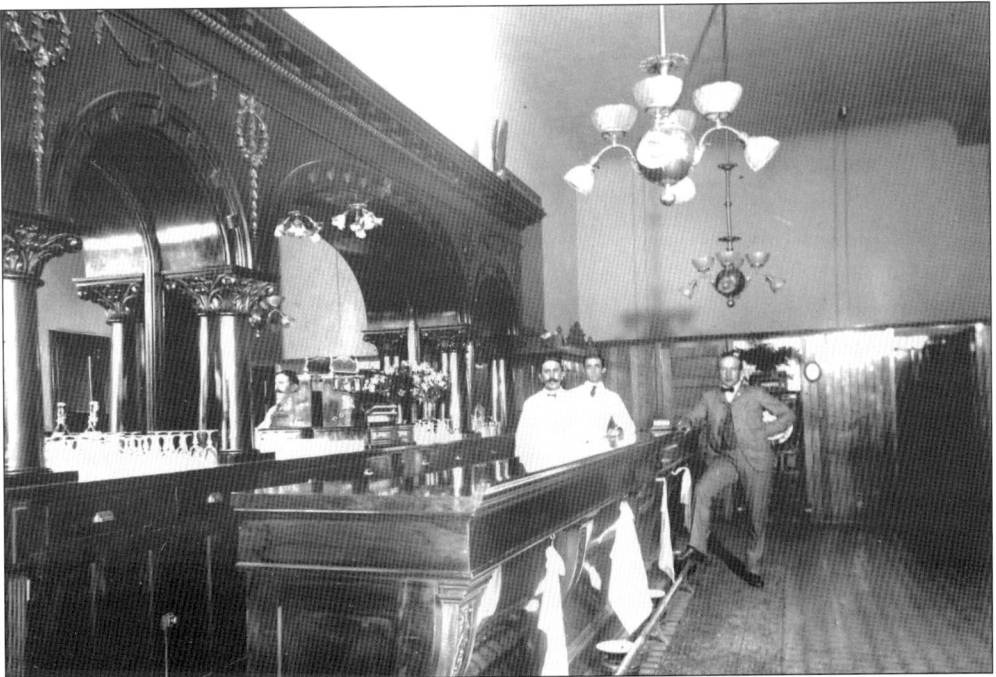

Tired travelers and salesmen found many comforts in the upscale Lorenz Hotel, including this saloon and billiard room.

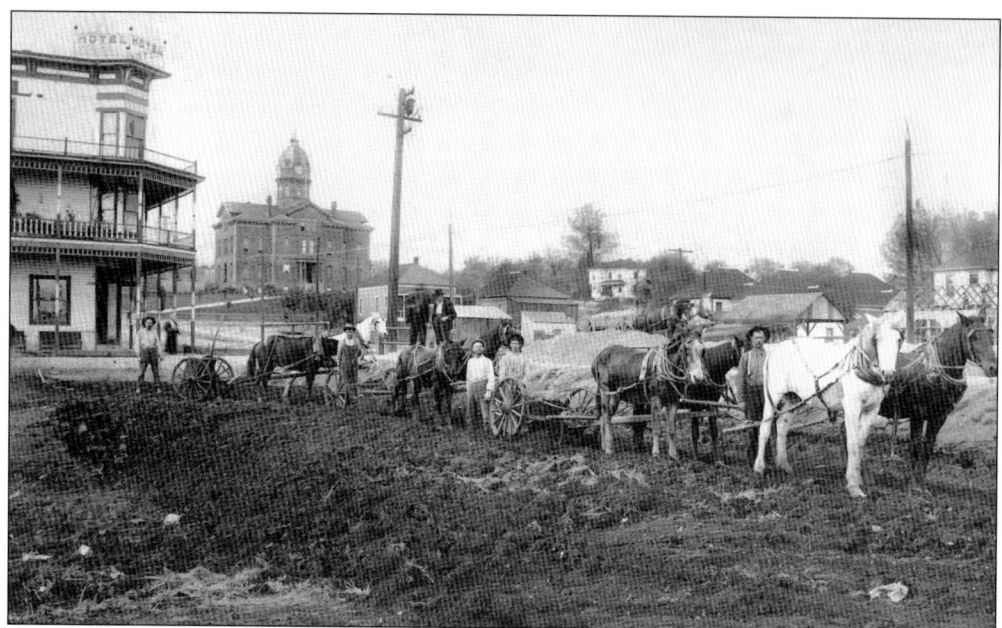

John Diestelhorst (center with white shirt) and son George (next to him), are shown with three teams of horses leveling land with "Fresno" scrapers near the site of the current U.S. Post Office on Yuba Street, c. 1910. The Western Hotel and Shasta County Courthouse are in the background. (Courtesy of Dave Scott.)

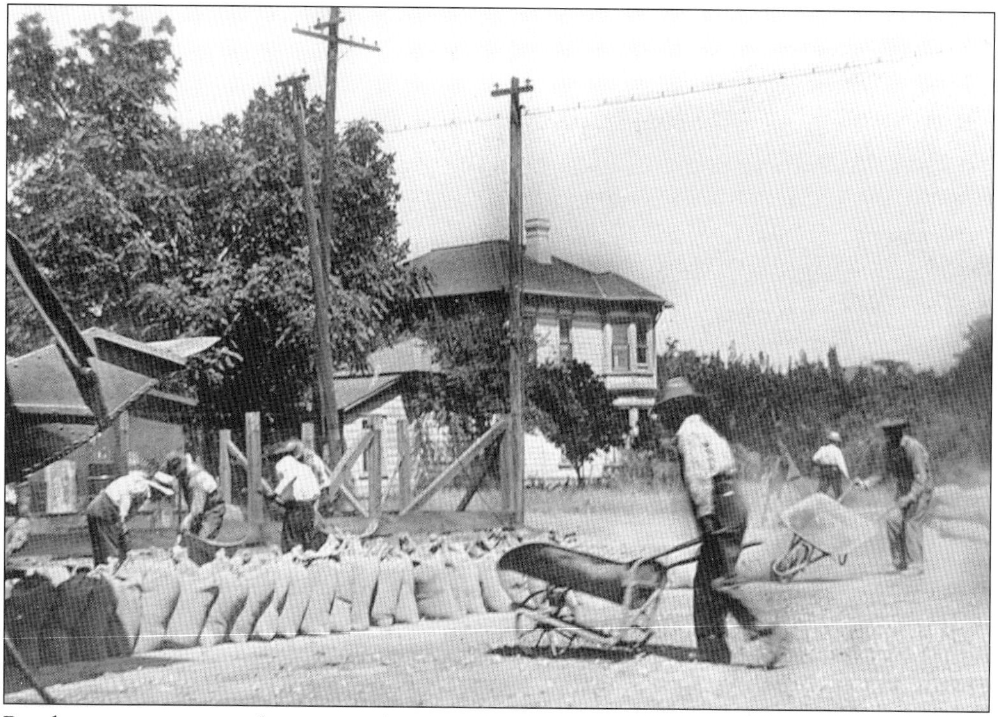

Road construction is underway on Placer Street between Market and Pine Streets. Not paved until the 1920s, the streets were muddy in the winter and dusty in the summer. When the first autos appeared, they sometimes got stuck in the mud.

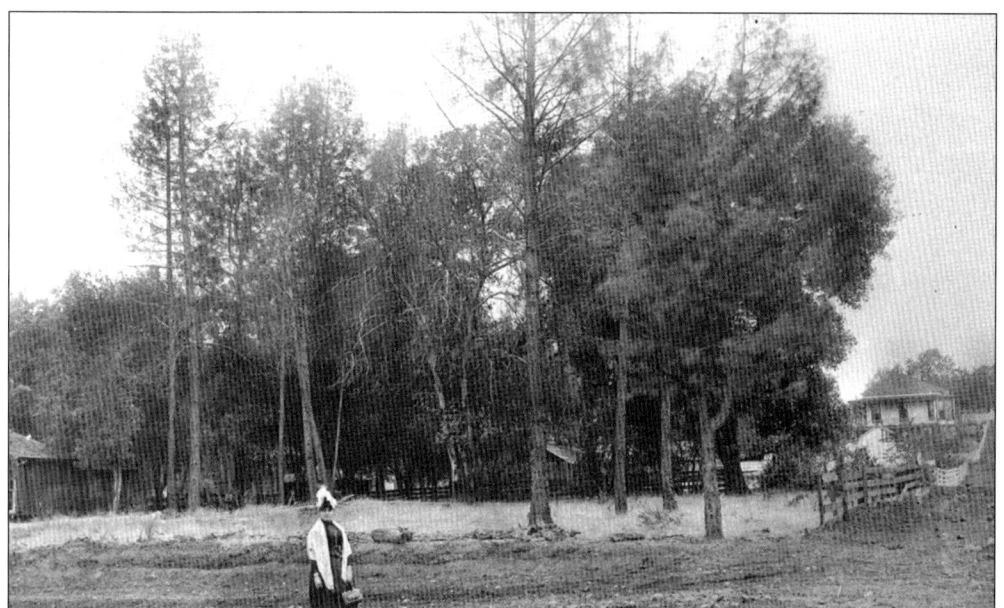

Miss Lillie Swain is shown at her family home on the corner of Oregon and Tehama Streets with Court Street in the background. Lillie was a very beautiful girl and had the honor of riding on a float in the first Fourth of July celebration in Redding in the 1870s.

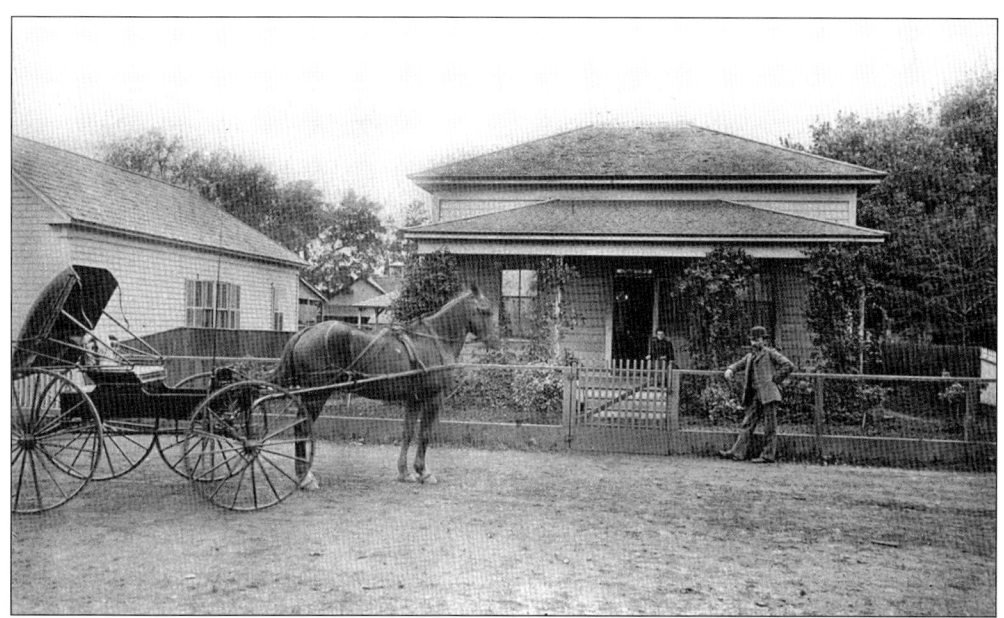

Newlyweds Carrie Scamman and Noble Russell pose for this photograph in front of their first home on East Street in 1889. Mr. Russell was a partner in Russell & LeFebvre Hardware. The horse's name was Frank.

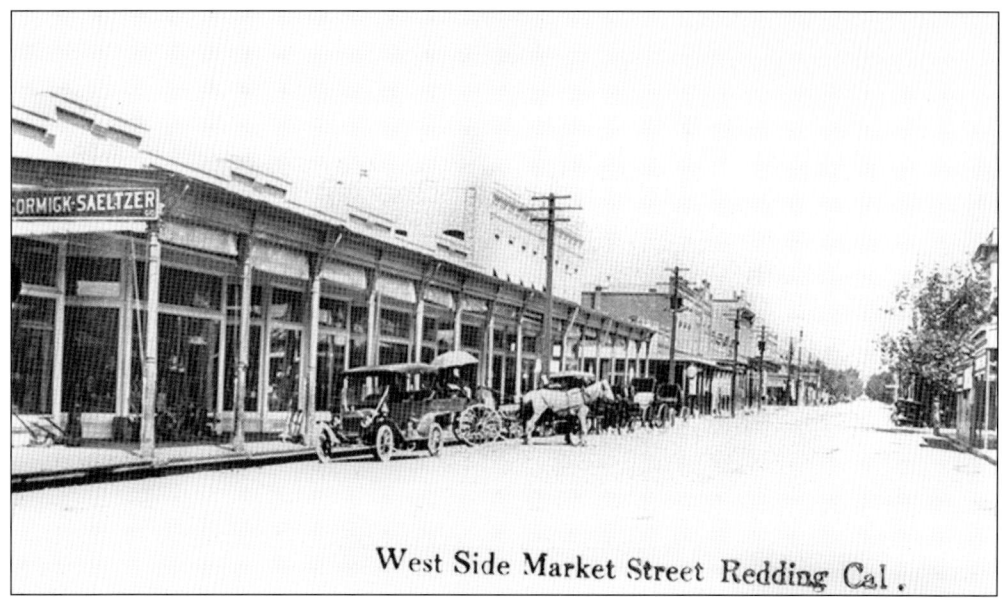

This c. 1915 view of the west side of Market Street shows the McCormick-Saeltzer store in the foreground. The change from the horse and buggy to the automobile is in evidence.

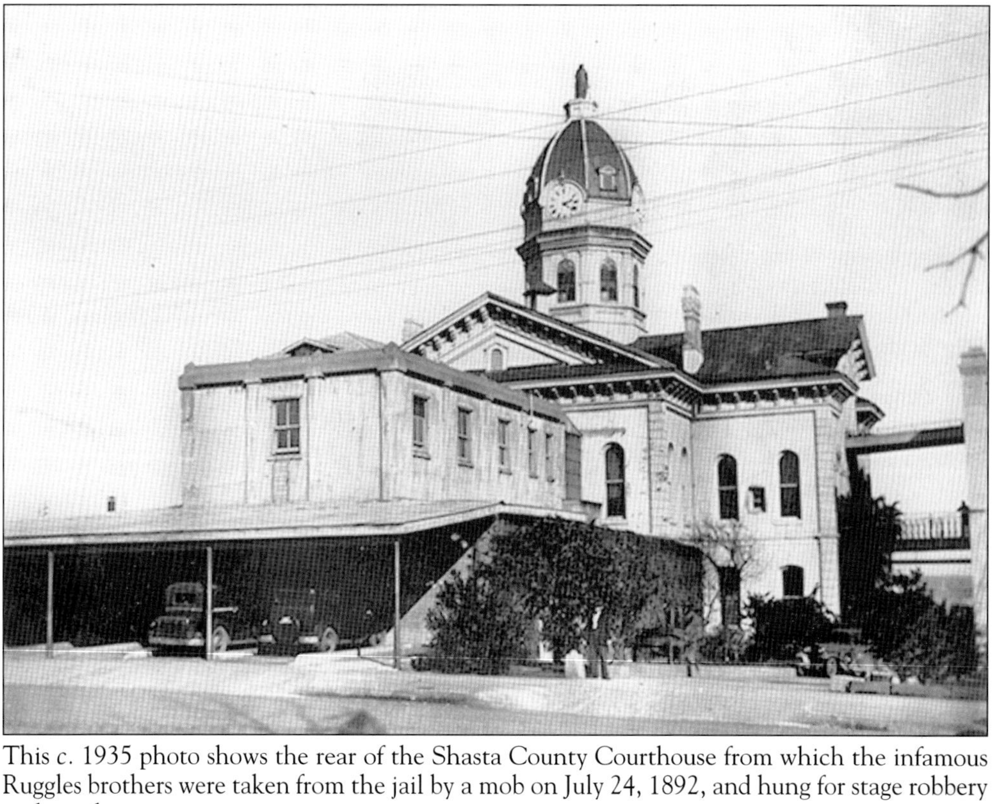

This c. 1935 photo shows the rear of the Shasta County Courthouse from which the infamous Ruggles brothers were taken from the jail by a mob on July 24, 1892, and hung for stage robbery and murder.

Two
HOMES AND EVERYDAY LIFE
1900–1930

With the dawn of a new century, city residents looked forward to a bright future. The town had grown substantially from its original plan in 1872 and was expanding west to Almond Street, stopping only because of the uneven and rising terrain. Homes filled in much of the area north of the train depot up to the Sacramento River as well as the low areas below the high bluffs of Pine Street. Development here extended to the Redding Cemetery and the Deakin's Riverside Farm. This lowland area is now occupied by Sequoia Middle School and the Park Marina Drive business and housing development. To the south, homes extended to Sonoma Street and to where Pine Street drops to Cypress Avenue.

Families in 1900 tended to be larger than today, with four to six children being common. To that end, Redding homes for the most part were two-storied and contained several bedrooms. Electricity had come to Redding as early as 1886 and by 1900 improved wiring and switches permitted ample outlets for each room. Much of the demand for electricity was, of course, for lighting, not appliances, which were only just becoming available. However, by 1920 most homes did have a telephone. Homeowners made good use of the telephone, keeping in touch with friends and relatives, but also ordering groceries or hardware. Pressure was on for local businesses to have their own telephone, or maybe two.

Much of the new growth in Redding was a result of mining opportunities—not gold, but copper. In fact, it was during the hydraulic mining of gold in the 1870s and 1880s that geologic engineers discovered that the foothills and mountains surrounding Redding on three sides contained large copper deposits. By 1910 a well-known "copper belt" ran from Keswick, northwest of Redding across Coram and Kennett directly north of the town, to Bully Hill and Ingot in the northeast. Foreign investors poured into Redding, using the Redding and Temple Hotels as headquarters for their field investigations. Soon, new towns sprouted around each of the large smelters; towns like Kennett eventually boasted worker populations almost as great as Redding's. Their hotels and business establishments rivaled Redding in size and popularity. The Keswick Hotel contained dozens of rooms in a sprawling, two-storied structure. The Diamond Restaurant in Kennett served some of the best food in the county and it was not un-common to see Redding residents make the long, 20-mile trip over a bone-jarring dirt road to dine there.

Despite all the hoopla over the new copper mining boomtowns, Redding continued to dominate the region and, more often than not, residents in the mining towns came into the "big town" for special occasions or major supplies. Market Street in downtown Redding in 1910 was still a dirt road, albeit covered with crushed rock to help keep the dust down. A steam-powered street grader billowing black smoke could often be seen moving slowly down one side of the street. Automobiles were making a debut in Redding, but without a doubt, horse-drawn carriages still ruled Market Street. Very few trees lined Market Street and the summer sun felt oppressive to shoppers and business owners alike as no one had air-conditioning systems. Instead, business owners hung huge canvas tarps from their overhanging front porches or heavy, dark curtains from the sun-drenched windows. In the winter the tarps came down and the curtains were drawn back, as homeowners and business owners relished warm sunlight during the short winter days of December through February. Market Street, like all the other roads in Redding, flooded during the winter season, slowing both horse-drawn and gas-powered vehicles.

Many found it hard to believe that Redding, a town located so far north, should have such hot summer temperatures, and residents were always searching for new ways to stay cool. Of course, the Sacramento River was a popular destination. Younger residents had their favorite swimming spots along both sides of the river, but the Diestelhorst Bridge area, just north of town, became the community swimming center. By the 1920s bleacher stands on the south bank of the river welcomed spectators to a variety of swimming and diving events, even local and regional swimsuit contests. For a few years the city sponsored a water carnival on the river where local businesses could build and launch their own highly decorated water float. Wherever one looked on the river, "water tents" could be seen. These canvas tents were erected on wood frames and served as changing rooms for swimmers.

The period from 1900 to 1930 was a time of proper, formal dress, both at home and while out and about. Cotton dresses, skirts, and blouses were the rule, while men wore full-length cotton shirts and wool coats. It is hard to imagine how women could have put up with such long, heavy dresses that fell almost to the ground. The sleeves of the dress ran the length of the entire arm, while the collar was properly buttoned or tied. Likewise, men continued to wear their coats during the summer months and many residents walking along Market Street wore ties and hats. Children, too, needed to dress appropriately and during school or anywhere out of the home they dressed just as formally as their parents. Before the 1920s, it was considered inappropriate for women to show "any skin" while swimming. Bathing suits looked like modified king-size bed sheets that had been wrapped around the swimmer. The Roaring Twenties changed all this and by 1925, hemlines had moved up and necklines dropped.

While much of the United States enjoyed a new economic prosperity during the 1920s, Redding did not. Actually, both the city and the county experienced the beginning of an economic downturn driven by the recent closures of the copper smelters. With World War I over and European countries in a major post-war depression, orders for copper plummeted. Hundreds, then thousands of mining and smelter workers lost their jobs and moved out of the area. Business profits in Redding dropped dramatically and few new homes or businesses were constructed during this time. Despite the copper plants shutting down and a resulting outflow of county residents, Redding remained the regional shopping and cultural center of the north valley. State transportation officials decided to construct a north to south highway to allow "automobiles a smooth and safe surface" on which to travel. The idea was to connect all of California's major cities and then link up with Oregon, where the road would continue through the Willamette Valley to Portland. This new highway, called Highway 99, was paved with blacktop, a new surface that had proved its worthiness on roads in the Bay Area and Los Angeles. The route for Highway 99 ran right along the rail lines and thus came through Redding. While the railroad had created the town of Redding and allowed it to prosper in the late 1800s and early 1900s, Highway 99 allowed Redding to remain a viable economic community. By the end of the 1920s, spur roads—all paved—ran east and west, connecting Redding with Trinity, Siskiyou, and Lassen Counties.

Everything changed during this time. Paved roads meant easier travel, and by the beginning of the next decade, it seemed everyone owned at least one automobile. This meant that the town could grow outward. No longer would Redding be a "walking town." Accordingly, Market, California, Placer, and Pine Streets, among other Redding roads, served as growing tentacles of new businesses and homes. City residents hoped that the new decade would bring new people and a new prosperity.

This 1886 photo shows a Shasta County cowboy dressed in his working clothes. Work duties consisted of driving cattle to different pastures and to water, marking and branding, and doctoring. Expert horsemen and fearless to a fault, these men were skilled with a lasso and in all areas of their work. A cowboy's life was hard work, long hours, unpredictable weather conditions, and little pay, but life suited him. The cowboy was loyal to the brand where he was hired and didn't ask for much in return for a full day's work. His belongings usually consisted of little more than a horse, a worn saddle, gear, and a few personal items.

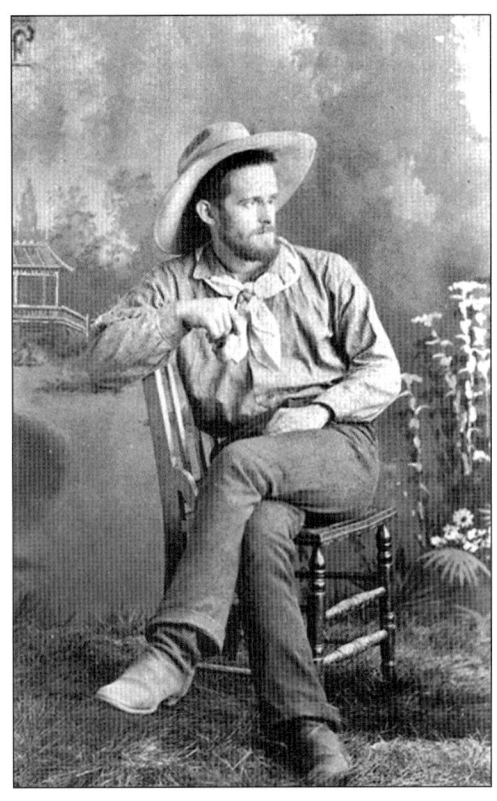

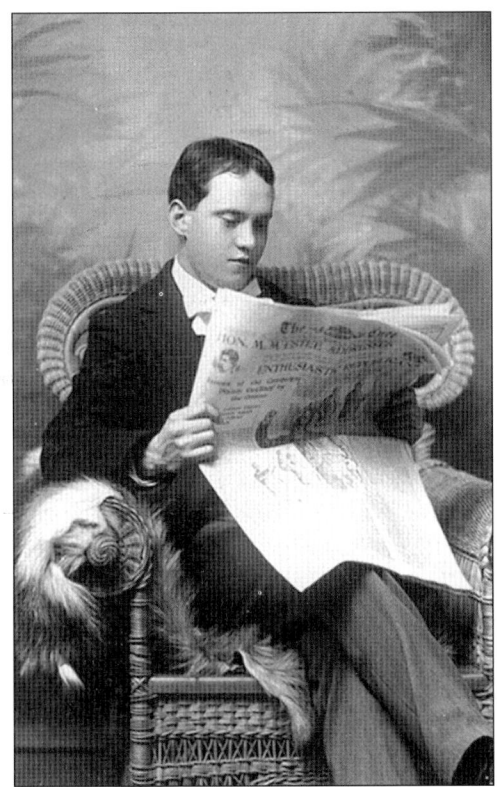

Lloyd Lee Carter, the son of William Carter, longtime proprietor of the *Shasta Courier*, is shown in this 1898 photo. Lloyd assisted his father as publisher until William Carter's death in 1901.

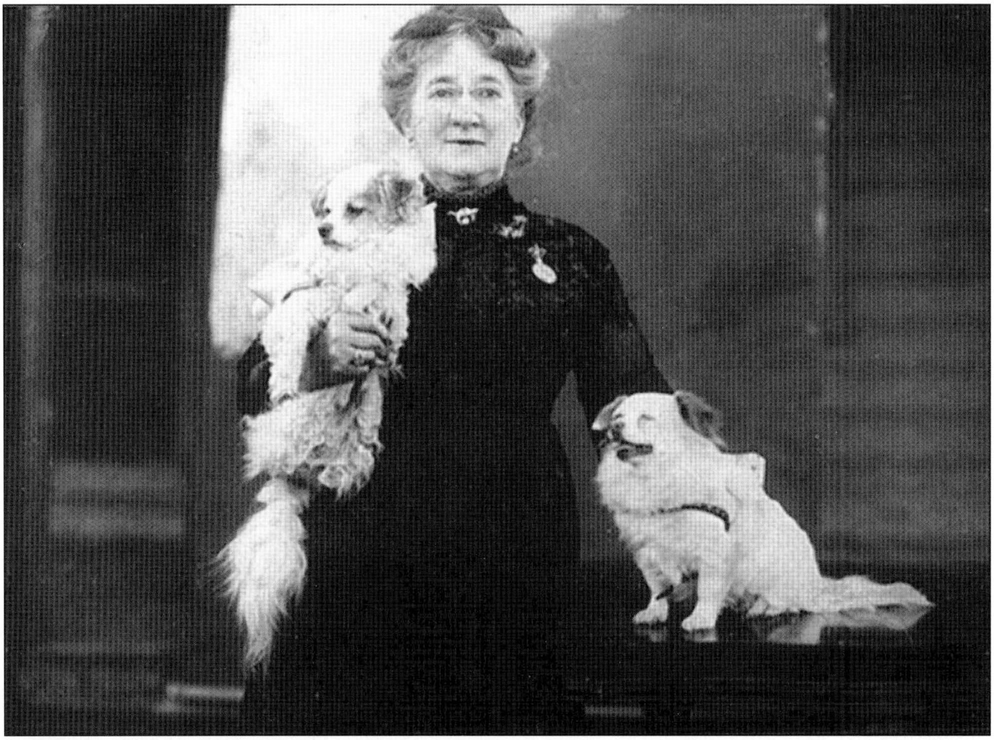

Mrs. Coyne and her precious pet dogs pose for the camera, *c.* 1900.

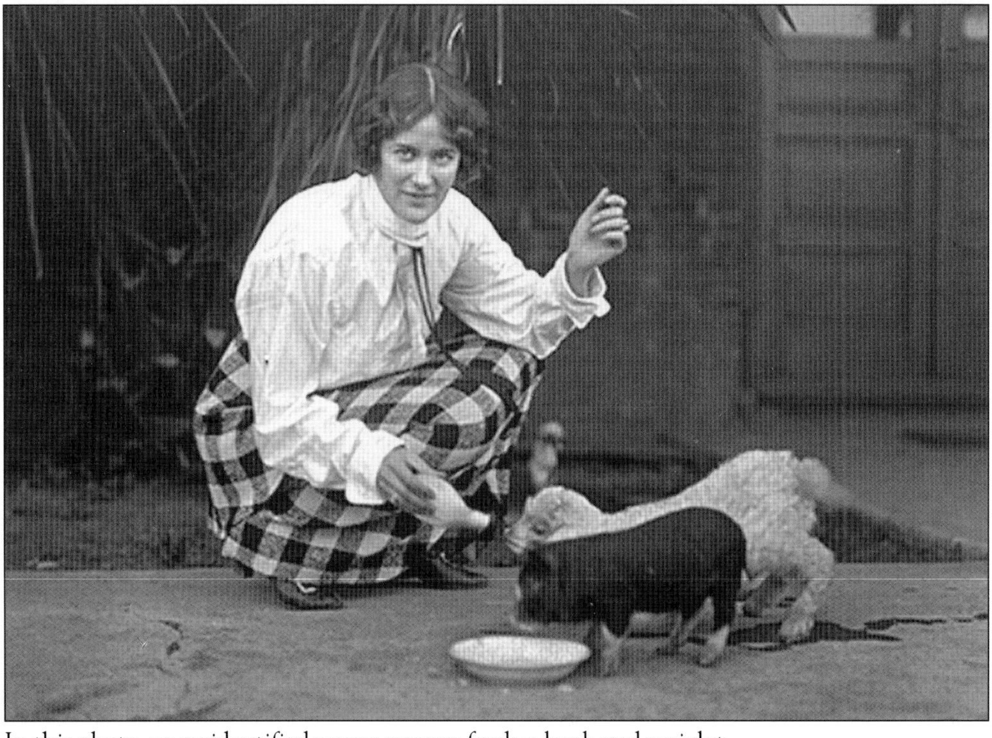

In this photo, an unidentified young woman feeds a lamb and a piglet.

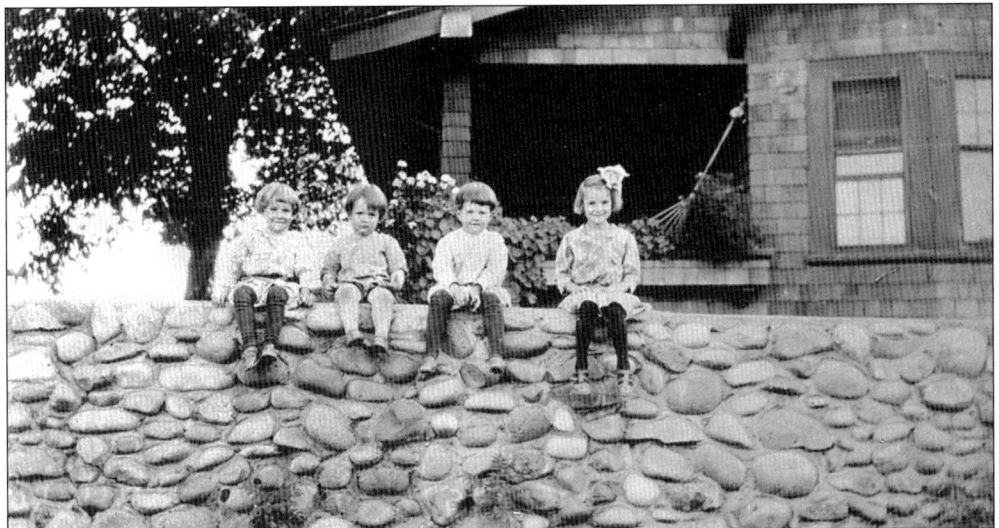

The four young children sitting on a rock wall at the Bush home at the northwest corner of Butte and Liberty Streets in this c. 1910 photo are, from left to right, George Bush, Alan Shirek, Rolfe Shirek, and Elizabeth Bush. The home is now the site of the Redding Medical Center.

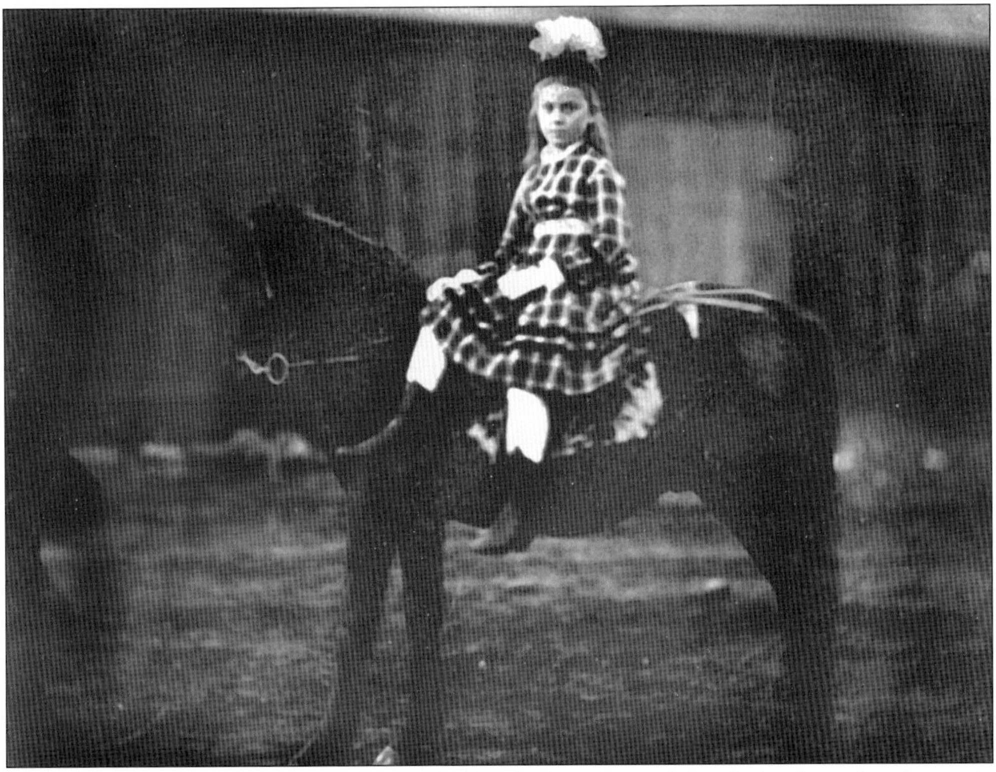

Jennie Bailey, shown here c. 1875, attended Little Pine Street School, the first schoolhouse in Redding, where she loved to dance and participate in theatrical performances. In 1883 she entered in the competition for the most beautiful girl in Shasta County. Jennie never married following the death of her fiancé, but worked as a janitor at the West Side Grammar School until it closed in 1937. She died in her family home on West Street at the age of 91.

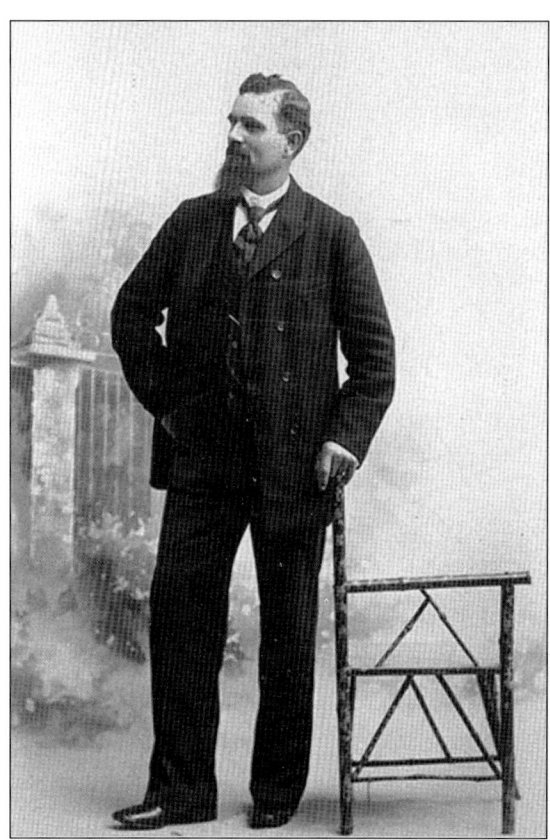

Herbert Bass operated a "tin" (hardware) store in the thriving town of Millville. He married Ida Powers in 1880 and the couple then moved to Montgomery Creek, where Herbert obtained a homestead and opened a hotel for teamsters and travelers. The Bass family moved to Redding in the 1890s and Herbert served two terms as a county supervisor.

Herbert and Ida Bass had five daughters. When the girls reached high school age, Bass built a home in Redding where they lived during the school term. The house still stands on Chestnut and Sacramento Streets.

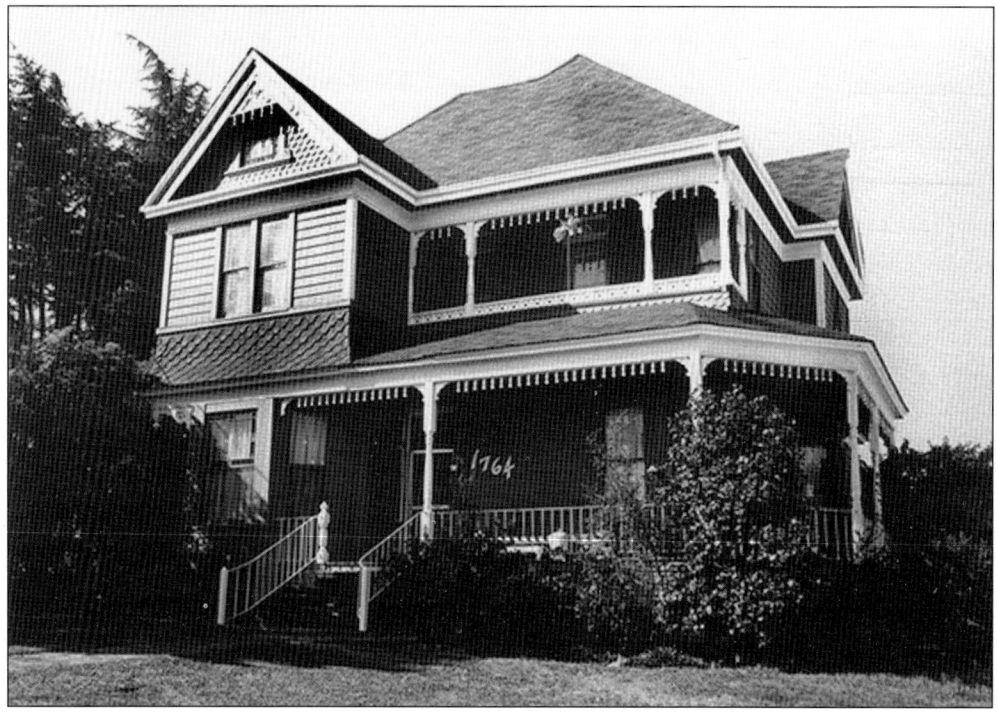

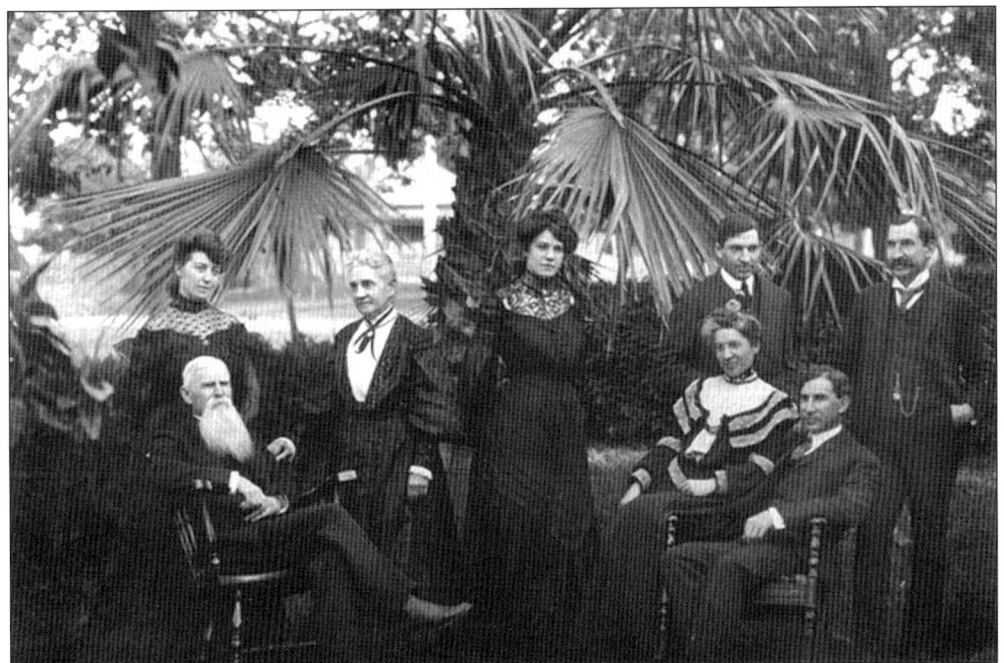

The Bass family, shown here in the front yard of their home on Chestnut and Sacramento Streets, are, from left to right, (standing) Annie Condon Bush, Eda Schroeder Bush, Tillie Helen Bush, Harry Bush, and Carroll Bush; (seated) Judge C.C. Bush, Eda Bush, and George Bush.

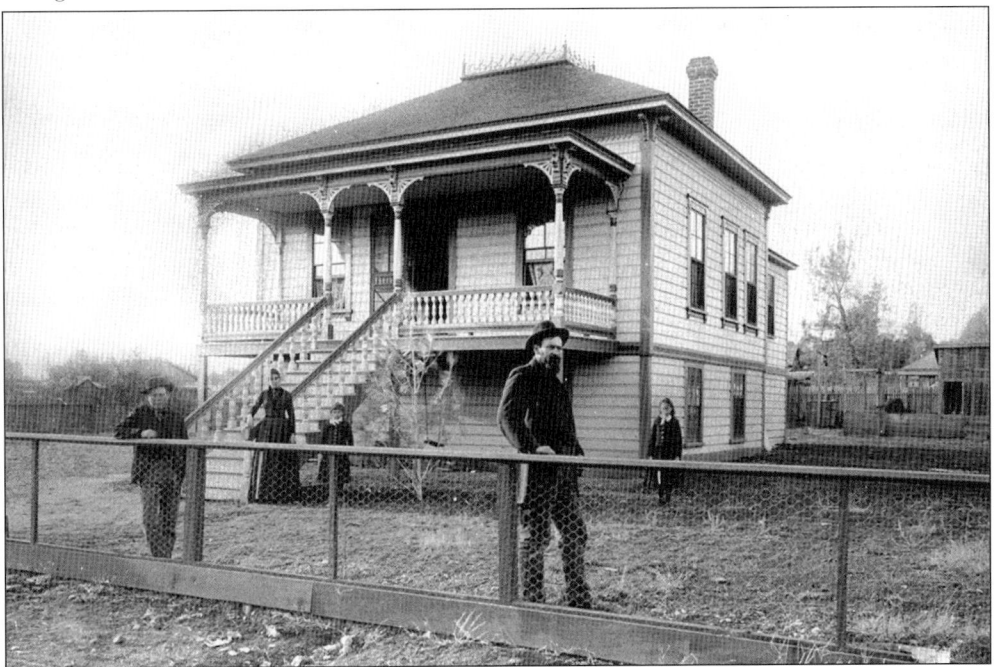

Mr. and Mrs. White and their children are shown in front of their Placer and Willis Streets home in Redding. The house was built around 1887 on three lots, which were purchased for a total of $50. Remodeled in 1978, the house is still standing.

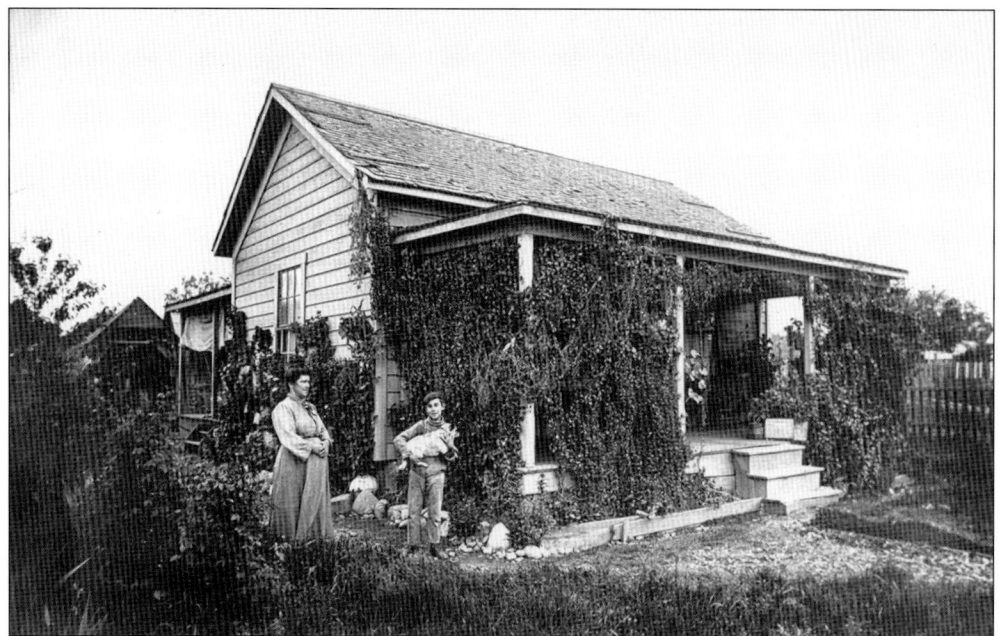

Edna "Frances" Orndorff Cantrell (holding dog) and her grandmother Victorine are shown in front of the Vige family home on Shasta Street.

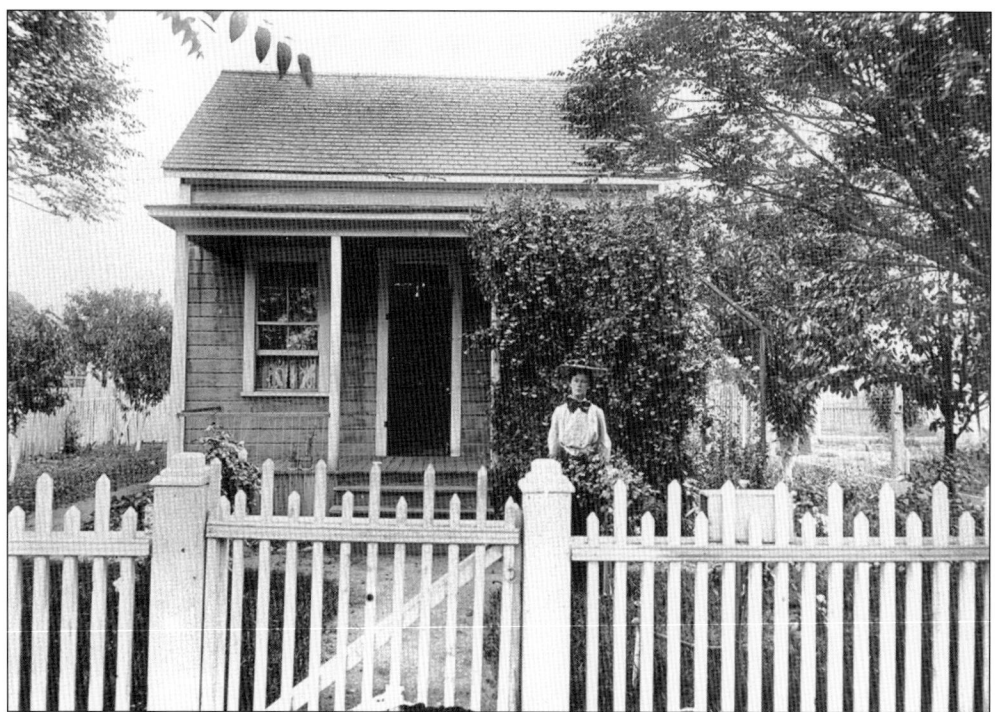

Christine Glover is shown in front of her first home on Pine Street in 1904. Her husband, Harry Glover, closed his blacksmith shop and opened a garage at Market and Placer Streets. Glover and Harry Cummings were Redding's first automobile dealers.

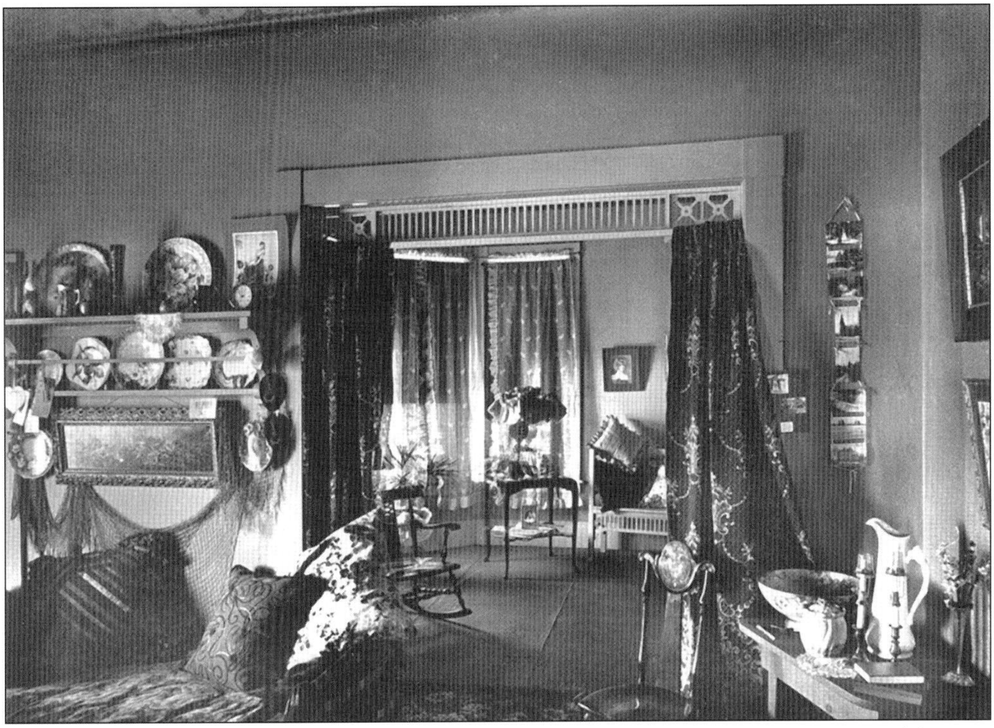

This rare 1900 photo of a home interior is of the Blodgett home on Gold Street in Redding.

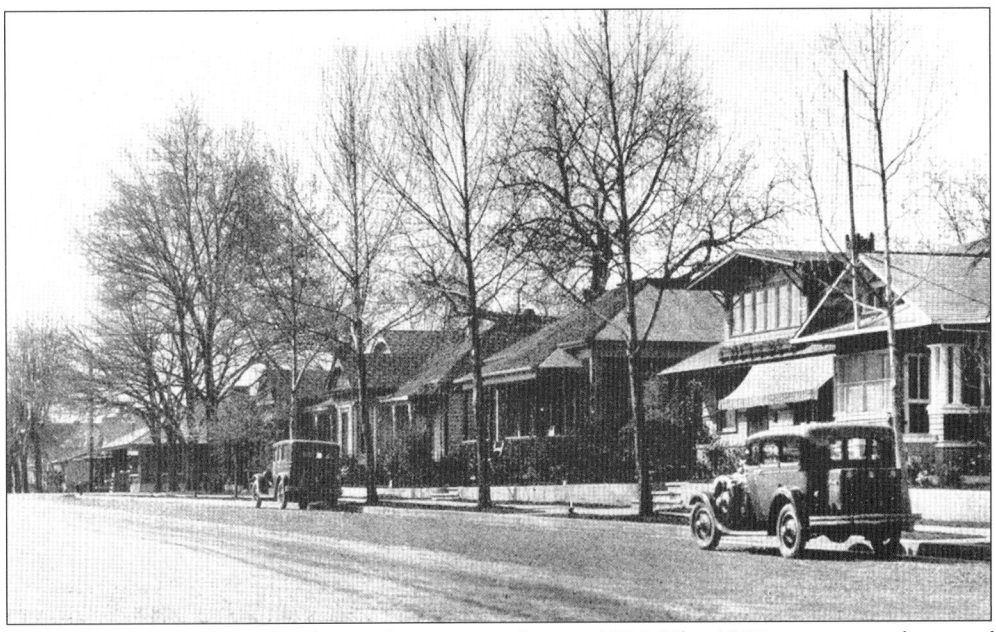

This view of the west side of Pine Street was taken c. 1926. The 1920s saw an explosion of automobiles on the streets of Redding. It became fashionable to own one or sometimes two cars.

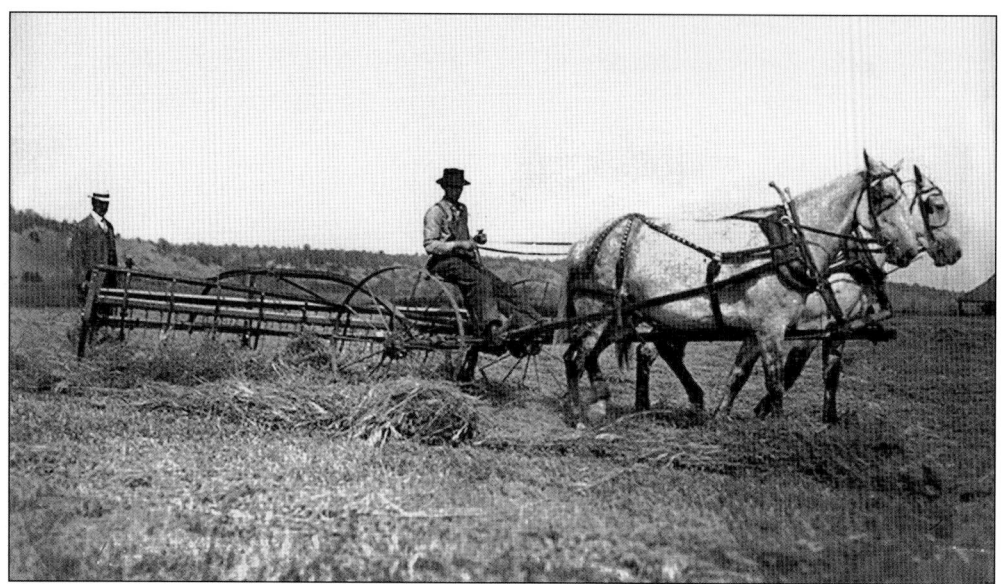

This 1920 photo shows crews haying on the Benton Ranch along the Sacramento River in Redding. The crews often boarded at the nearby Idanha Hotel.

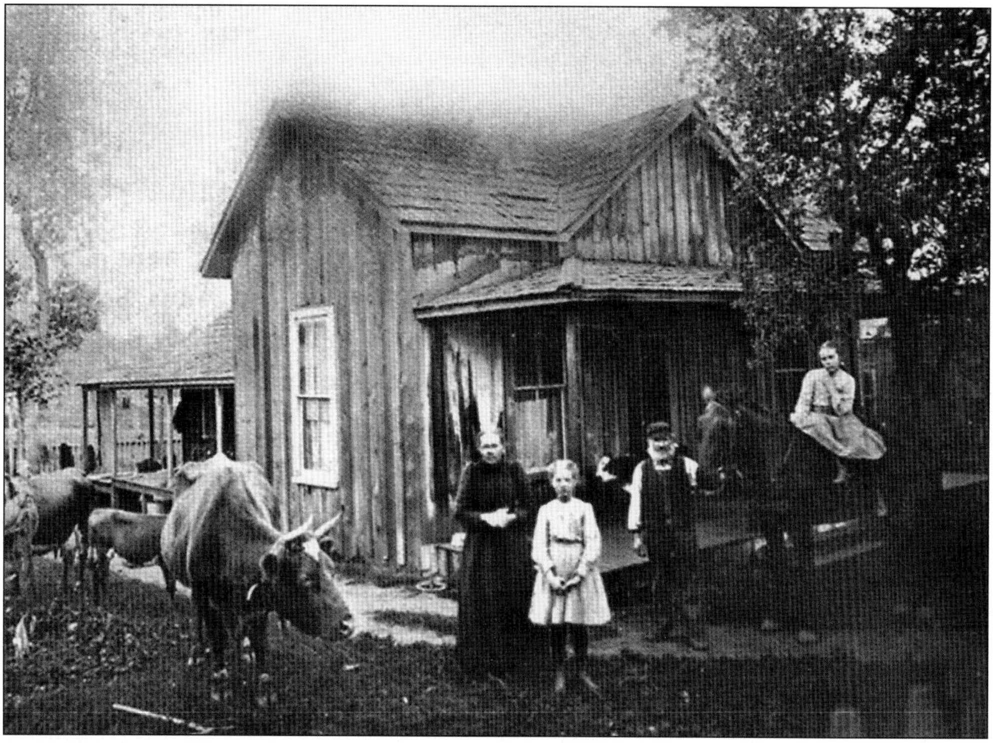

Anna Nottleman (center), daughter Frieda, husband John, and daughter Emma (seated on Prince) are seen at their Redding home in 1910. Shortly after the city incorporated in 1887, Nottleman settled on the property, where he built a house and barn, bought some cows, and began Nottleman's Dairy. Prince pulled the wagon that delivered the milk, which was kept in tin containers. Customers paid 5¢ a pint and 10¢ a quart.

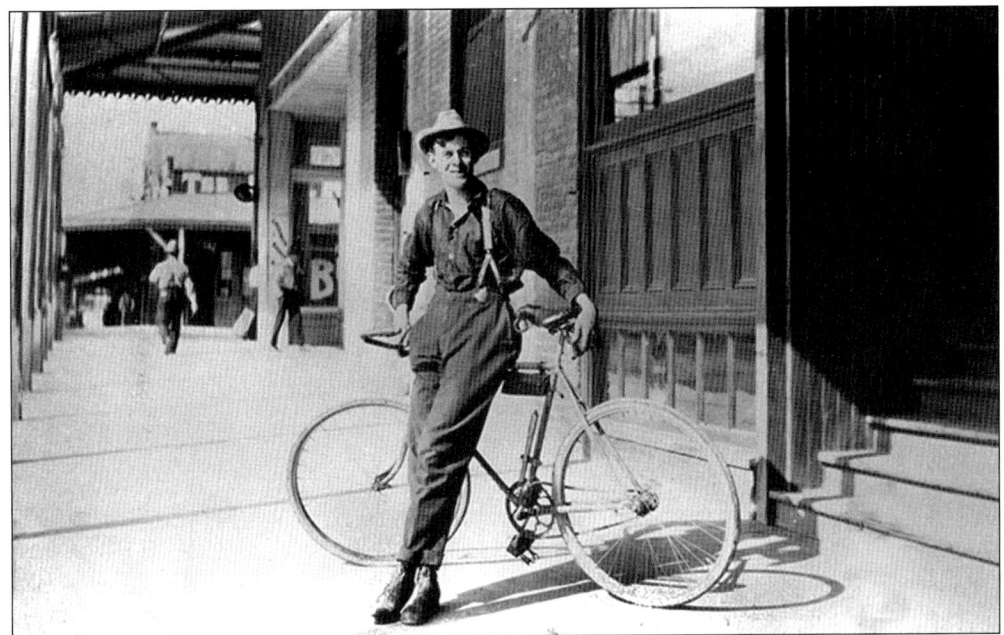

This 1910 photo shows telephone company linesman Jesse W. Moore in front of the telephone company office on California Street.

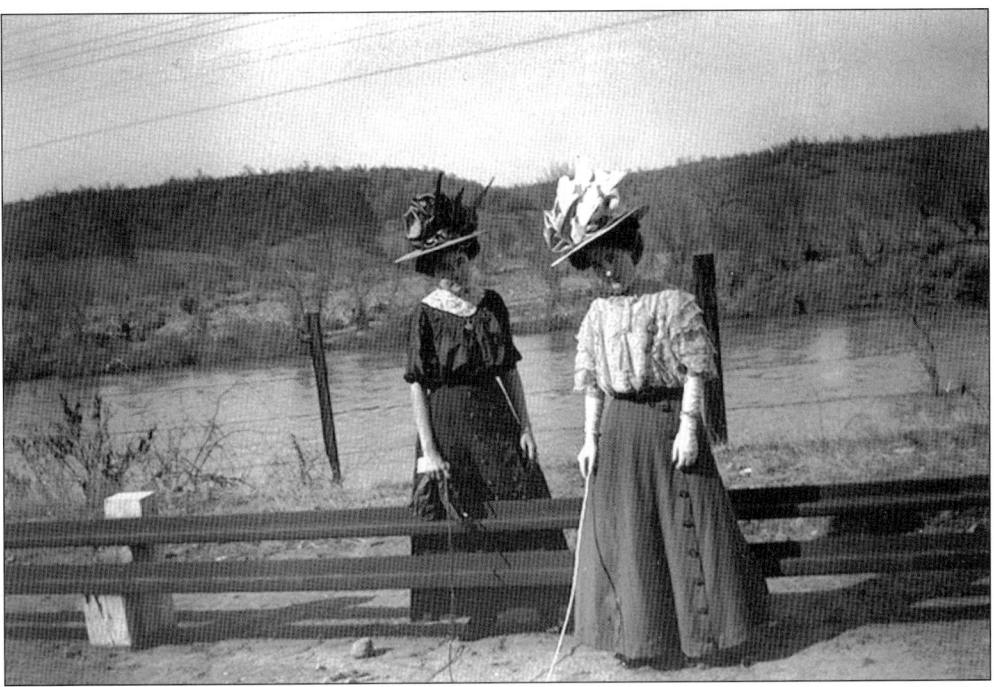

These two ladies are very proud of their fancy hats as they walk along the south bank of the Sacramento River above the Diestelhorst Bridge.

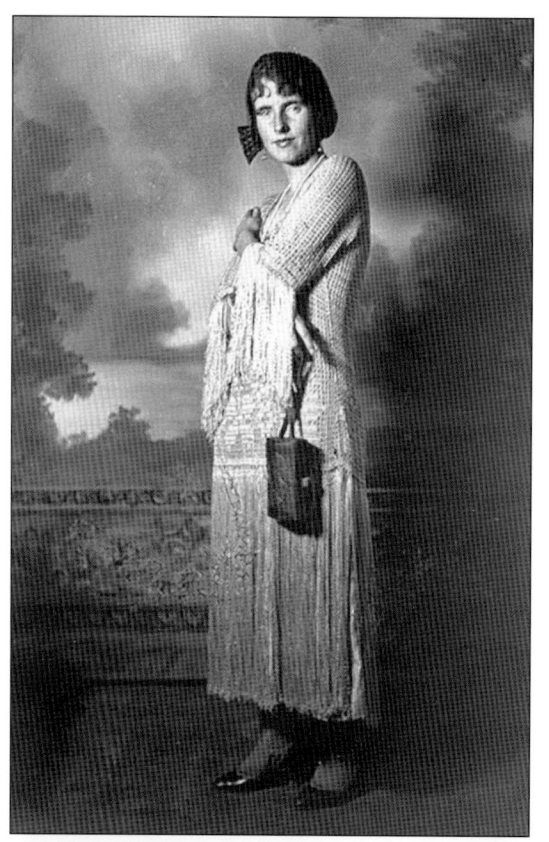

This 1924 photo is of Melba Quirk Neal, a member of a pioneer family in Shasta County who was born in Ono. Melba was a 1923 graduate of Shasta High School and two years later married Virgil Neal. In the 1920s and 1930s she was employed by the *Courier-Free Press*, later the *Shasta Courier*. In the 1940s she worked for the draft boards of Redding and Northern California and was a dispatcher for the California Highway Patrol until her retirement in 1969.

The Frank and Anna Sprague Rose home at 1444 Chestnut Street is shown here with a 1925 Chevrolet in front. Frank was a miner before he came to Redding.

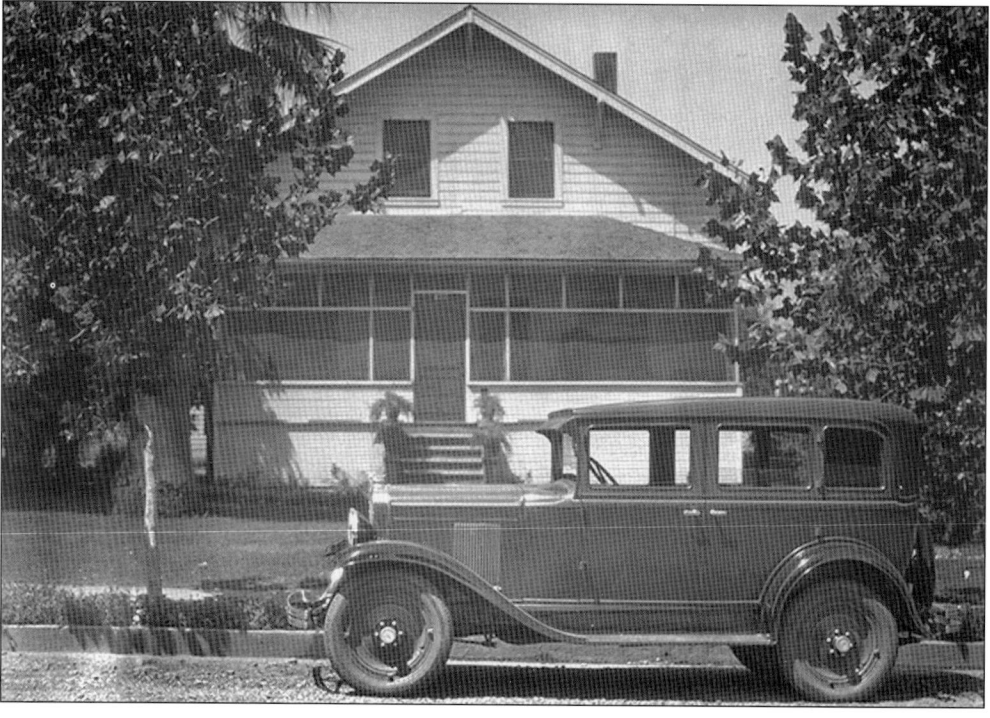

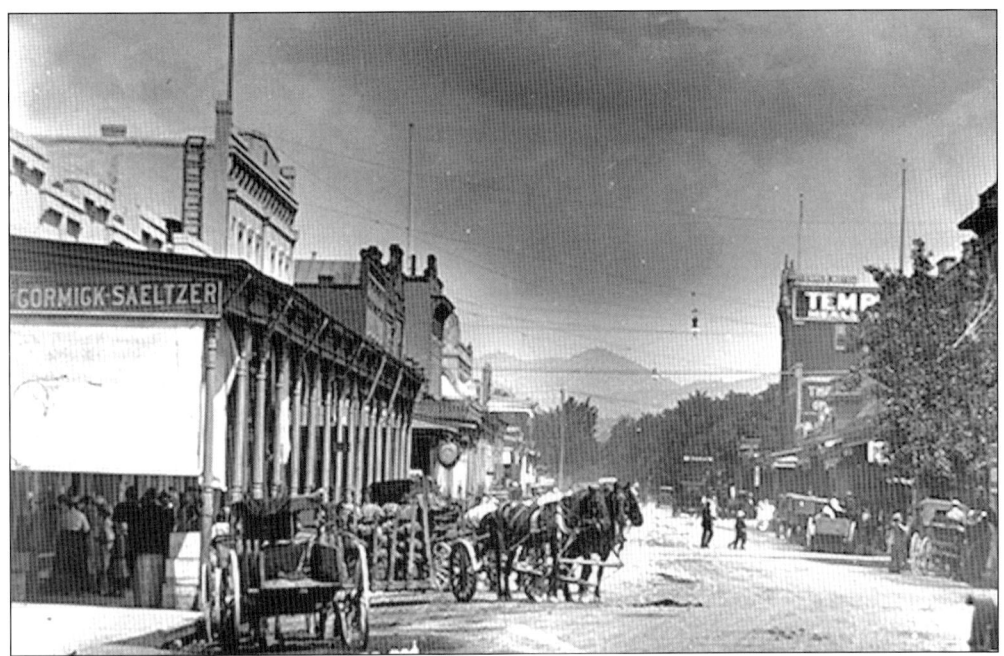

This photo of Market Street, taken before 1915, shows the McCormick-Saeltzer store on the west side of the street and the Temple Hotel on the east side. After the turn of the century, the first automobile appeared. By 1906 there were six automobiles in Redding; the first one was owned by Supervisor Ferdinand Hurst.

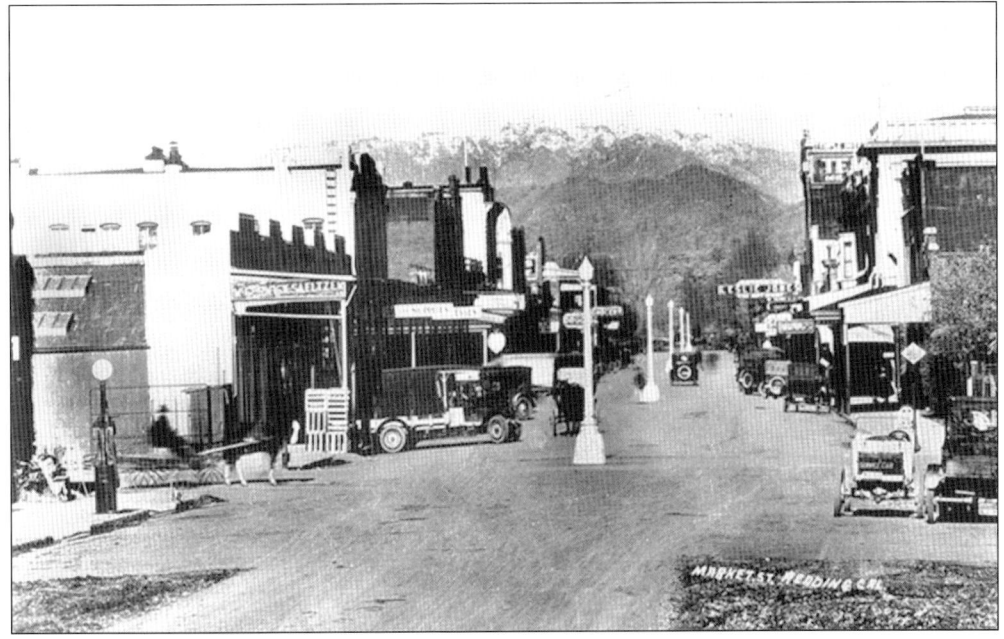

Market Street after 1915 was still unpaved and had streetlamps down the middle. The first automobiles were serviced in blacksmith shops, but in 1908 James Wright, a former machinist with the Mountain Copper Mining Company, opened Redding's first garage just south of the city hall.

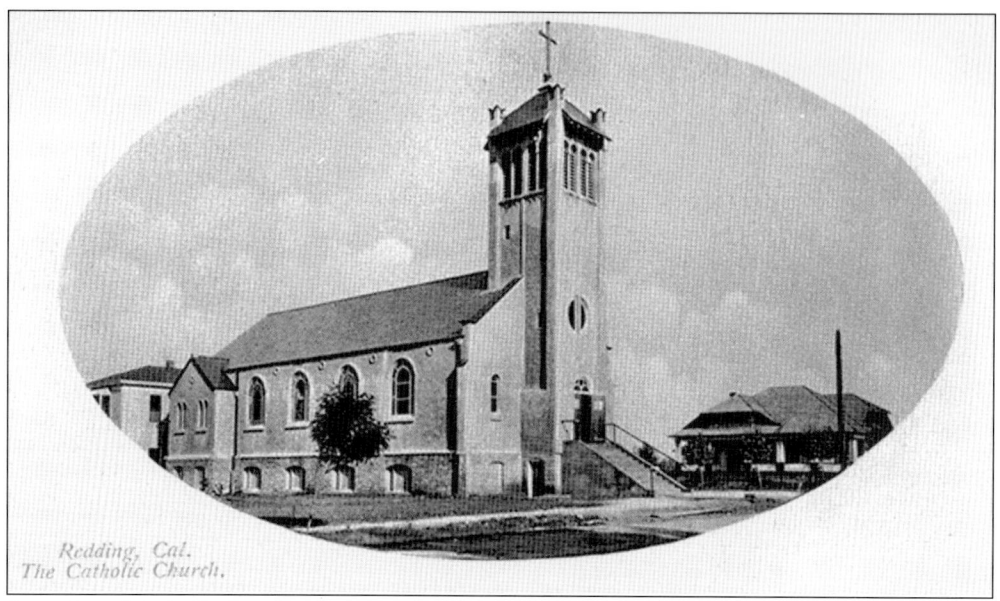

Saint Joseph's Catholic church was erected in 1884 at a cost of $2,000. The first mass was celebrated there in 1885. In 1905 a second Saint Joseph's church was built and had a steeple that soared 100 feet into the air. The building was destroyed by fire in 1908. The church pictured here was built in 1910 and burned in 1964.

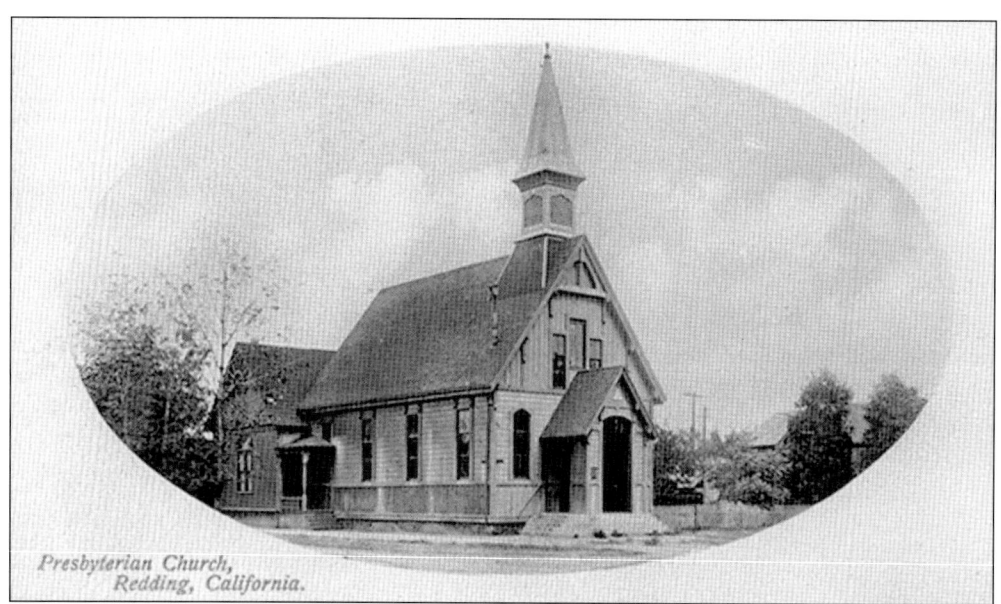

This Presbyterian church was dedicated in 1881 and had a 300-pound bell that was donated by B.B. Redding, the railroad agent for whom the town of Redding was named. The church burned in 1915 and was rebuilt in 1916; meanwhile services were held in the Pine Street schoolhouse. Judge C.C. Bush's wife led the choir.

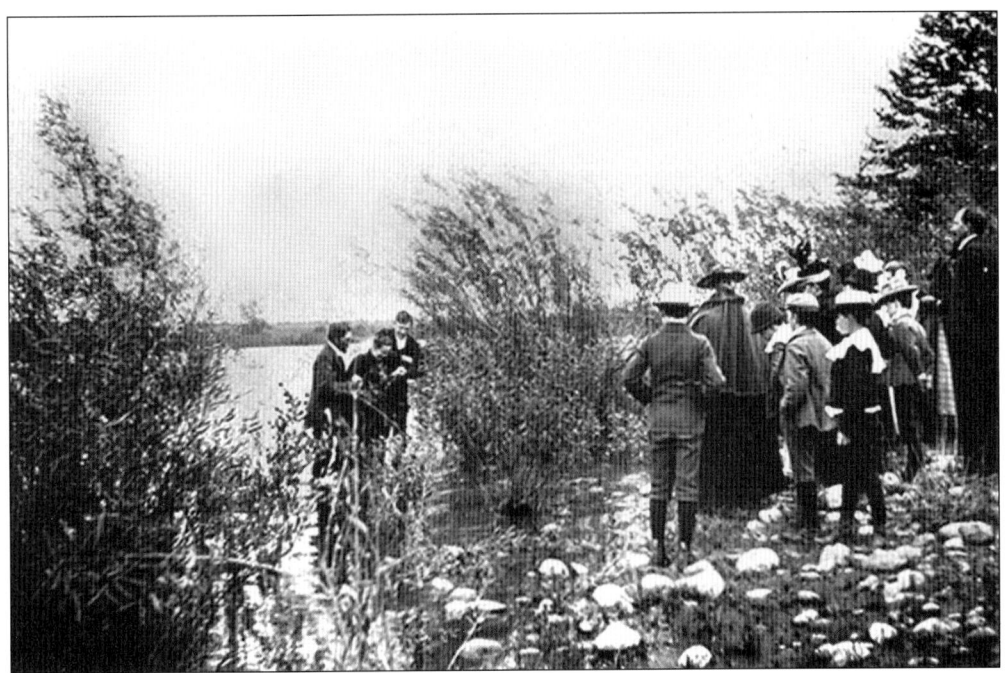
A spring baptism is performed in the cold Sacramento River, c. 1910.

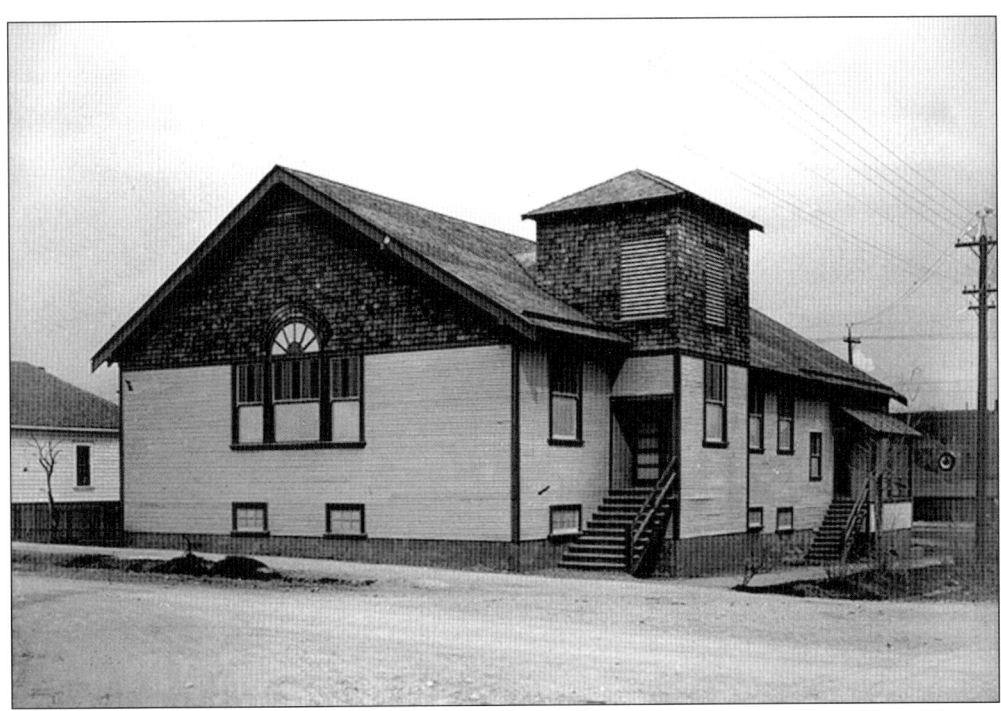
The first Baptist church of Redding was organized in 1887 by Rev. W.S. Kidder of Ono. He was the first pastor and, along with his wife and several of their children, was a member of a Baptist church organization called "Ono." This photo shows the Baptist church c. 1920.

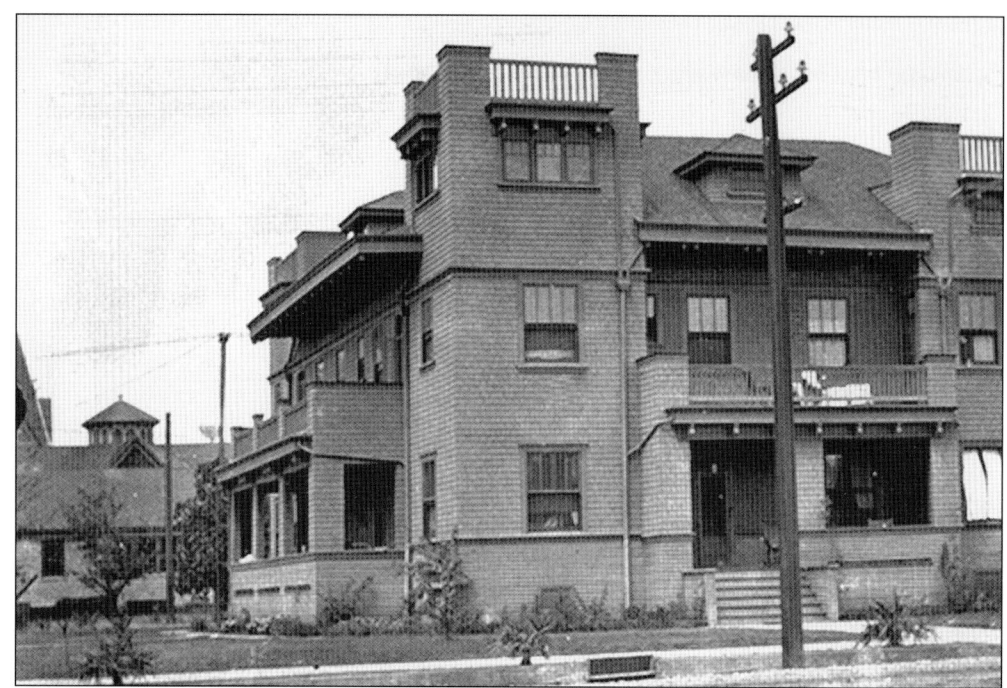

Saint Caroline Hospital and Training School was built in 1907 at Sacramento and Pine Streets in Redding. The $25,000 building was financed by Redding business owners and named after the mother of Dr. Ferdinand Stabel, one of the hospital's founders. Fire destroyed the building in 1909, and it was rebuilt at the same location in 1910. In 1944 the Sisters of Mercy, which operates Mercy Medical Center in Redding, bought the hospital.

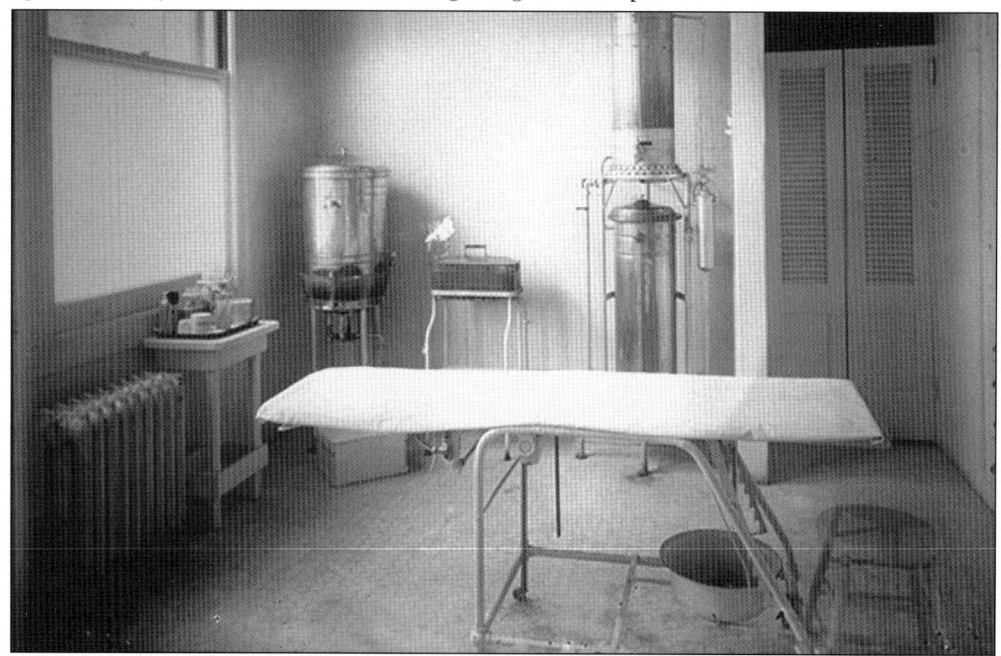

This photo shows the antechamber to the surgery room at Saint Caroline Hospital, a far cry from the modern facilities we enjoy today.

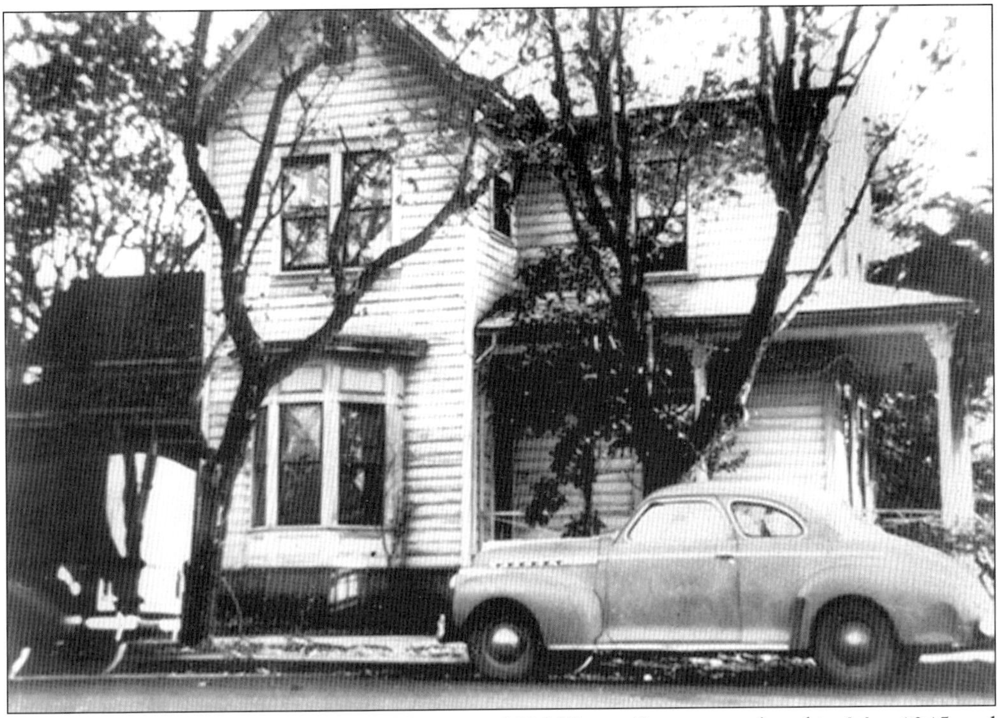

Mrs. Anderson's Redding Maternity Home on 2009 Placer Street was closed in May 1945 and converted into an apartment house when Dr. Wyatt's Memorial Hospital opened on the corner of East and Butte Streets.

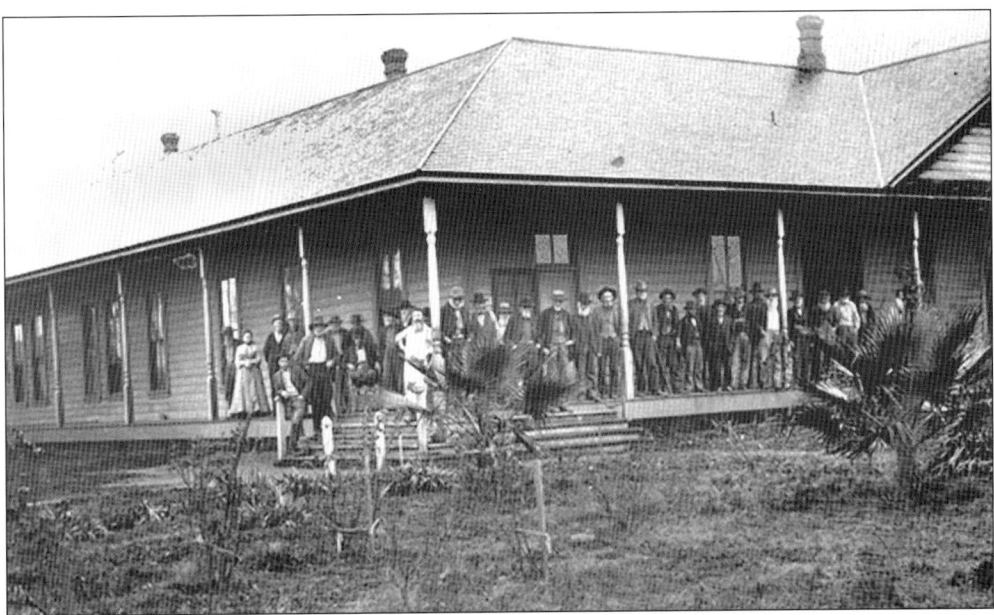

A crowd gathers on the porch of the Shasta County Hospital in this 1902 photo. In 1898 the county board of supervisors bought land south of Redding for the hospital, which cost $9,400 to build. The facility served the county as a hospital until 1934 and then as an almshouse until 1957. The county health department building, completed in 1959, now stands on the site.

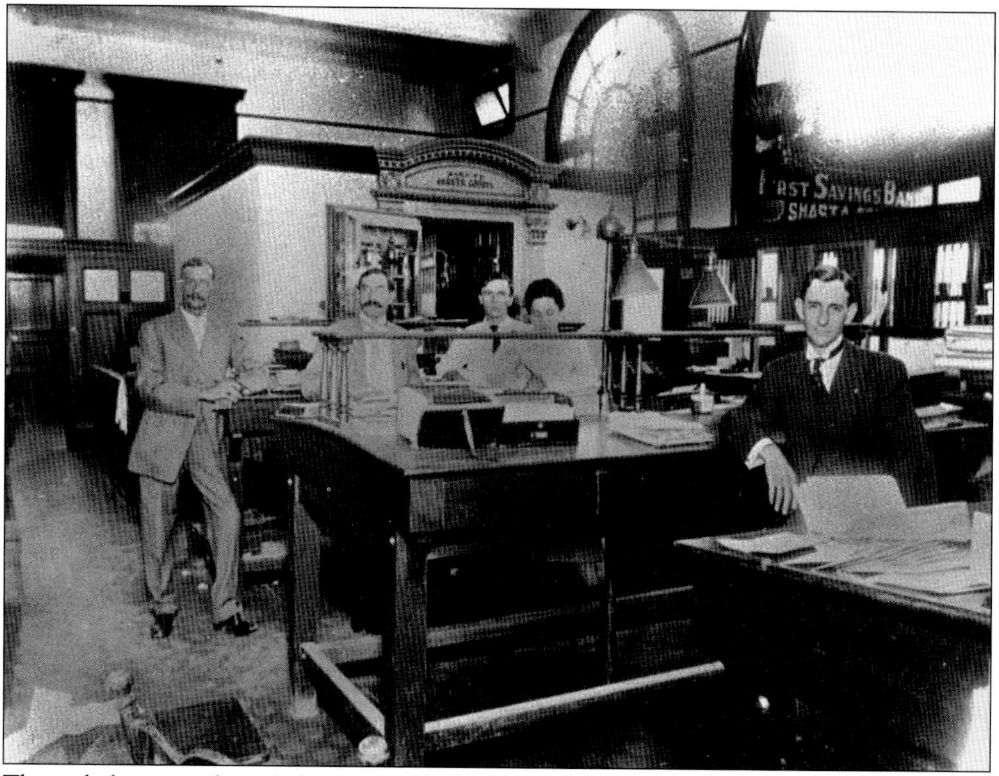

These clerks are ready to do business as they wait for customers in the Redding National Bank, c. 1912.

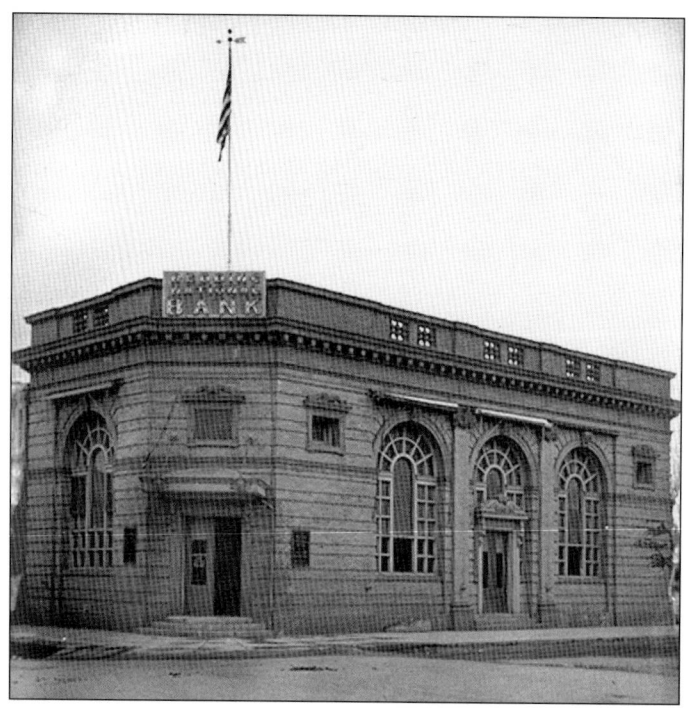

Redding National Bank was built in 1901 by the Holt and Gregg Brick Company. The building still stands at 1459 Market Street. Failing in 1911, it was purchased by the Bank of Italy, which later became the Bank of America. Pictured here in 1914, the building is the second oldest in Redding.

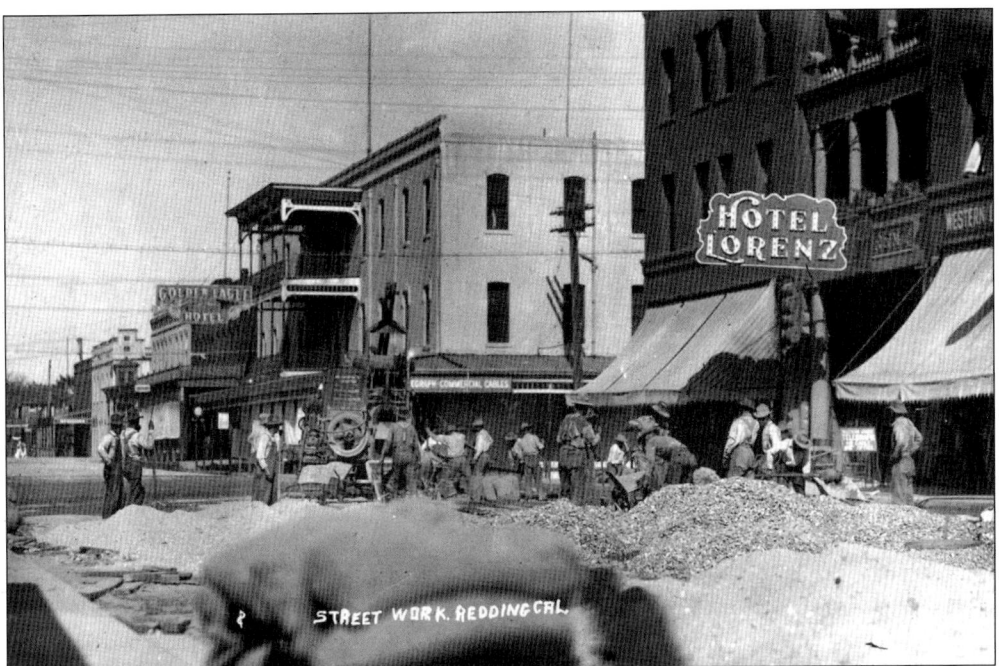

Street work with a paving machine is conducted on Yuba Street in front of the Lorenz Hotel, c. 1920. Note the man on the left leaning on his shovel. (Courtesy of Richard Lorenz.)

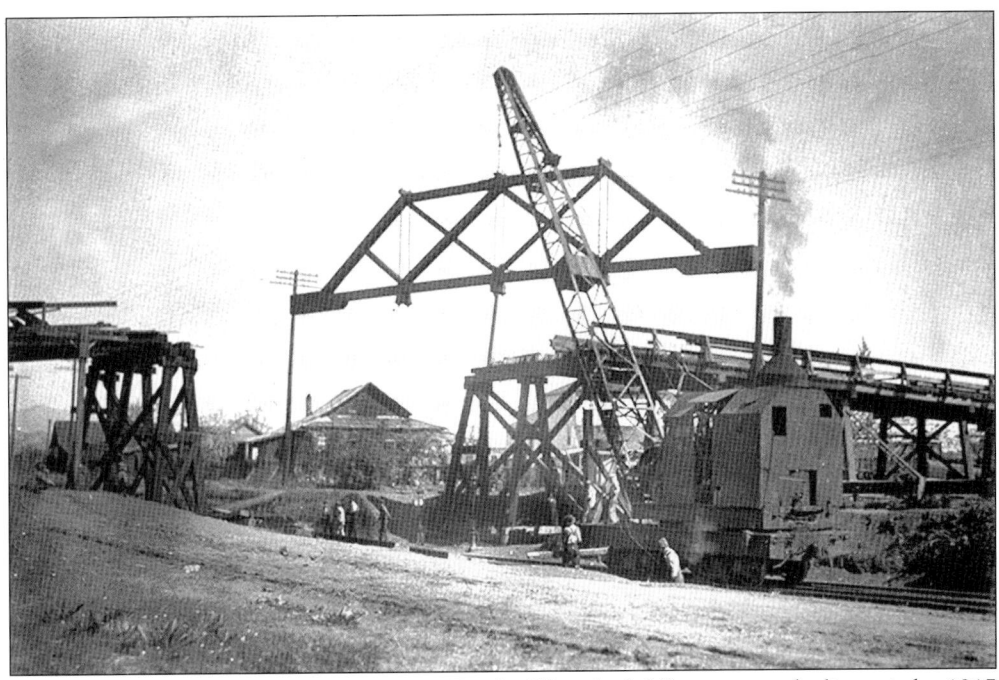

The over-crossing on North Street, now Eureka Way, had fallen into such disrepair by 1917 that it had to be rebuilt. A steam-powered crane was used in the project. Originally built in 1903, the Redding bridge was designed only for horse-drawn vehicles.

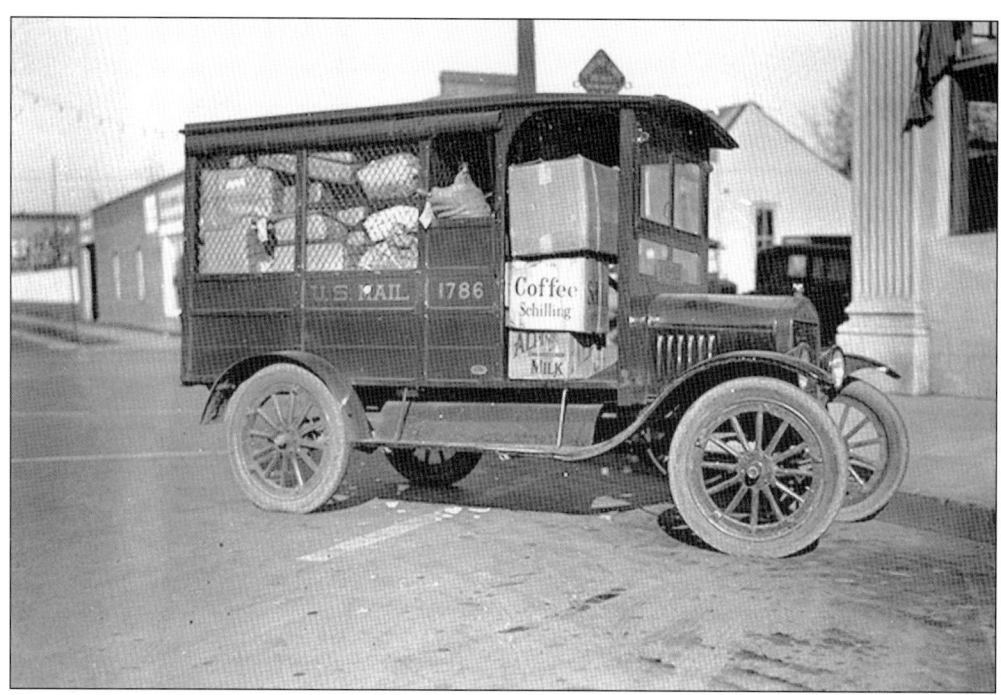

This Ford Model T mail truck, laden with packages, stands in front of the Redding Post Office at the southeast corner of California and Tehama Streets, c. 1920.

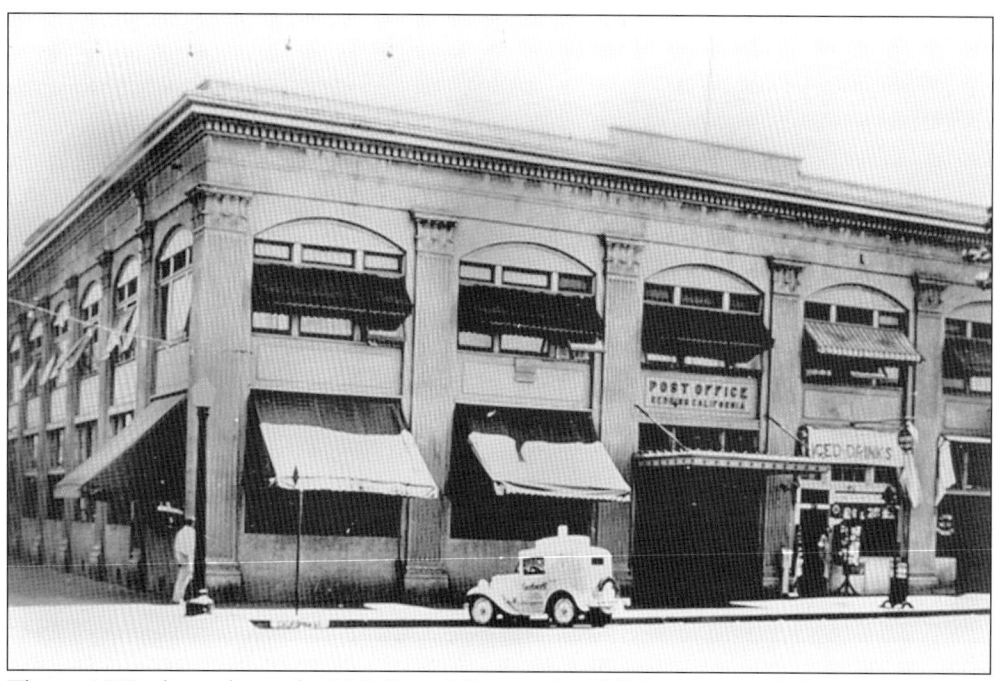

This c. 1920 photo shows the U.S. Post Office in the Hill Building on Tehama Street. The truck in front has a "Gerbers" iced drinks sign painted on its side.

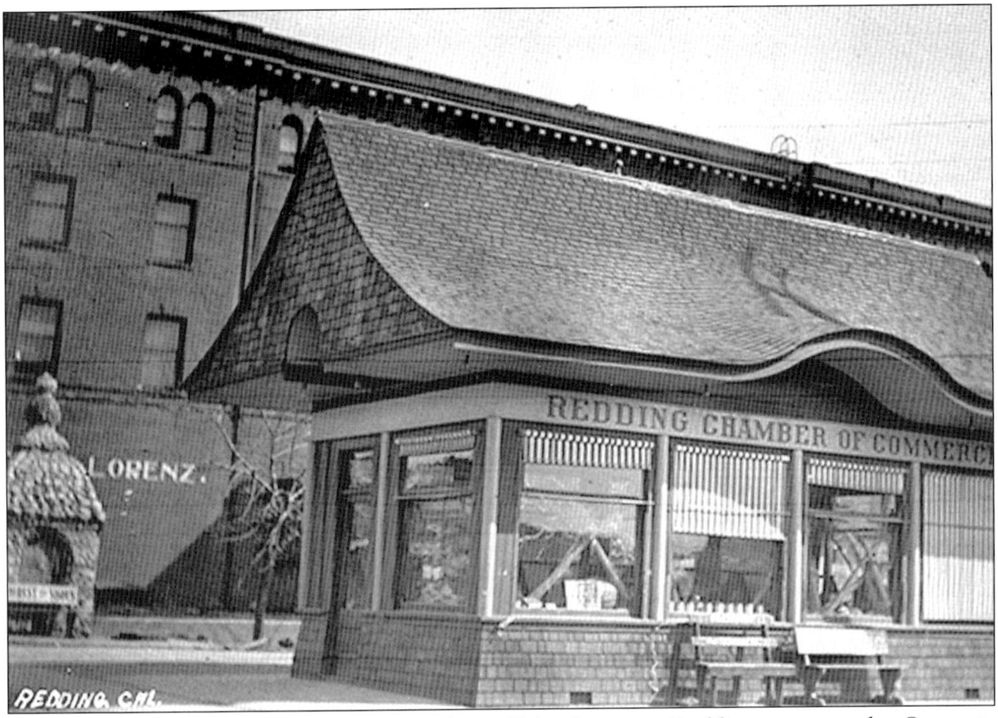

The chamber of commerce building stands on Yuba Street in Redding, next to the Carnegie Library. The chamber was organized in 1910, with Dudley Saeltzer as its first president. The Lorenz Hotel is in the background.

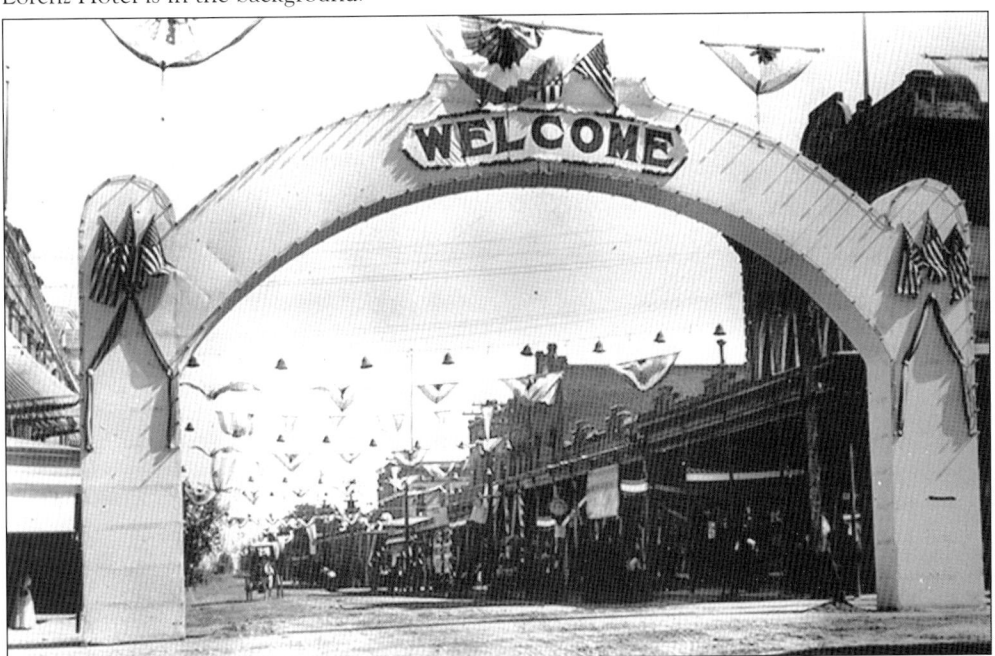

The "Welcome to Redding" arch on Market Street, looking south from Butte Street, was erected by the Fraternal Order of Eagles for their convention, c. 1895. The IOOF building on the right is still in use today.

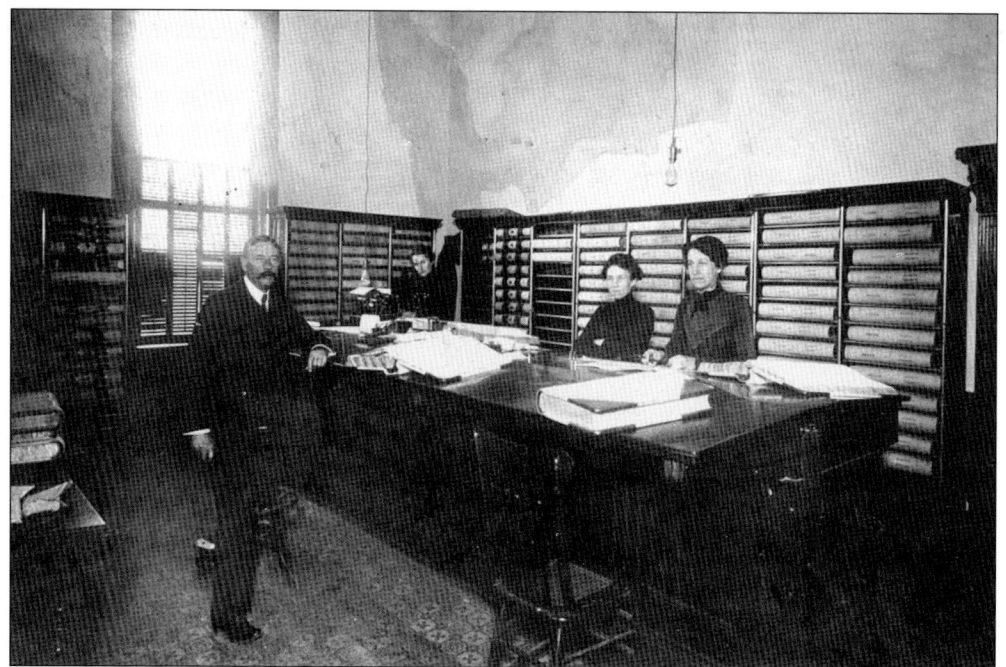

John R. Lowden, county recorder, is shown in the old courthouse before the hall of records was built, c. 1901. The women in the photo, from left to right, are Martha Moss, Stella Breslauer, and Jennie Thompson.

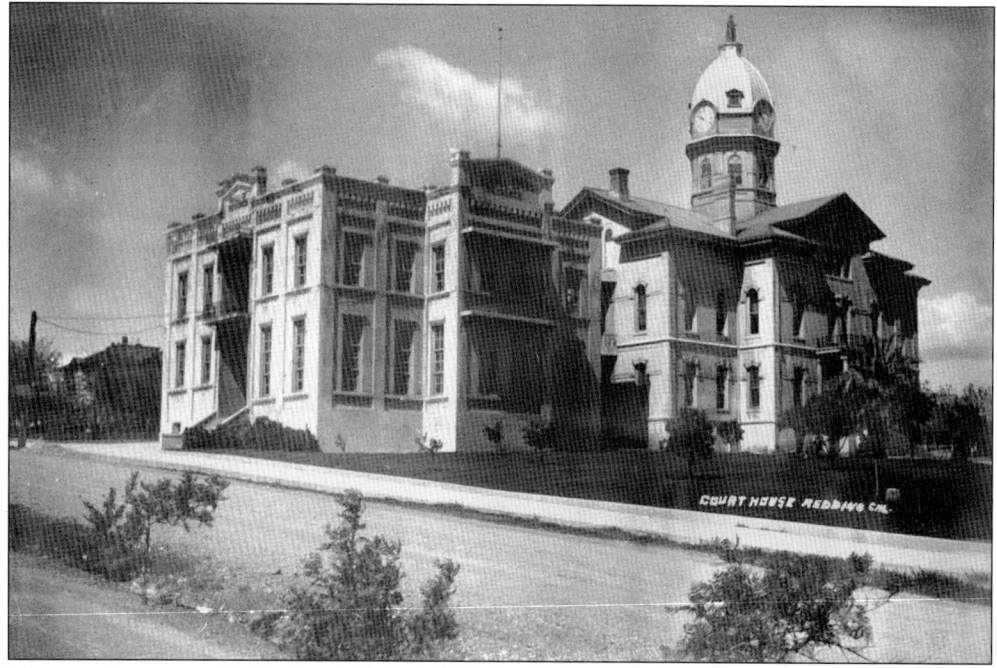

The courthouse and hall of records stood on Court Street with Lady Liberty atop the clock tower. The hall of records was built in 1906 at a cost of $35,000 and was designed by Robert Reading. The Redding Brick & Tile Company used this photo in a promotional album extolling "the clay found in this district."

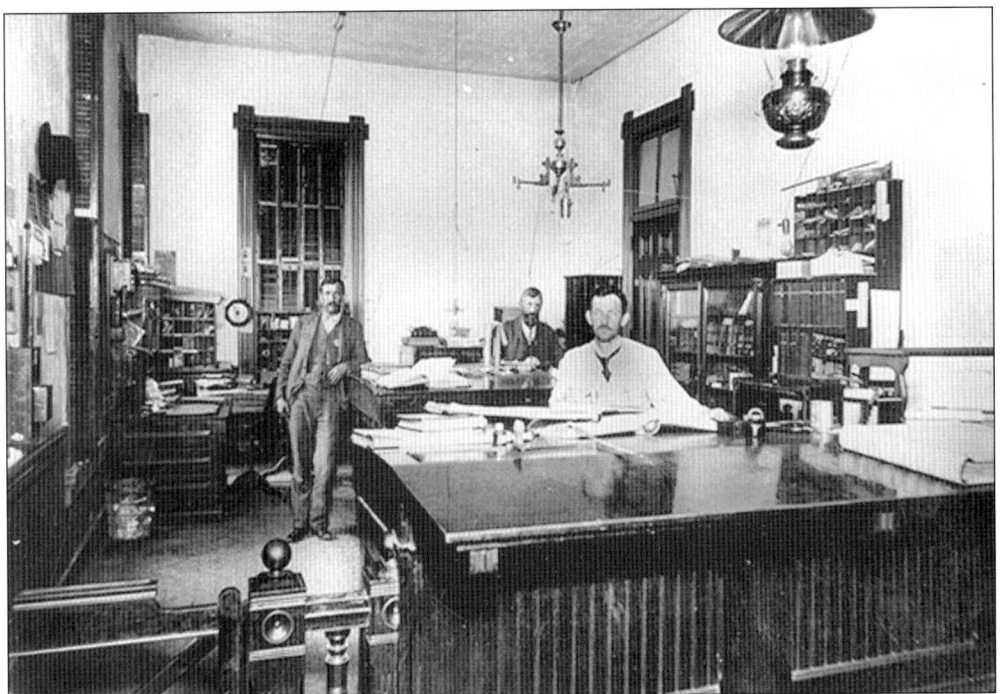

Charles Behrens (left) was sheriff of Shasta County between 1899 and 1903. Undersheriff James Richardson is in the background of this c. 1899 interior view of the Shasta County Sheriff's Office.

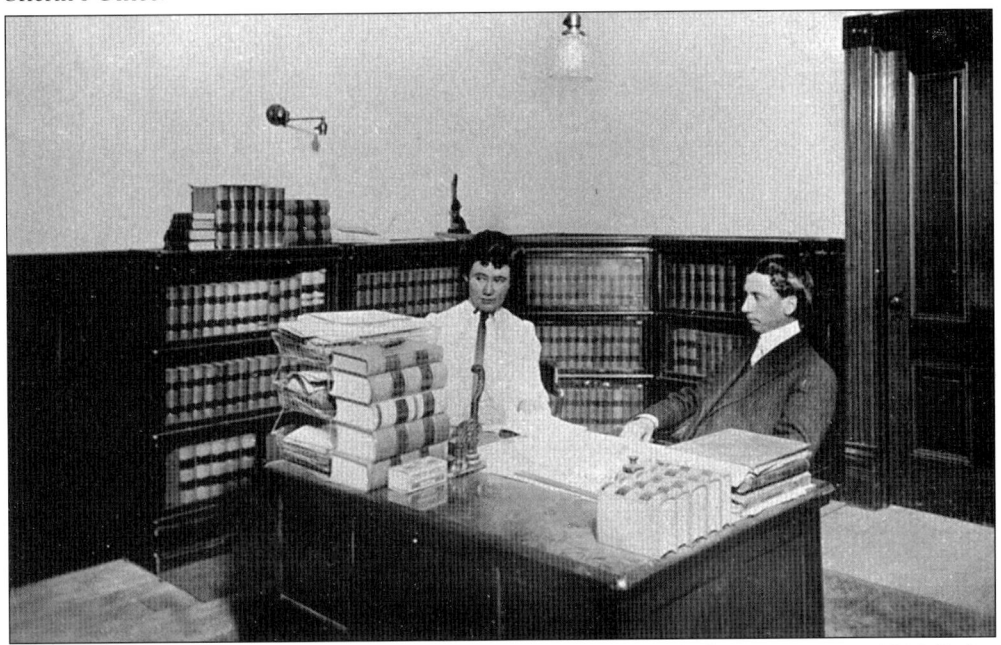

Judge Francis Carr is shown seated at his desk with Jennie Woods, his secretary, in 1908. Judge Carr participated in the litigation involving water rights that followed the early hydro-electric power development. He and his firm served as council in many cases in which the principles of water law in California were settled by the Supreme Court.

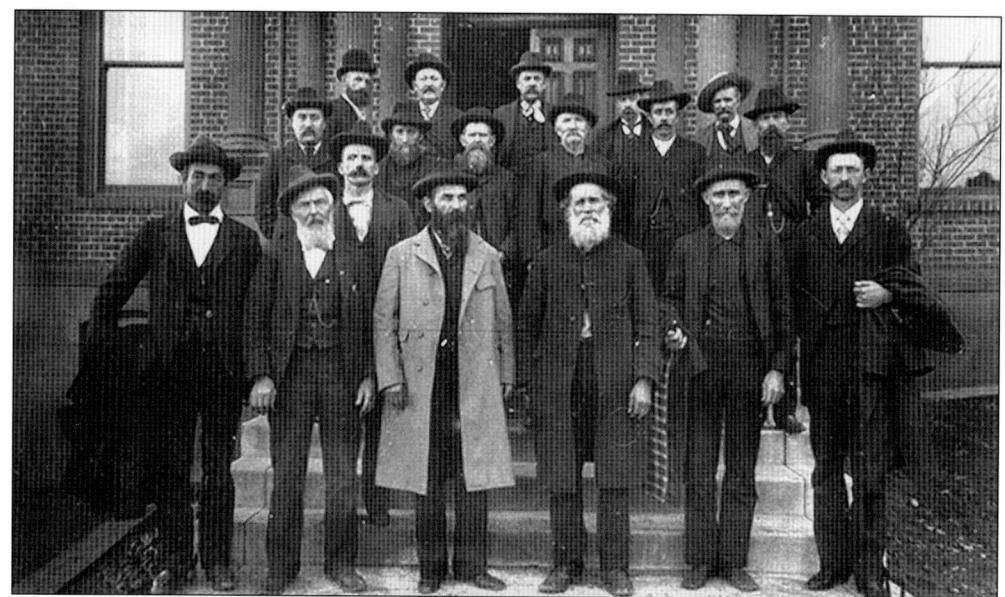

The Shasta County Grand Jury is shown in front of Redding City Hall on December 19, 1897. Bernard Klukkert is on the left in the front row.

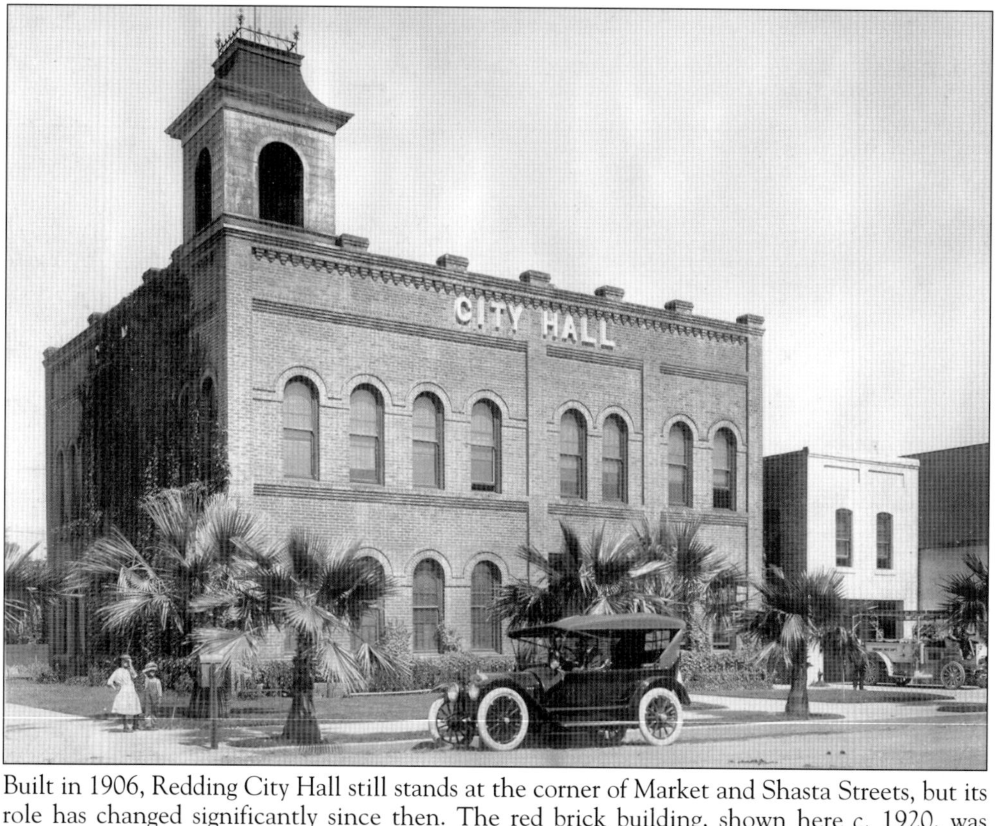

Built in 1906, Redding City Hall still stands at the corner of Market and Shasta Streets, but its role has changed significantly since then. The red brick building, shown here c. 1920, was restored in 1987 and is now used as an art gallery and theater. It once housed a jail, the police department, a wedding chapel, city council chambers, and all of the city's offices until 1979.

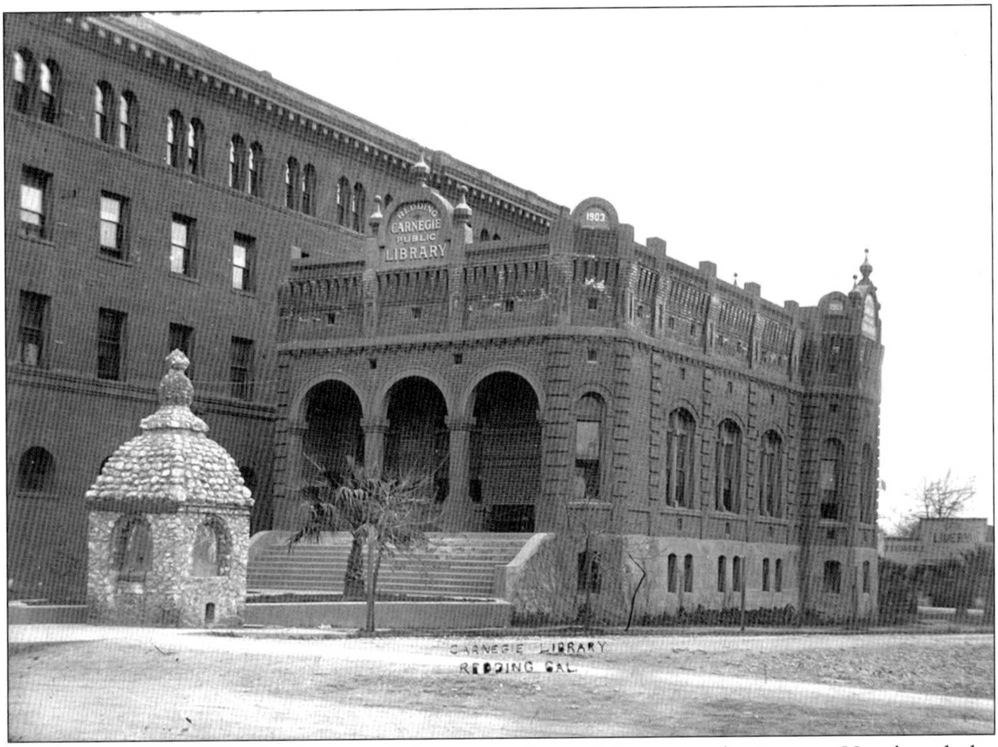

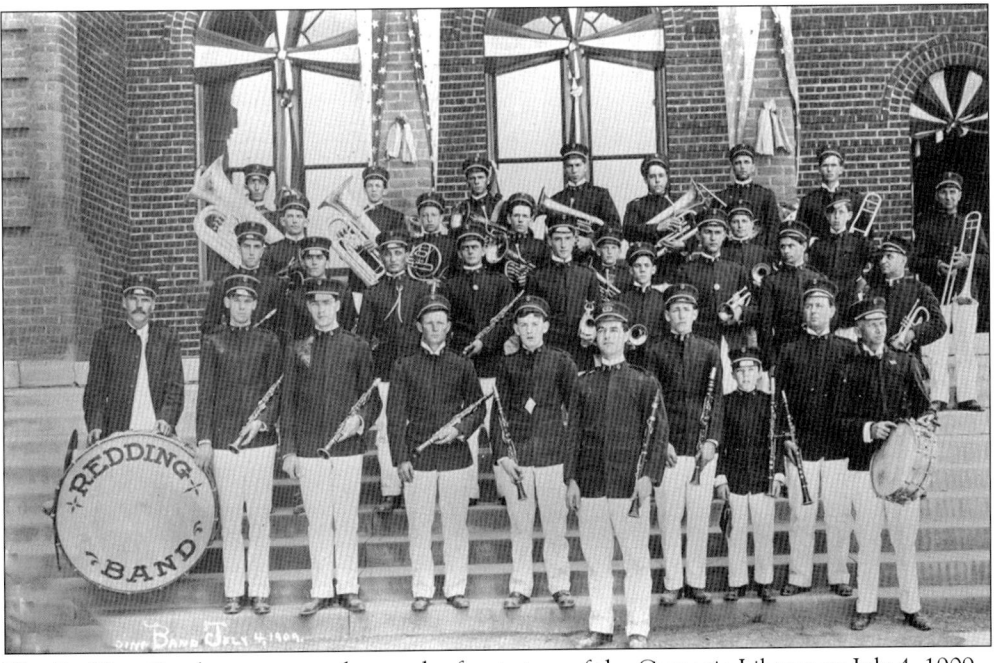

Built in 1906, Redding's Carnegie Library was located between the Lorenz Hotel and the chamber of commerce building on the south side of Yuba Street between California Street and the railroad tracks. In 1962 the library moved to its present location at 1855 Shasta Street.

The Redding Band prepares to play on the front steps of the Carnegie Library on July 4, 1909.

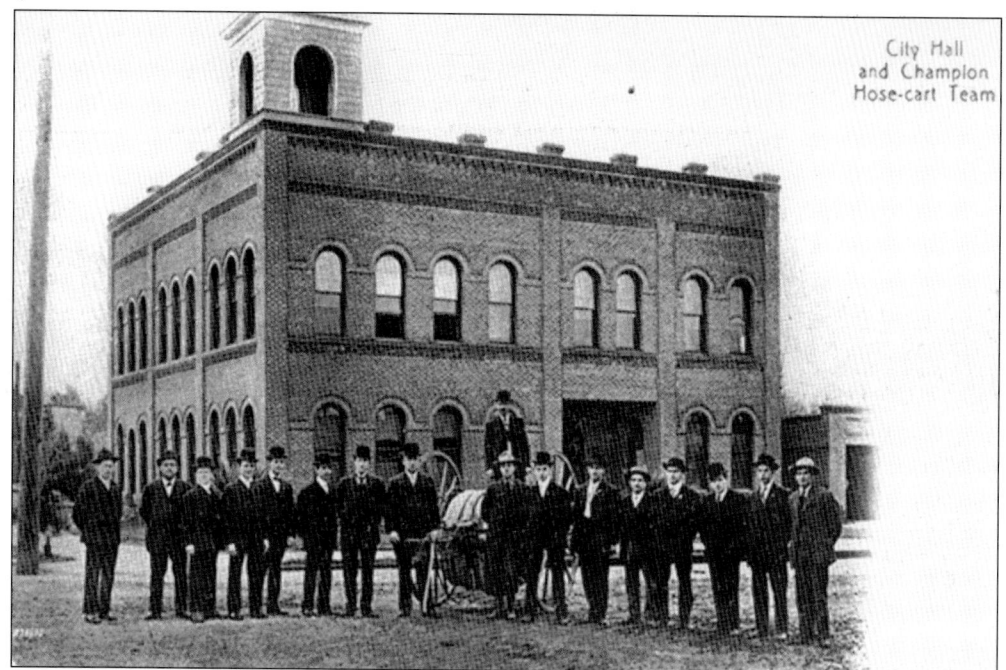

The men of the Champion Hose-Cart Team pose with their wheeled hose cart in front of city hall, c. 1906.

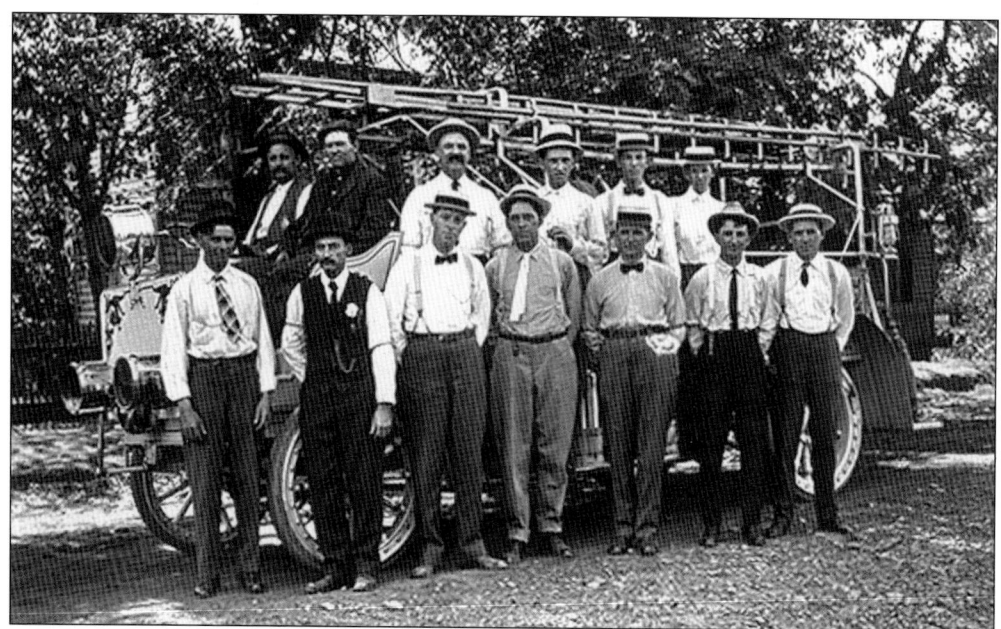

The Redding Fire Department Hose Company poses with its truck, the first automotive fire rig owned by the department, c. 1920. Shown, from left to right, are (front row) Joe Streife (grocer), A.M. Dick (Elbert's father), Pop Smith (police), Camille Brouillard (Redding Laundry), James Glazer, unidentified, and Dudley Saeltzer; (back row) Jim Wright (driver), Chief Poole, Ralph Saeltzer, Harry Glover, two unidentified men, and Frank Dick (Elbert's brother).

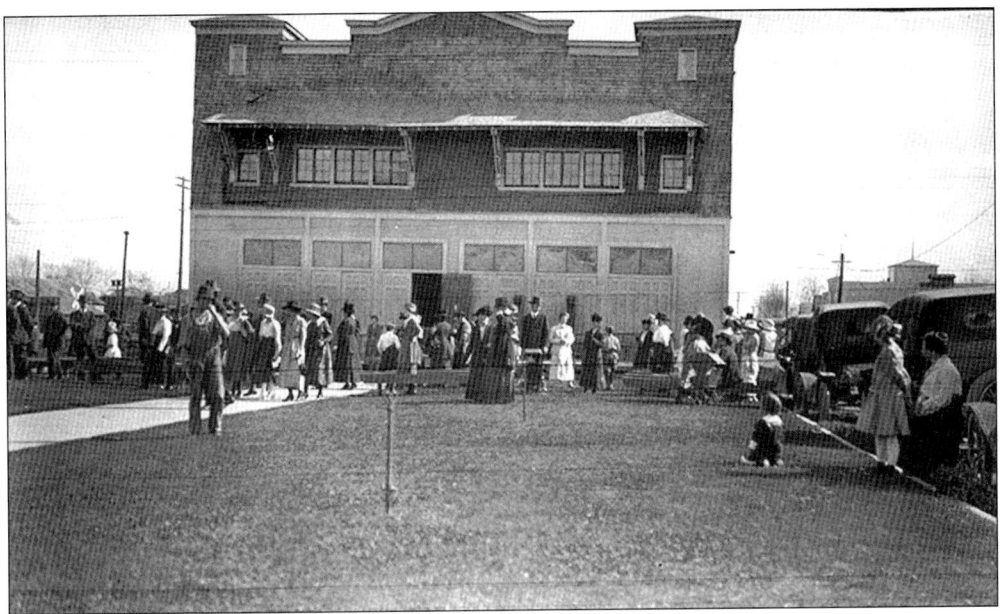
The band pavilion, Yuba Street at the railroad tracks, was built in 1910 and was torn down in the 1930s.

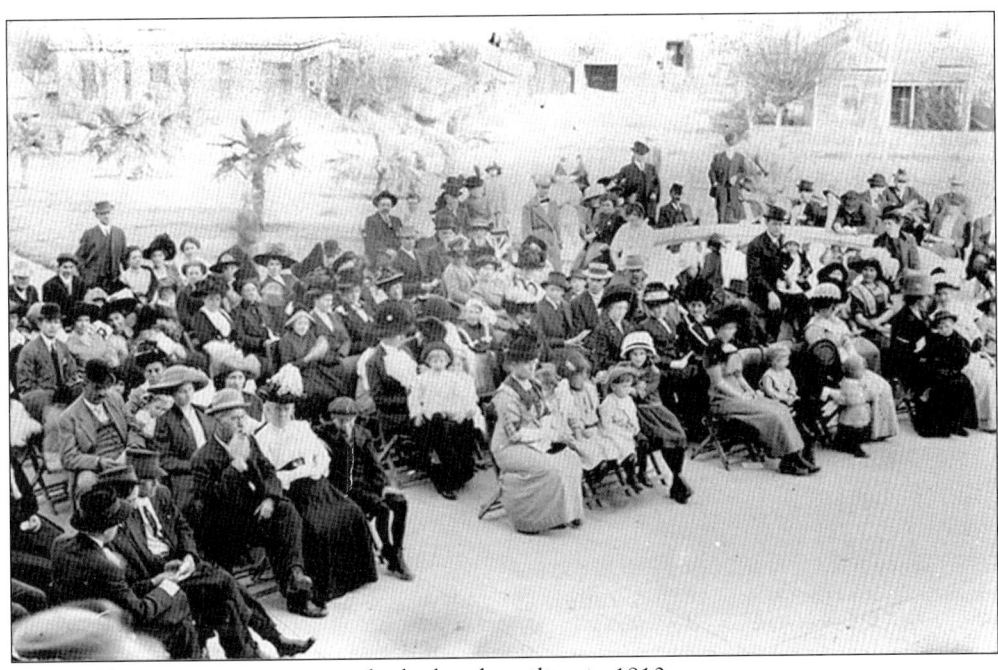
A crowd listens to a concert outside the band pavilion in 1910.

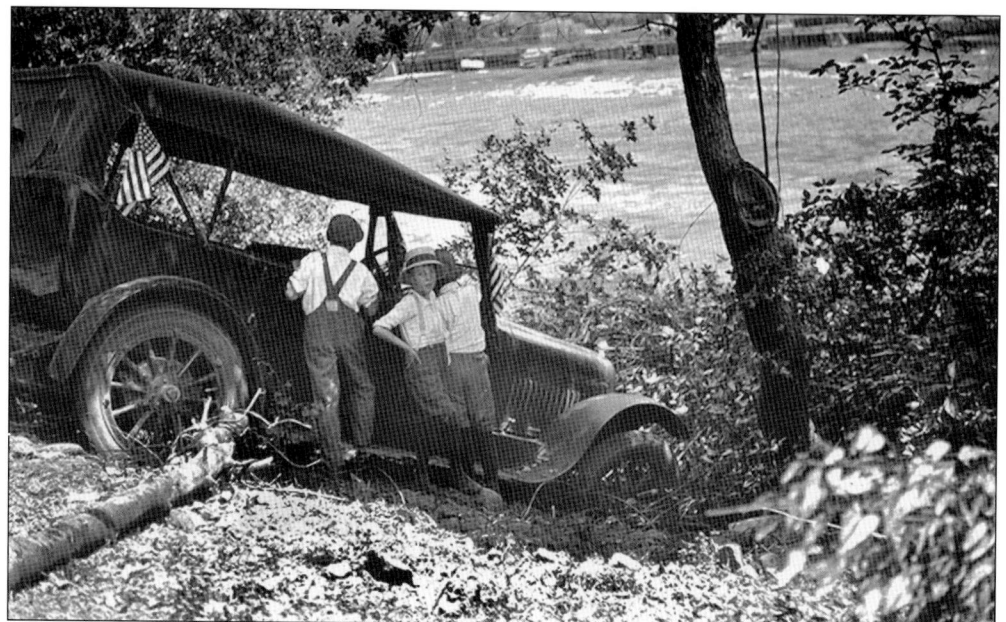

Three boys inspect an automobile accident in 1915. The Sacramento River is in the background. In 1907 an automobile enthusiast predicted that "some day there would be 1,000 autos in the town of Redding."

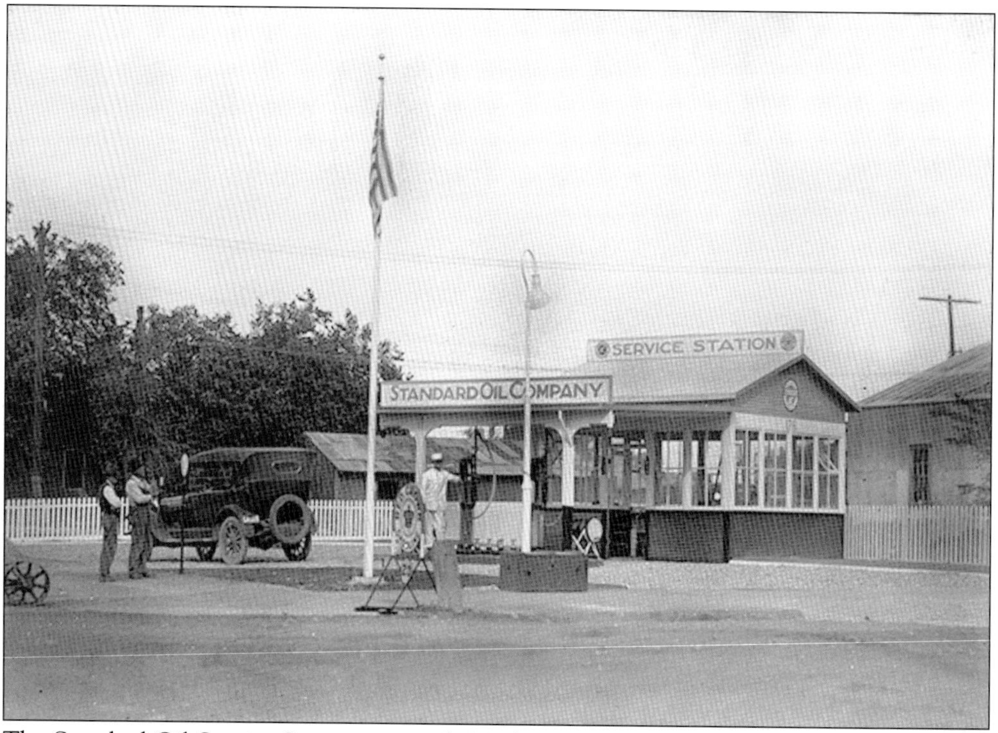

The Standard Oil Service Station on north Market Street is shown here, c. 1940. Before the days of self service, the uniformed attendant stood ready to assist by checking the oil, water, and tires, and washing the windshield.

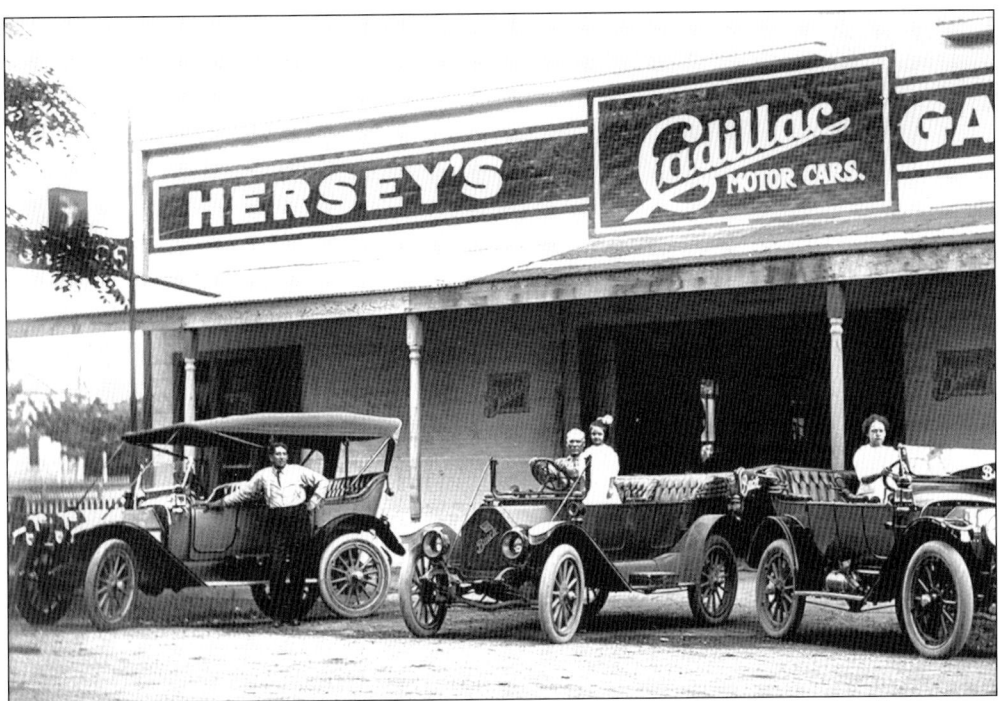

Hersey's Garage, shown here c. 1915, was one of the earliest of Redding's garages. Located on Yuba Street, Ed Hersey's garage supplied gasoline and oil, as service stations had not yet developed. The garage also supplied tires; rough and rocky roads were a constant problem.

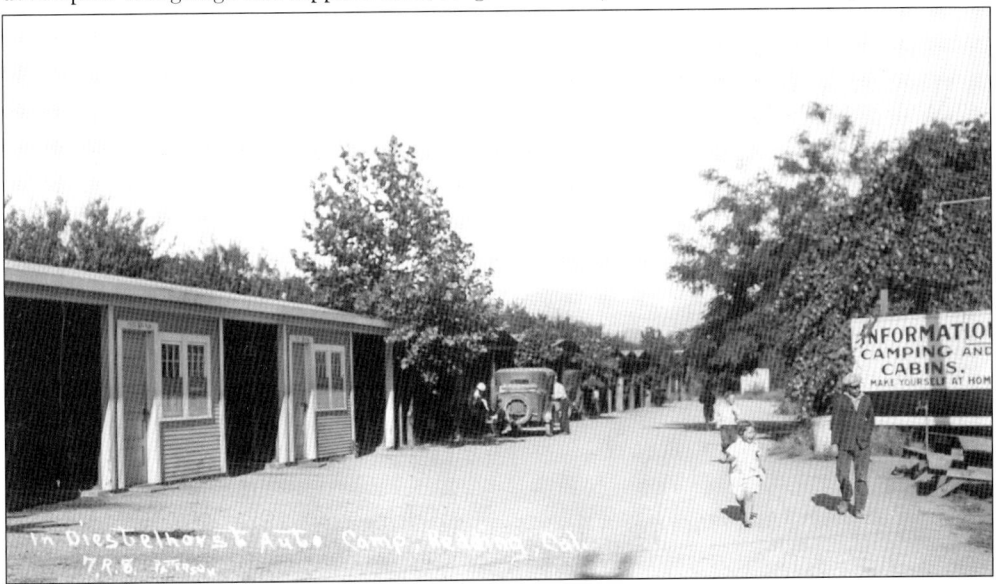

Diestelhorst Auto Camp, established by John and Charles Diestelhorst, was part of the Diestelhorst Resort located near the Diestelhorst Bridge. The resort included a gas station, overnight campground, and a store. It was also the location of Redding's "swimming hole" from 1915 until the building of Shasta Dam. The water became icy cold when the "bottom" water of the dam was released. The large concrete steps leading to the river's edge still remain in Caldwell Park.

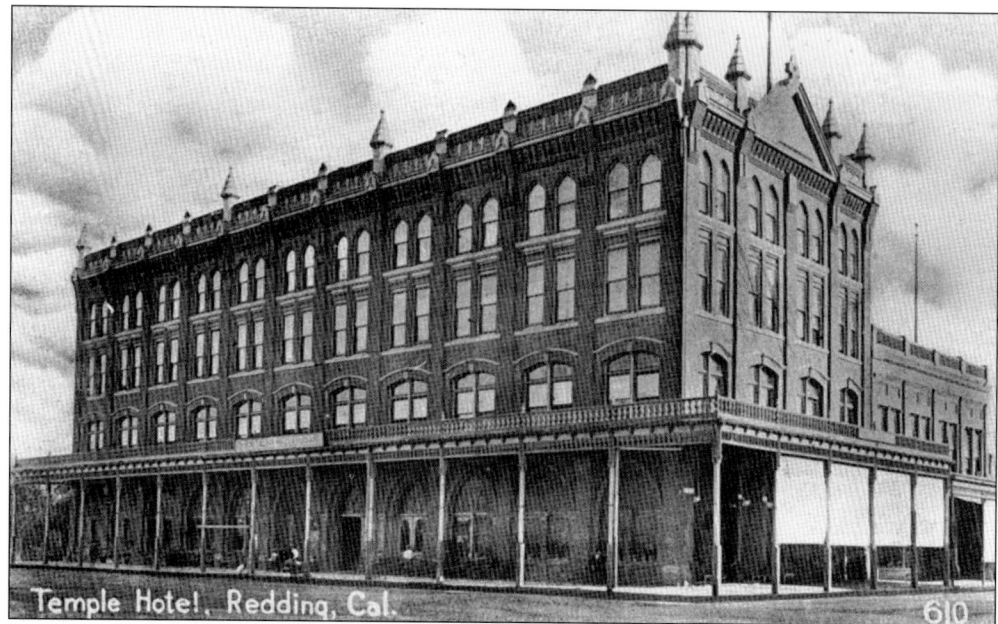

The cornerstone of the Temple Hotel was laid on August 19, 1891. The hotel was built by the Redding Lodge of Masons on the corner of Tehama and Market Streets was completed in 1894. At the time it was built the Temple was the tallest California building north of Sacramento. It had 100 rooms but only one bathroom. In the early days most people bathed once a week, and on Saturdays the rush was on. The hotel was torn down in 1964 to make way for the downtown mall.

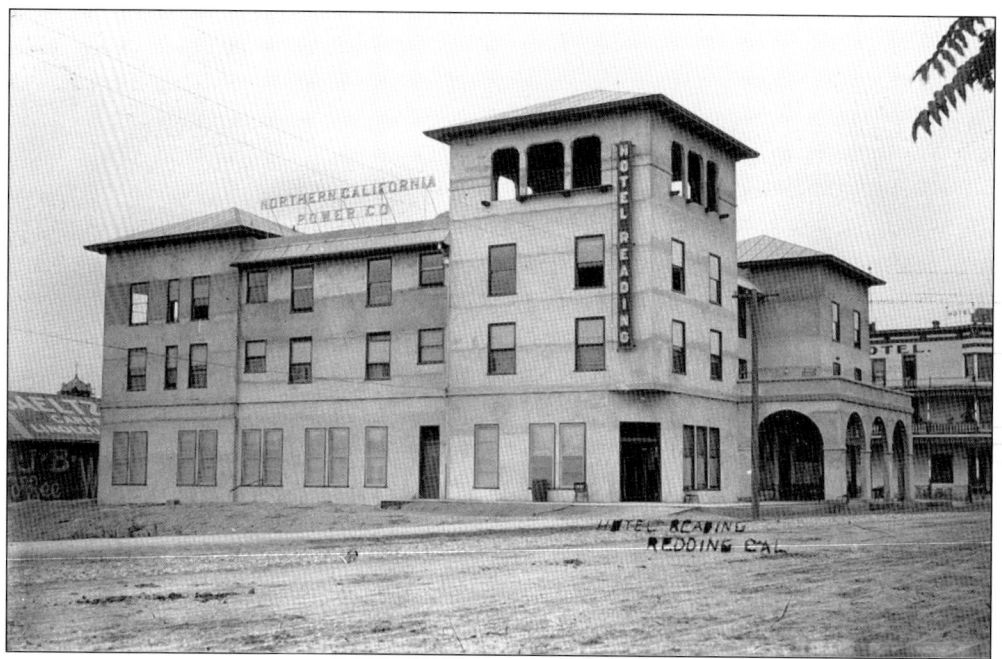

Reading Hotel, c. 1915, was located on Yuba Street on the site of the current post office. The hotel was owned by the Gillespie family and burned November 25, 1917.

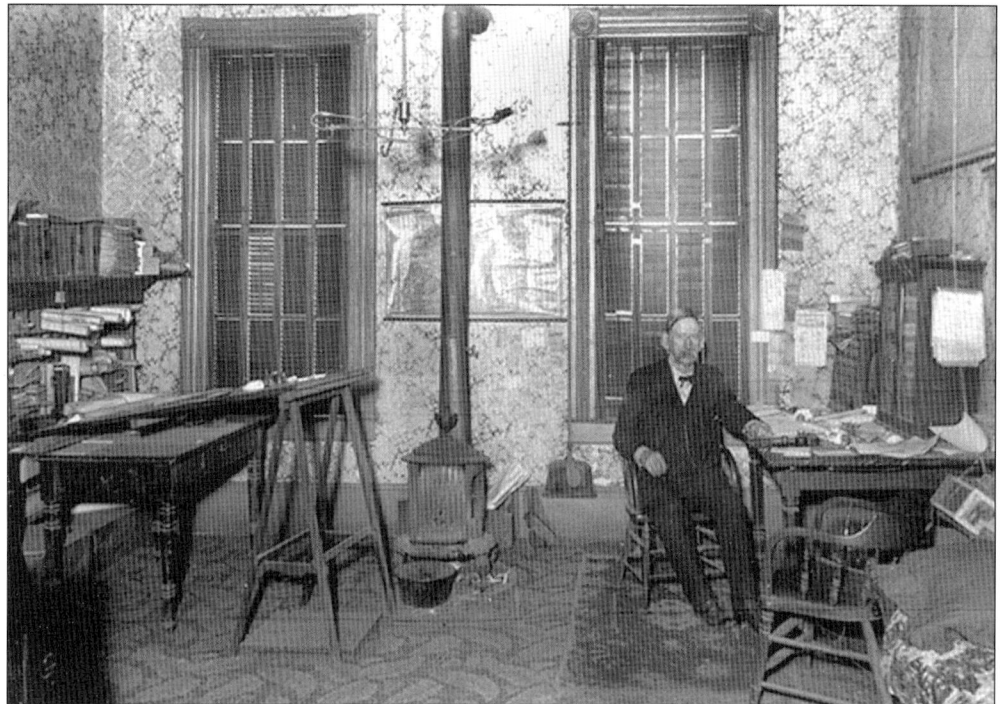

William H. Bickford was clerk for the Redding Land Office. Following the removal of the county seat to Redding in 1888, the land office also moved from Shasta to Redding in 1890. It was located upstairs in the old McCormick-Saeltzer building on Yuba Street.

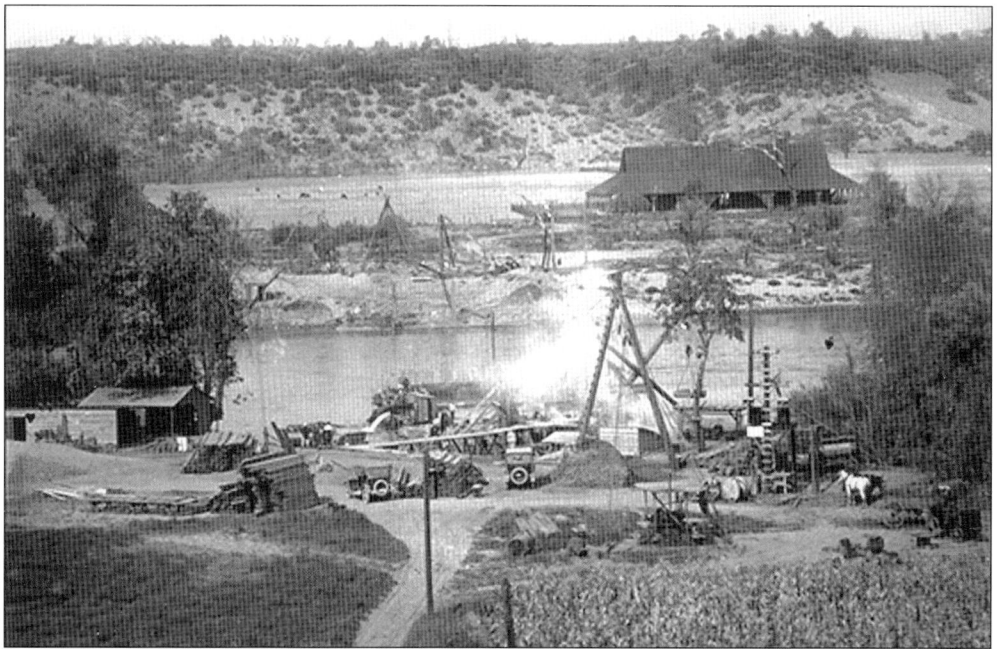

This 1916 photo shows the start of work on the Anderson Cottonwood Irrigation District's diversion dam across the Sacramento River near the present Market Street Bridge in Redding. Across the river, cattle graze in what is now Caldwell Park. Menzel's barn is located to the north.

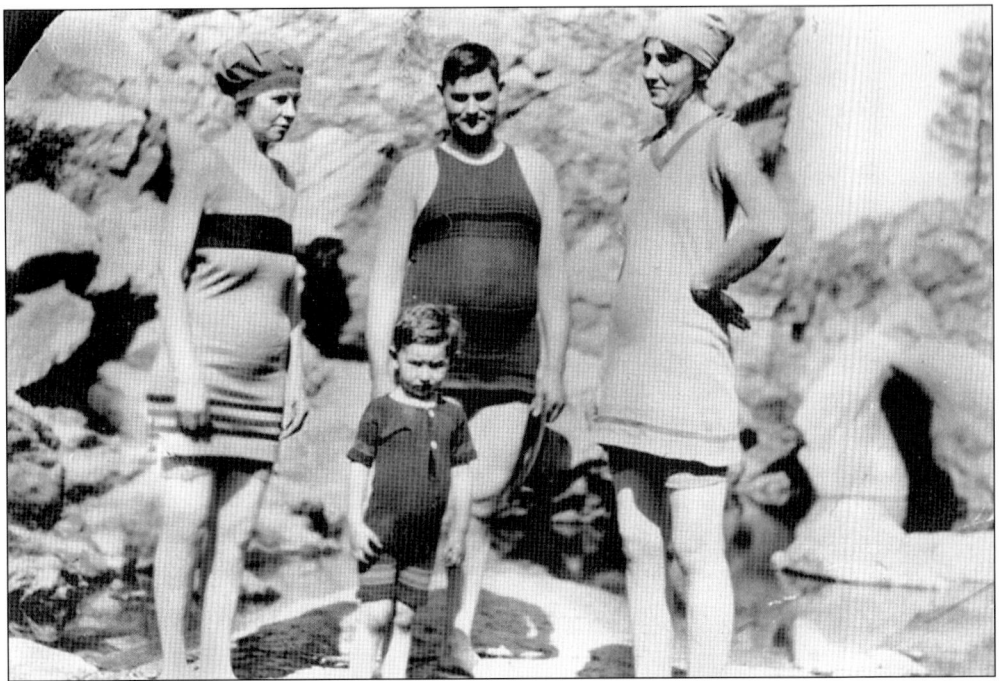

Out for a swim c. 1915 are, from left to right, an unidentified woman, Ben Klukkert, Winona Robinsin Klukkert, and their son Jack. Ben Klukkert worked with his father, Berend, at Klukkert and Sons Bakery in Anderson. Later, he and Steve Coughlin owned the Klukkert City Bakery on Market Street. Ben Klukkert was an avid golfer and hunter and organized the Redding Golf Club.

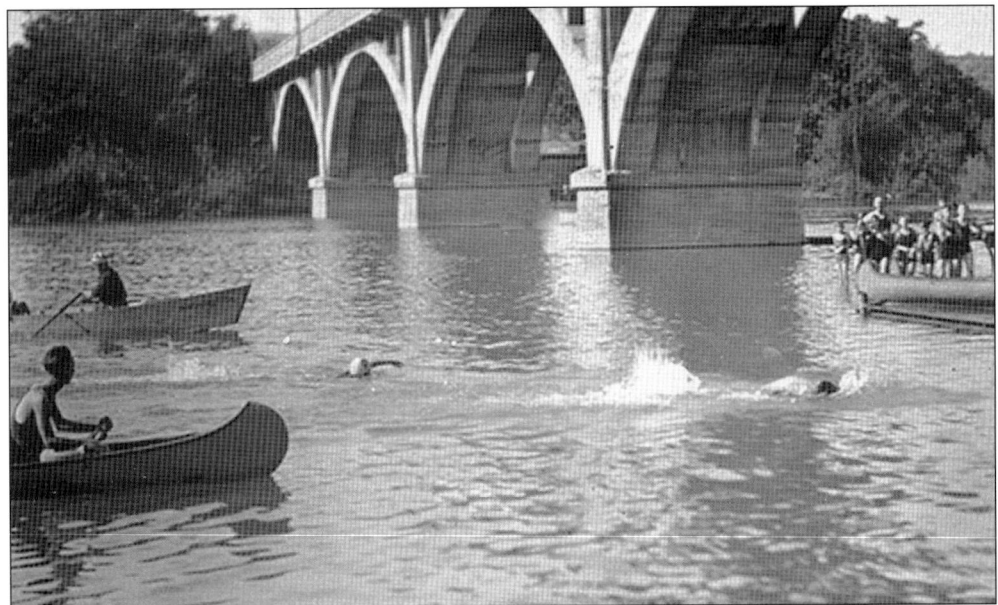

This c. 1920 photograph shows the Water Carnival at the Diestlehorst Bridge with the finish line of the one-mile swim at Lake Redding. The 1915 highway bridge became a focus of community recreation.

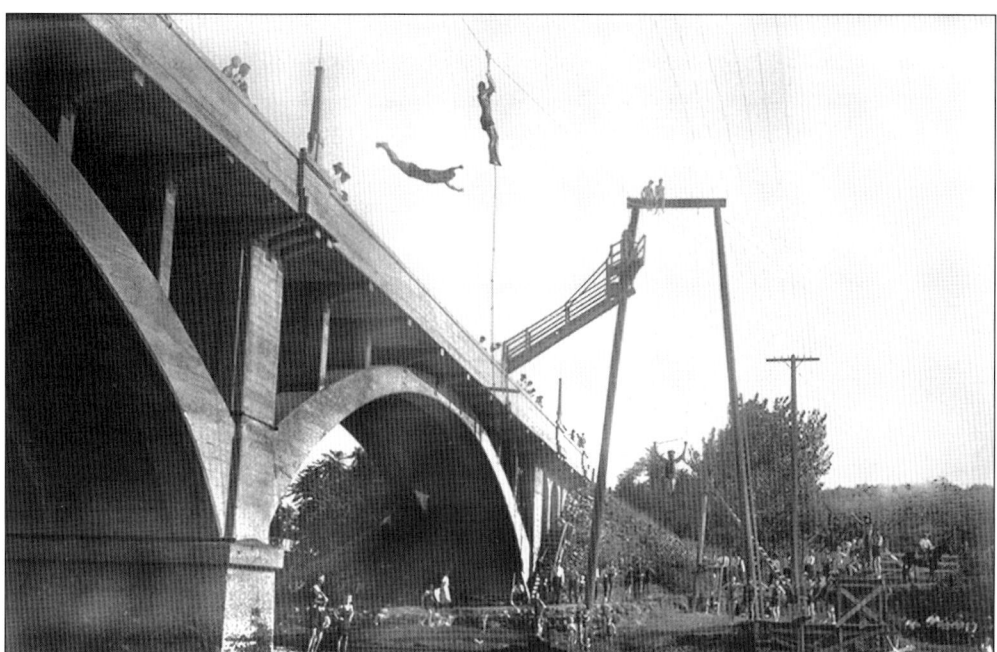
A diver jumps from the Diestelhorst Bridge into the Sacramento River in this 1930 photo. The higher the platform, the higher the diver's status. The elite were those who not only could dive off the bridge railing, but also could shinny up the light pole and then make the leap.

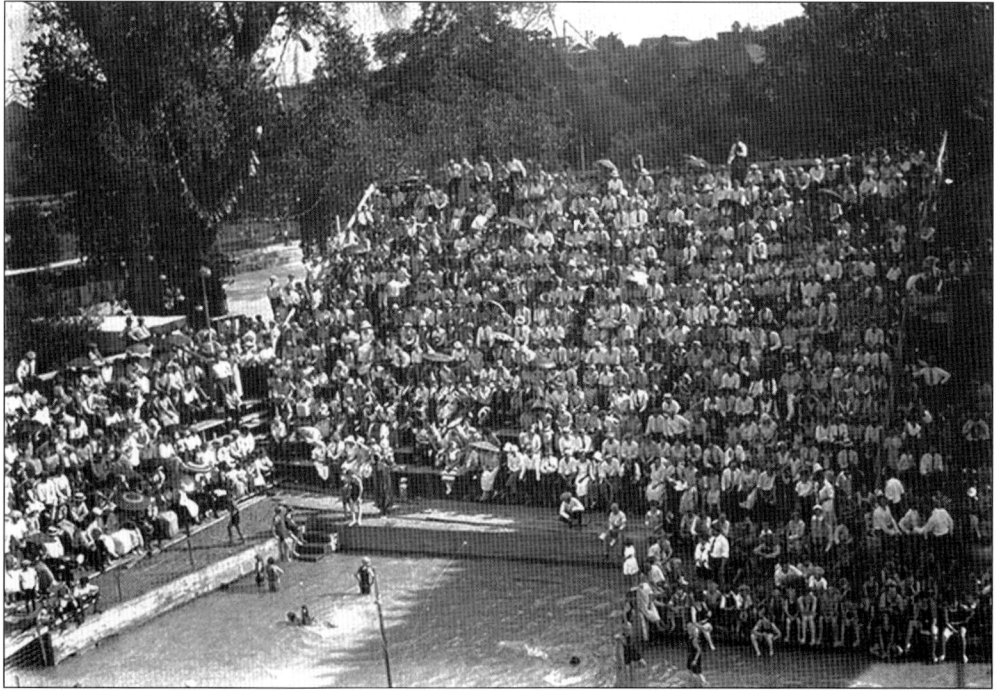
The Water Carnival at the Diestlehorst Bridge included beauty pageants, swim contests, and boat races. This c. 1930 photo shows the grandstand.

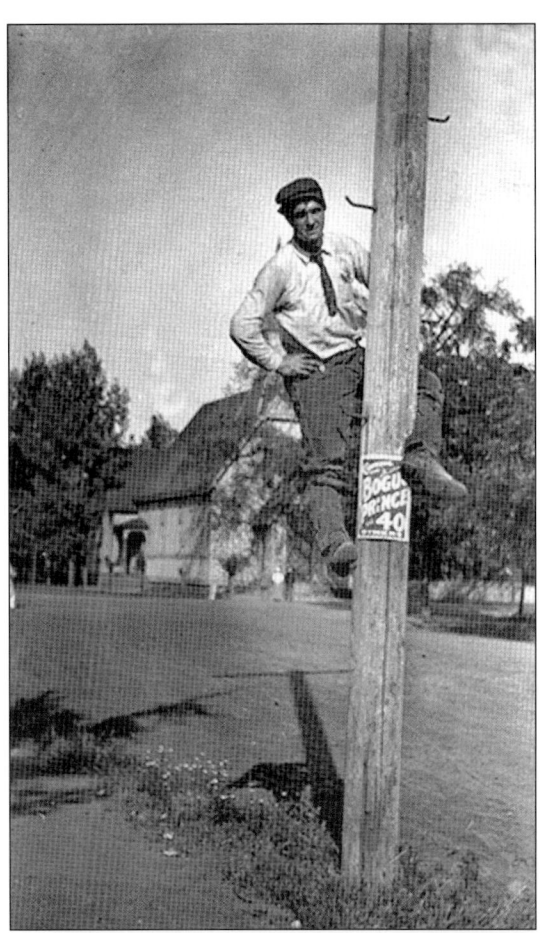

A lineman for Northern California Power Company demonstrates how to climb a power pole.

These c. 1920 employees for the Northern California Power Company stand outside the office on California Street. The company was established in 1902 and sold to PG&E in 1919. Assistant general manager Wade Moores is second from right.

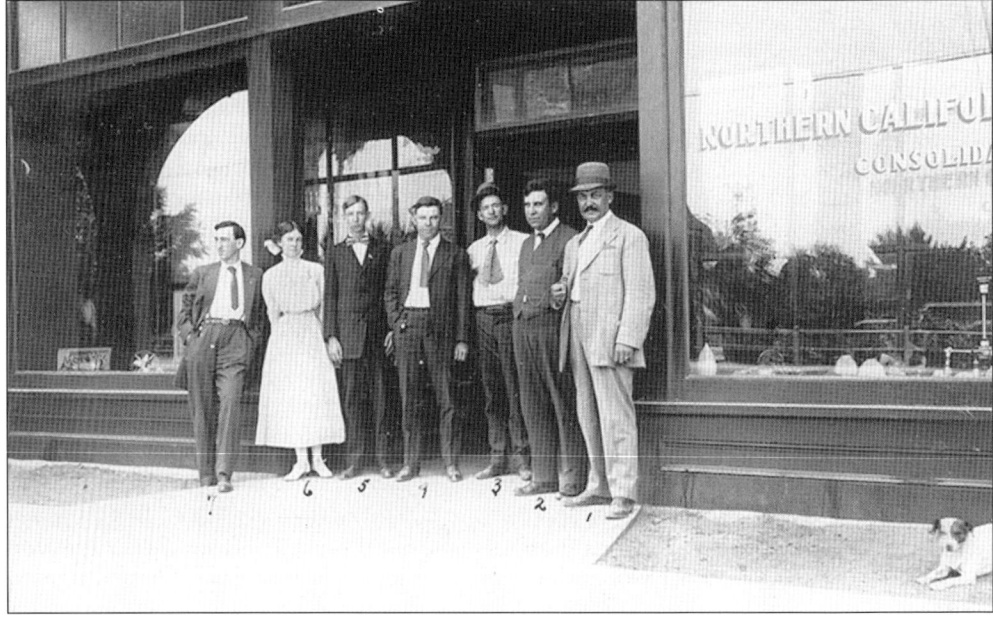

Three
BUSINESS AND WORK
1900–1930

The key to Redding's success as a regional commercial center lies in the fact that the town took the lead early in its history to develop a wide variety of businesses. These shops, markets, livery stables, hardware stores, restaurants, and hotels grew in size and number during the first part of the 20th century. A brief look at some of these businesses in the early years of the century provides a good understanding of the variety of goods and services available.

The McCormick-Saeltzer store, still popular and expanding in the early 1900s, offered a full line of produce and dry goods, including Jesse Moore Whiskey, a favorite drink for special occasions. The Redding Lumber Yard, one of several lumber outlets in town, sold rough and finished lumber. They also did millwork and provided many of the finished wood boxes and fencing material for homeowners. Thomas McLaughlin, owner of the City Livery & Feed Stables, had his stables located just behind the Hotel Lorenz. McLaughlin prided himself on offering "horses accustomed to all roads and travel." Roads were a problem, and the state of city streets tended to be almost as bad as the county roads used less often. Chuckholes appeared overnight during wet wintry months and keeping up on road maintenance proved difficult. Citizens of Redding could often be seen repairing downtown ruts and draining waterholes.

Another popular store in Redding was Russell & Lefebvre Dry Goods. With a full line of stoves and ranges, the proprietors challenged the McCormick-Saeltzer store. The Russell store, which sat opposite the Temple Hotel on Market Street, sold hardware, agateware—even doors and windows. On the side, they offered to do in-home plumbing. The idea of selling goods and also offering in-home repairs and services appeared to be commonplace in the first two decades of the 20th century. Lumberyards would offer home construction as contractors, paint stores would sell the paint, then come and do the painting. Clockmakers, furniture makers, and retail grocery stores offered free home delivery of purchased meats, vegetables, fruits, and canned goods.

Along with Redding's large commercial stores was a long list of individual entrepreneurs who worked out of their homes or apartments. A Mrs. Neeler lived at the Ivers Apartment House in Redding where, for a fee, she would shampoo or "singe" your hair. She also did facial massages and manicuring. For a slight additional fee, Mrs. Neeler packed her shampoos and cutting tools and came to your home. Her phone number was "608." J.H. Houston, another industrious business owner, borrowed money to start his own hauling firm in the city and, by 1910, he had several wagons and was quite busy. Houston would haul "anything within the city limits," including heavy packages and boxes from stores to homes. His wide assortment of barrels, from small to large, assured customers that he could safely haul any item they needed.

Then as now, restaurants were quite popular, and Redding was no exception. Many families would save up money just to go out on the weekends, and this usually meant dinner at a good restaurant. Gambrinus Hall, located in the Litsch Building on Market Street, employed many cooks and served hearty and delicious meals for years. Proprietor Tony Jaegel offered perennial favorites such as steak and potatoes, but also trendy new dishes like oysters. For some reason, oysters were quite popular in most of the other restaurants around town, including the eateries in the Hotel Lorenz and others on Market Street. During a city-wide scare concerning tainted oysters in 1906, Jaegel spent time and money to assure his customers of the quality of his oysters. His advertisement in the local newspaper was more of a warning, reading, "Look Out, and be careful not to eat any of the inferior grades of oysters. We sell and serve only the best—the Eagle Brand of Fresh Frozen Oysters. Served any style by competent cooks."

Another interesting business in Redding in the early 1900s involved the use of young men and women to deliver light packages and letters. Known as "express runners," these fit employees would sit at the express office of J.H. Hall and wait for a telephone call and subsequent order request. Attired in a smart uniform, the runners listened carefully as the pickup and destination locations were given to them, then they hurried out onto the busy streets of Redding. Mr. Hall ran this business out of Buck's Shoe Store during business hours—and from his home at night. To do this, he maintained two phone numbers. Promising fast and safe deliveries, for pennies an order, the express business thrived until the large-scale use of automobiles in the 1920s.

Looking clean and proper was the style of the day in early Redding, and cleaning and dye establishments were quite numerous. John Bonnett owned the Redding Cleaning and Dyeing Works, which operated from a building on south California Street. Clothes were carefully washed in large metal basins using various strengths of detergent. Since cotton fabrics were by far the favorite of Redding residents, Bonnett and his employees spent most of their time washing, drying, and ironing cotton shirts and pants. Wool was used in the wintertime, especially in coats, and a special cleaning process was used for these garments. Employees transformed newly arrived bolts of cotton into a variety of color-dyed materials, with brown, blue, and black being the most popular.

The business world of Redding had its share of college-trained professionals during this time. Lawyers and doctors were the largest group of professionals and were scattered throughout the downtown area. Attorneys such as William F. Aram and John J. Dailey called themselves "counselors," taking on a wide variety of legal problems. Dailey specialized in mining claims, which were still a major source of client interest at this time. Water rights played big at this time too, with county ranchers and farmers continually defending existing water rights patents or seeking new rights. Many of these claims were against the county and state government. Another area of rising need was that of corporation law. New businesses sought the legal protection and advantages of incorporation, and they continually needed legal advice as their businesses grew.

Doctors were in high demand and provided services from offices all over the city or made house calls. Surgeon C.E. Boynton worked from the First Building on Butte Street across from the Novelty Theater. Dr. C.E. Reed placed his office inside the McCormick-Saeltzer store. He rented and lived in a room at the Hotel Lorenz, where he also accepted patients. Sherman T. White, another physician and surgeon, advertised working from Eaton's Emporium, while R.F. Wallace lived and worked out of the Temple Hotel. Dentists were no different than physicians and C.C. Corriere pulled teeth from a small office over the top of the McCormick-Saeltzer store.

A multitude of other jobs and careers were seen in Redding. Southern Pacific Railroad employed track repairmen, engine maintenance workers, and railroad tie haulers. The railroad also hired women to cook for the men who left the city to work in camps up and down the rail line. Railroad sales agents kept busy at the depot selling tickets for destinations close and far away. A trip to Red Bluff cost $1.80, Chico $3, Sacramento $3.70, and San Francisco $7.20. Grocery store stockers, sales persons, and meat sellers worked hard at their jobs every day so city dwellers and persons from around the county could come in to stock up on food supplies. Redding offered the largest and highest quality foodstuffs available anywhere in the North State. The Jacobson Grocery Company took pride in having the best produce and meats in town, with a "no questions asked" return policy. This held true for the Menzel & Milnthrop Meat Market, which sat opposite the Temple Hotel on Market Street.

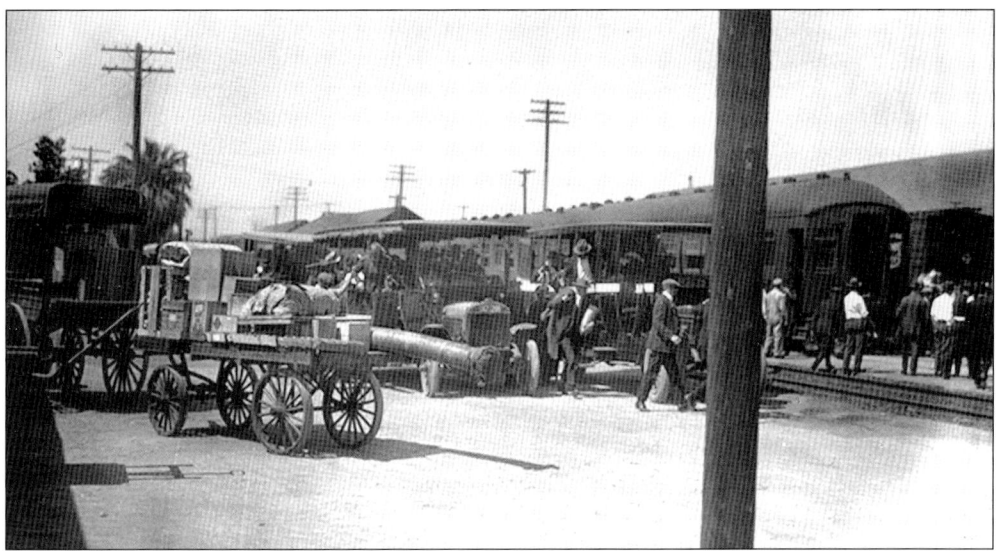

The train depot, shown here c. 1915, was made from California redwood. All of the hotels were within a block or two of the railroad station. The hotels met all passenger trains with a horse-drawn bus. On warm summer evenings the fashionable thing to do was to walk down to the depot to see the train come in.

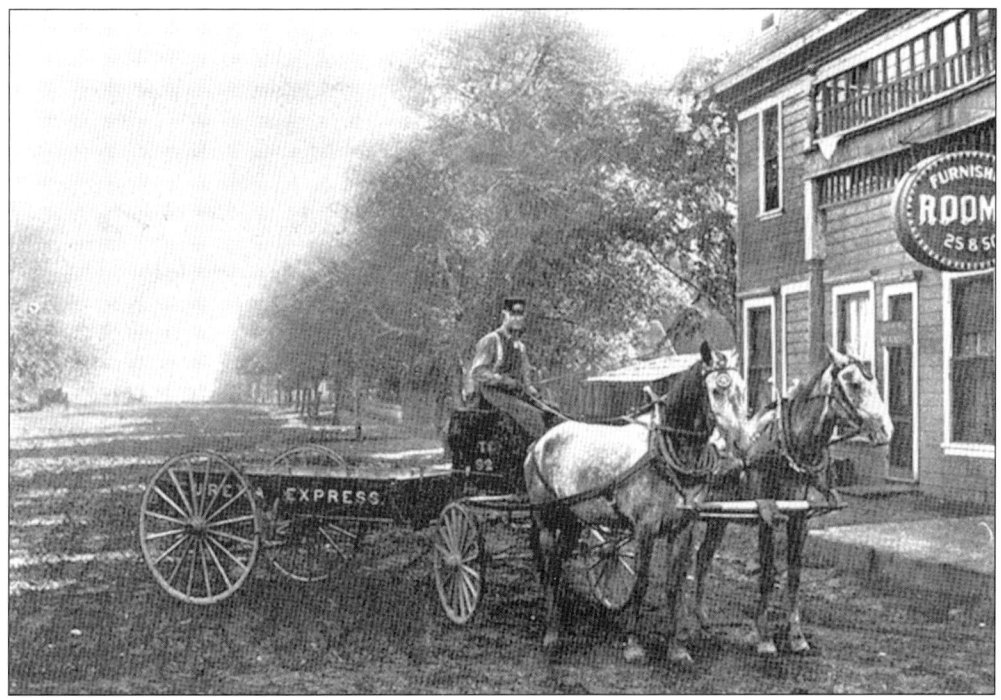

Eugene Bainbridge, driving a two-horse team for the Eureka Express freight line, is shown here on his way to meet the train, c. 1900.

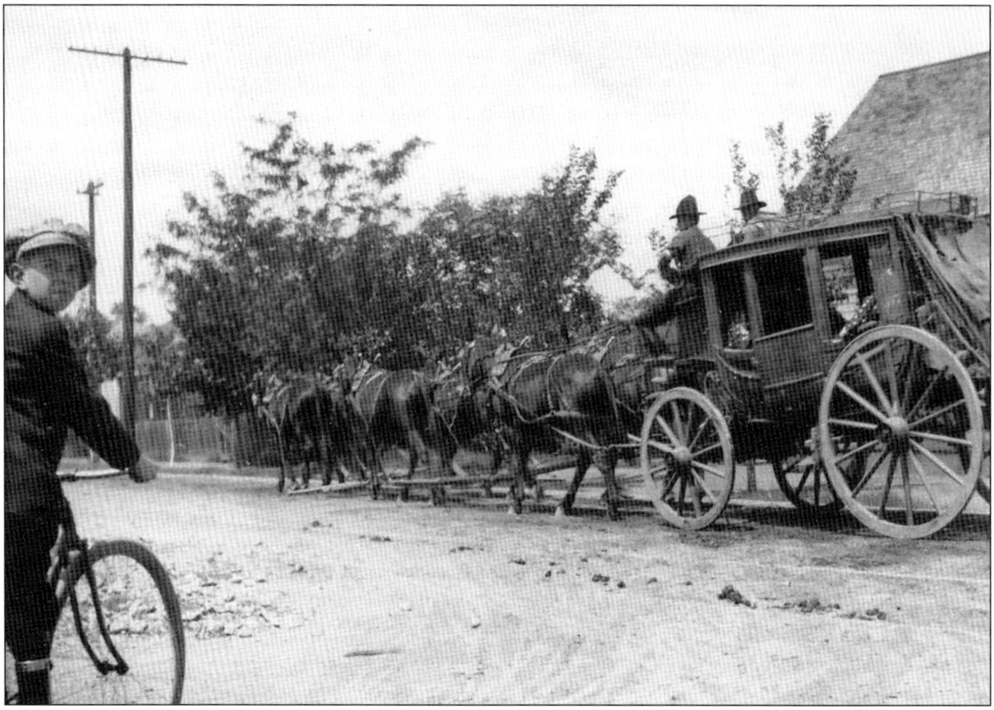

The Weaverville to Redding Stage, c. 1900, had bells on the lead horses announcing its arrival. Often male passengers were asked to get out and push regardless of their clothes, while the ladies walked behind. (Courtesy of Richard Lorenz.)

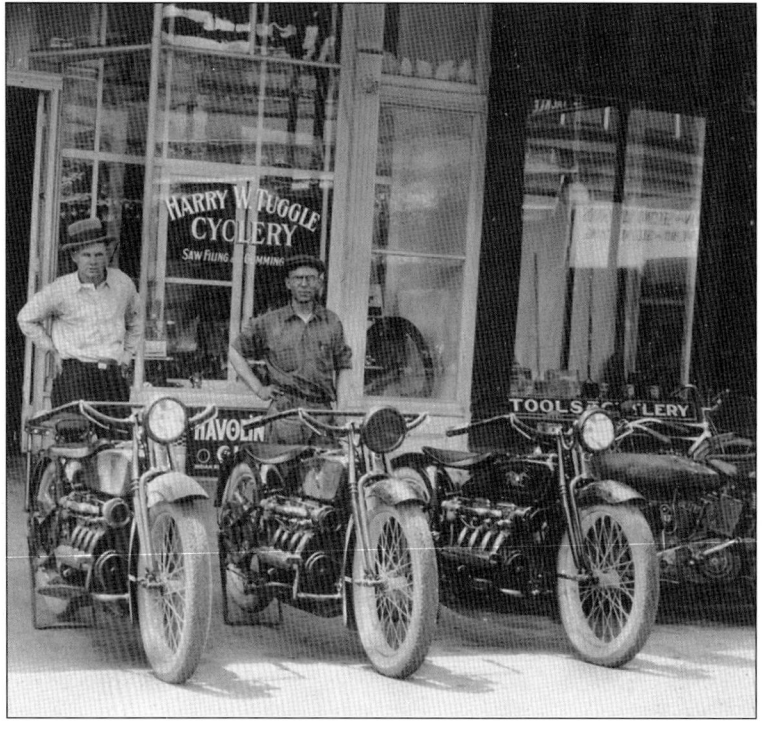

This c. 1900 photo shows Tuggle's Cyclery, which was on the west side of Market Street between Shasta and Tehama Streets in Redding. Pictured are Hime Klakins (left) and Harry Tuggle.

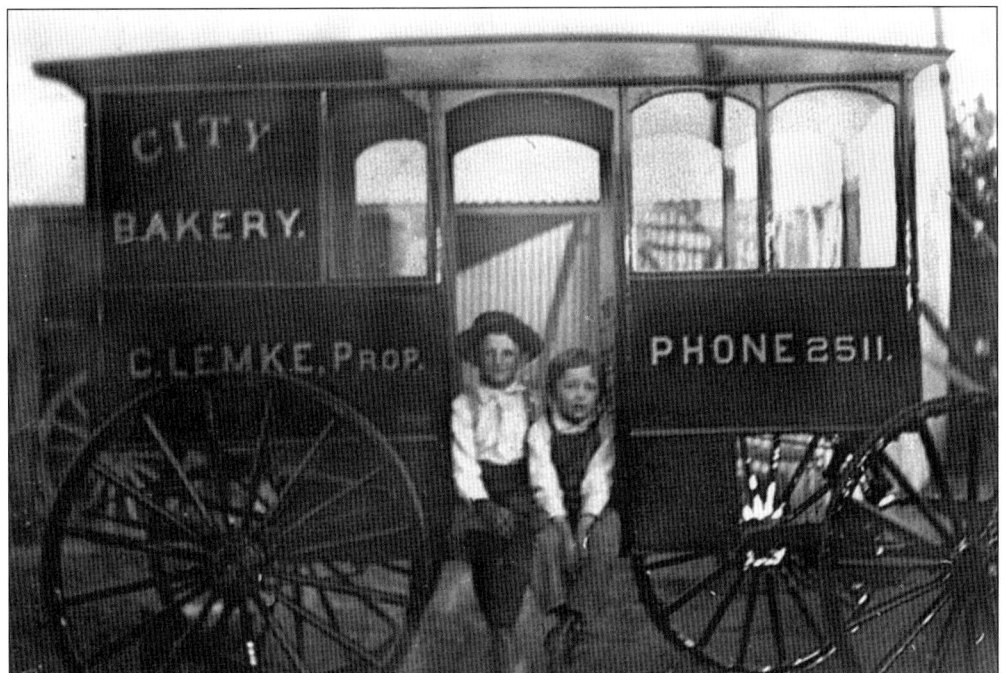

The City Bakery was built in 1888 and was owned by Joe Shafter, who sold it in 1916 to Coughlin & Klukkert. The bakery also contained the lodge hall of the American Order of United Workmen. This photo shows the City Bakery delivery truck, c. 1915.

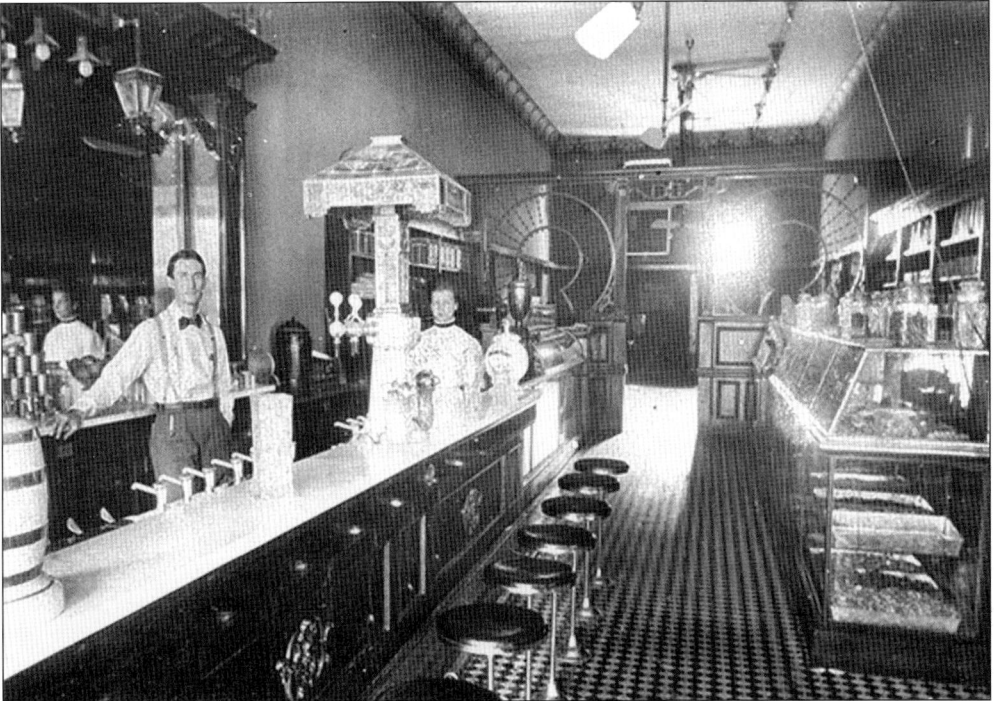

Eaton's Drugstore & Soda Fountain was built in 1903 by J.P. Eaton. A cherry coke could be had for 5¢ and was mixed and flavored from the spigots behind the marble counter.

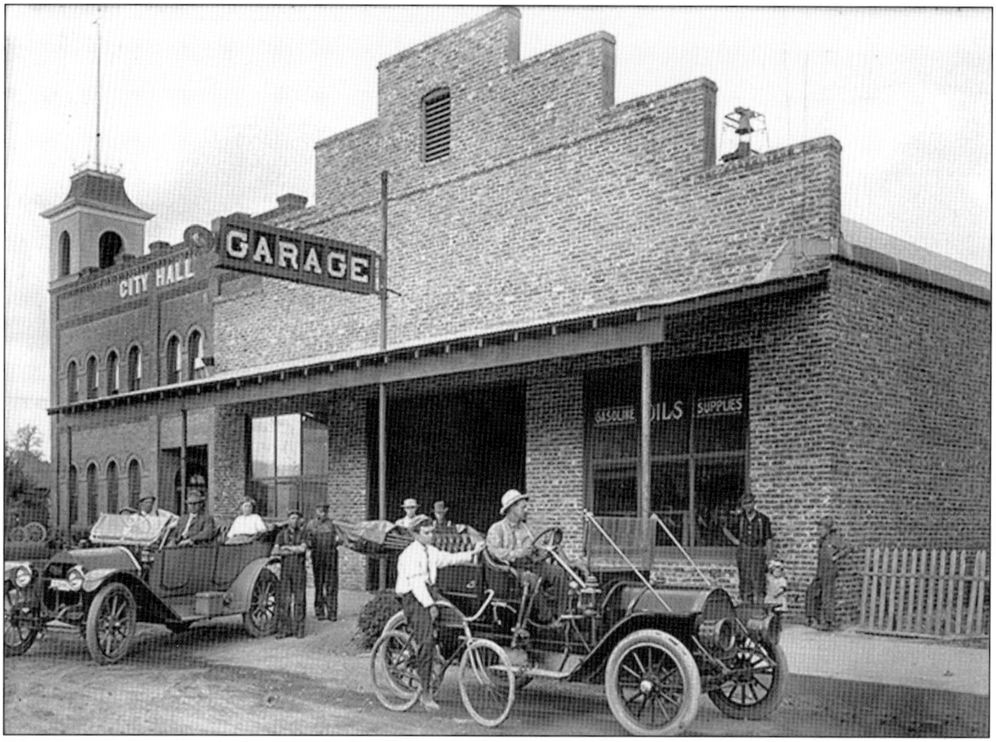

Wright's Garage and the city hall, shown here in 1911, stood on the 1300 block of Market Street. James Wright owned and operated the first automobile garage in Redding in 1908.

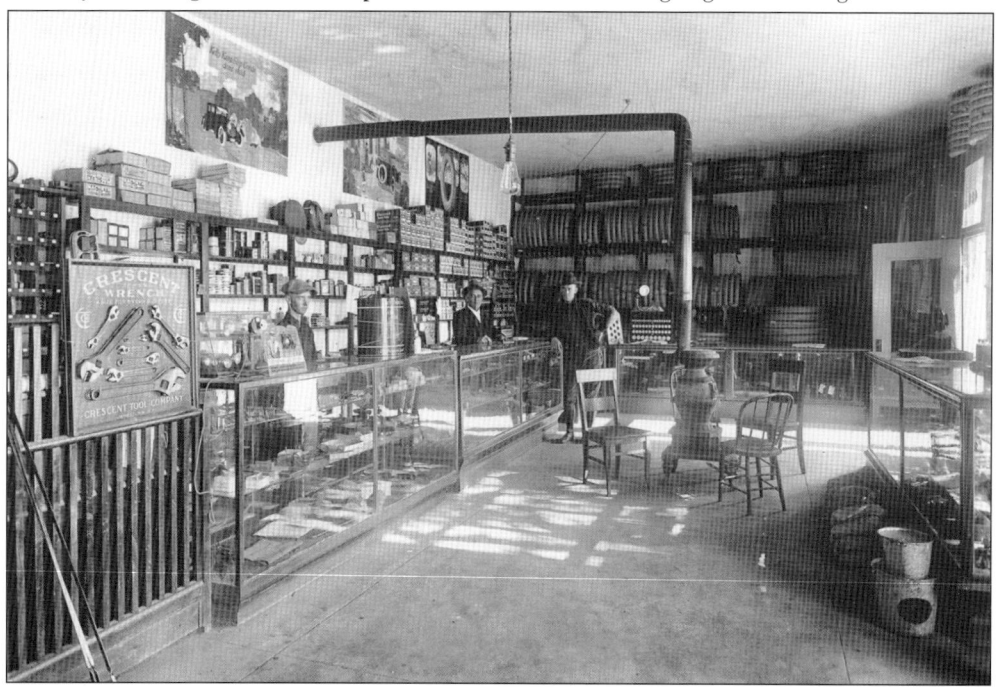

Frank Freitas is shown here in his vulcanizing shop off Placer Street in 1922. Frank sold tires, auto supplies, and had gas pumps in front of his store.

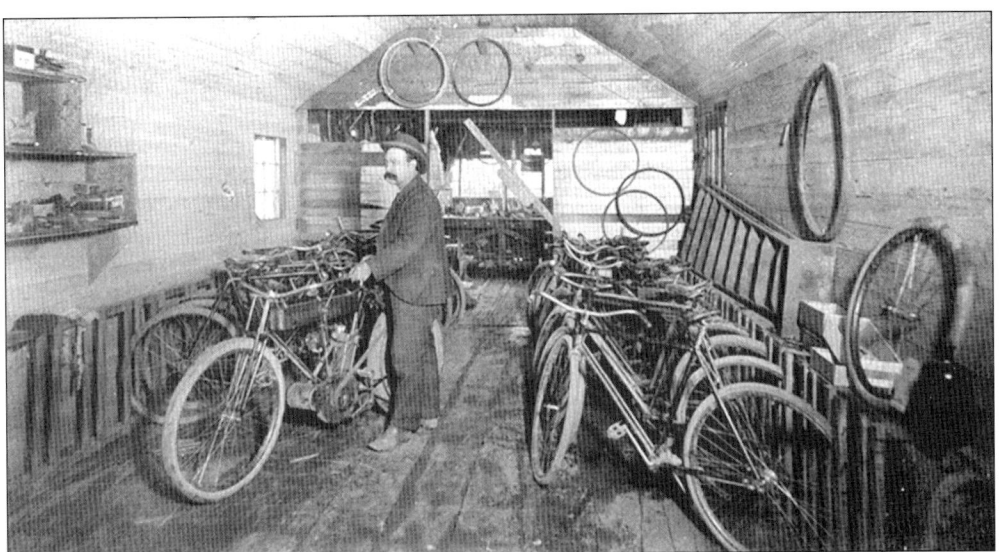

George Dix is holding one of the bikes in the bicycle shop on California Street in Redding, c. 1910. Before coaster brakes were invented, a cyclist had to walk down the mountain as well as up. Sometimes they could ride downhill by cutting a small fir and tying it behind the bicycle so that it would act as a brake.

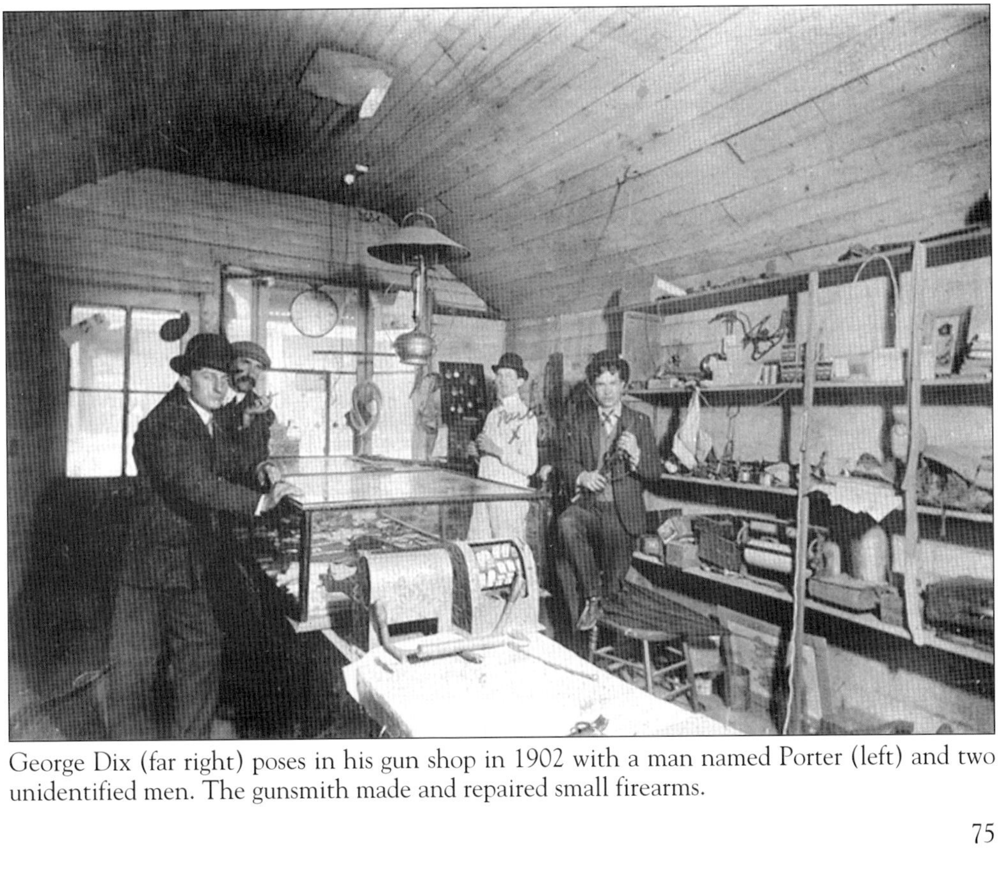

George Dix (far right) poses in his gun shop in 1902 with a man named Porter (left) and two unidentified men. The gunsmith made and repaired small firearms.

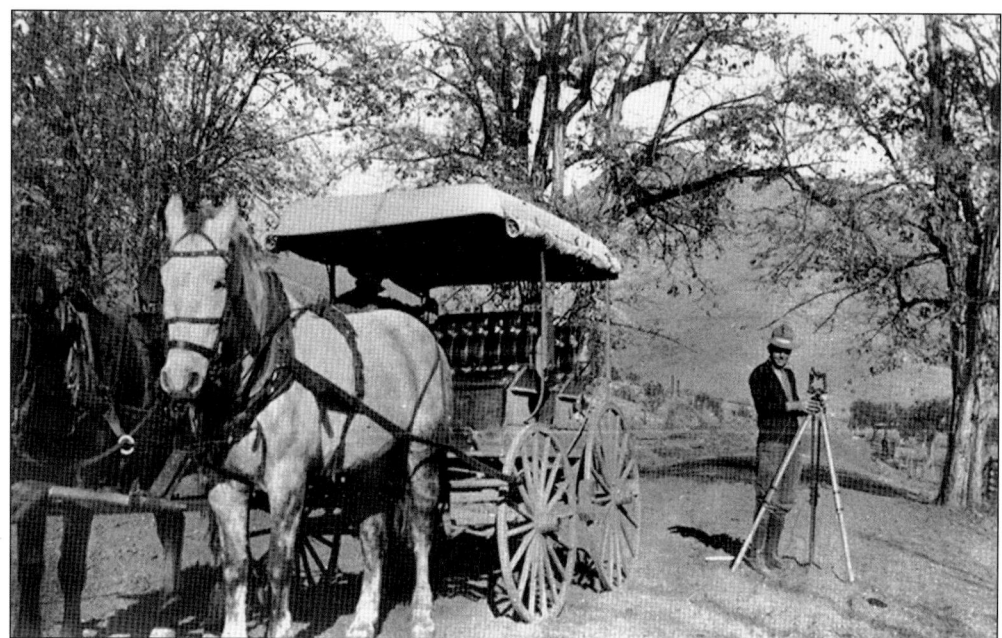

A California Highway Commission surveyor takes measurements on a road in the Sacramento River canyon north of Redding, c. 1912. Back then the pace was set by horses rather than barreling semis.

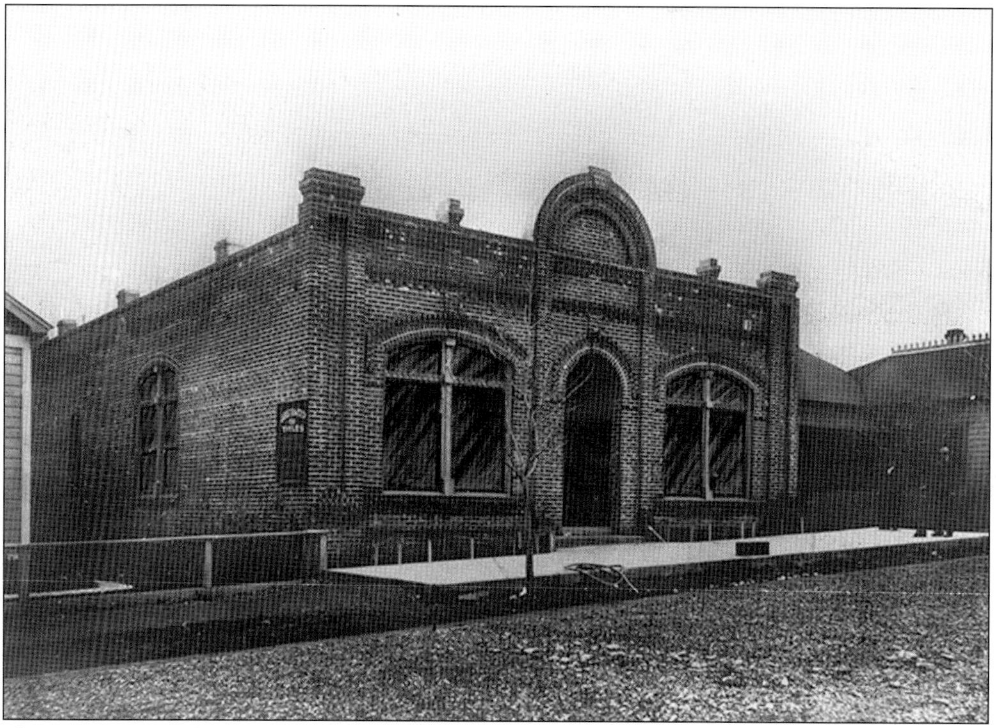

Shasta County Title Company, owned by Carl R. Briggs, is pictured here, c. 1900.

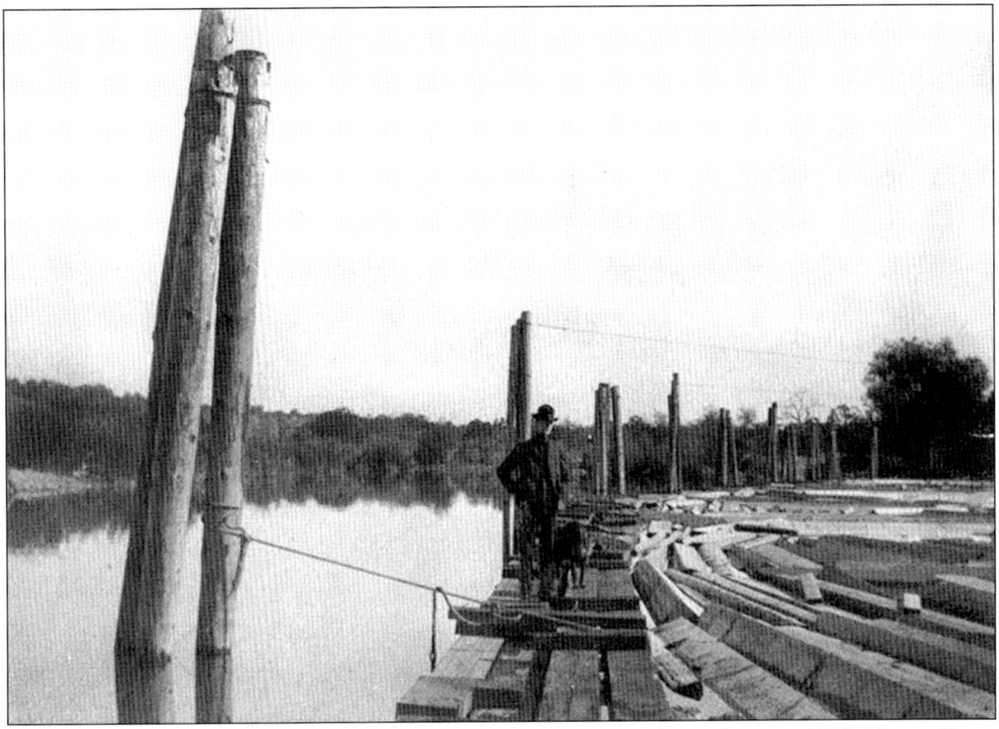

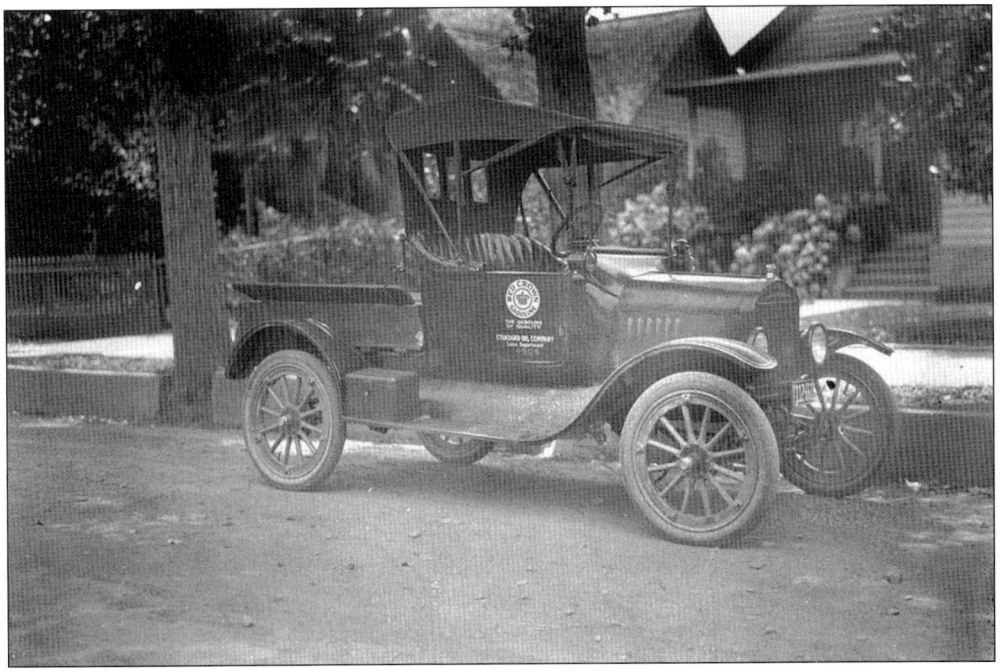

The Benton sawmill at Turtle Bay on the Sacramento River is shown here in 1908. The mill was closed down in 1916 and moved to Siskiyou County after a flood took a season's worth of logs.

A Standard Oil Zerolene delivery pickup truck is parked on Market Street, *c.* 1920.

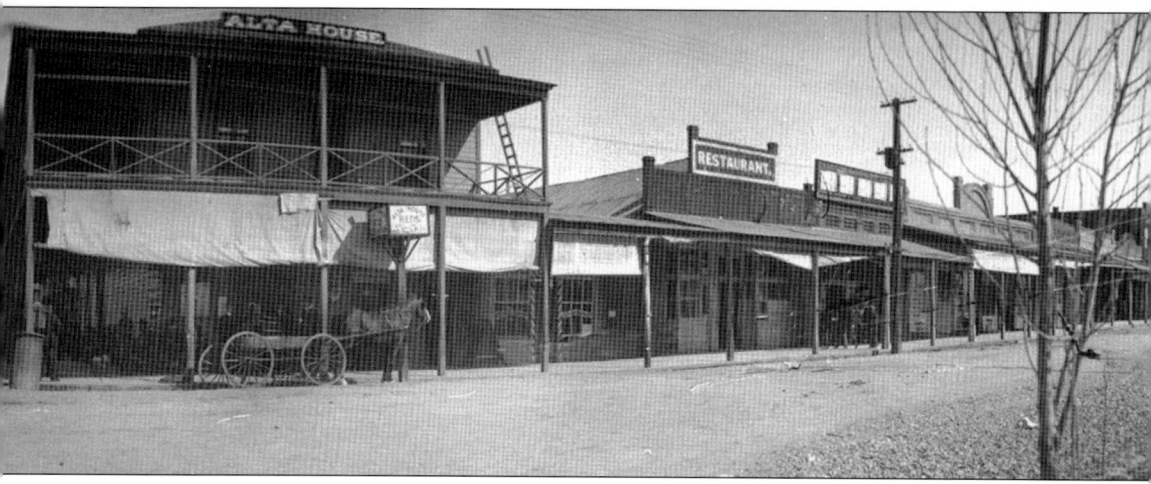

At the Alta House Hotel, on the east side of California Street between Yuba and Butte Streets, beds cost 25¢ and 50¢. Alta House was managed by August Henry Gronwoldt who, along with his brother George, had been a miner in Harrison Gulch in 1887. August was elected to the city council in 1921. He also served as mayor in the 1920s through the 1940s and was on the board of supervisors.

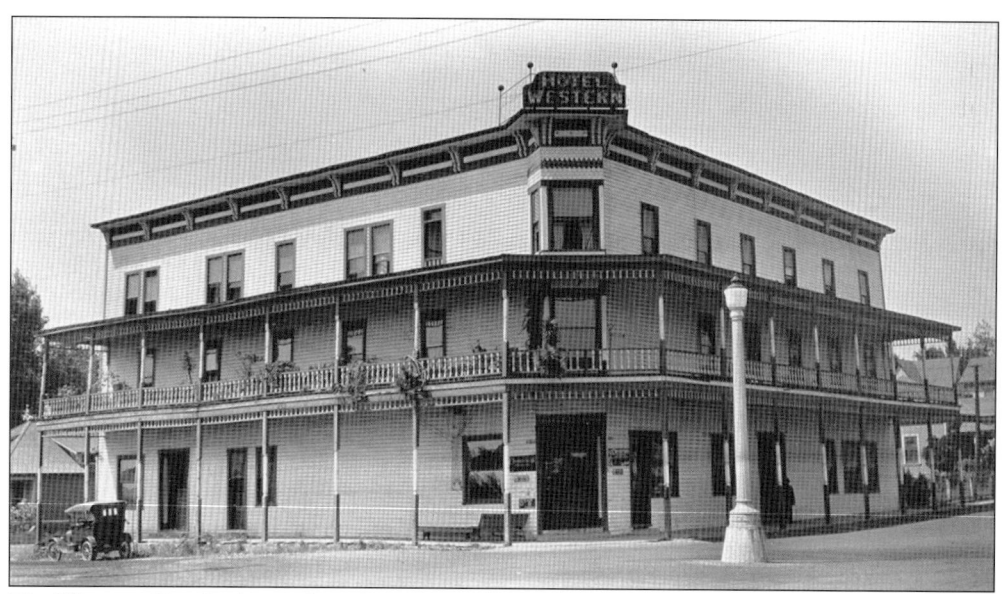

The Western Hotel is located on the southwest corner of Yuba and Oregon Streets, shown here c. 1915. It was built on a swamp that was a breeding ground for frogs and mosquitoes. The top floor later burned and was not replaced although the building is still in use today.

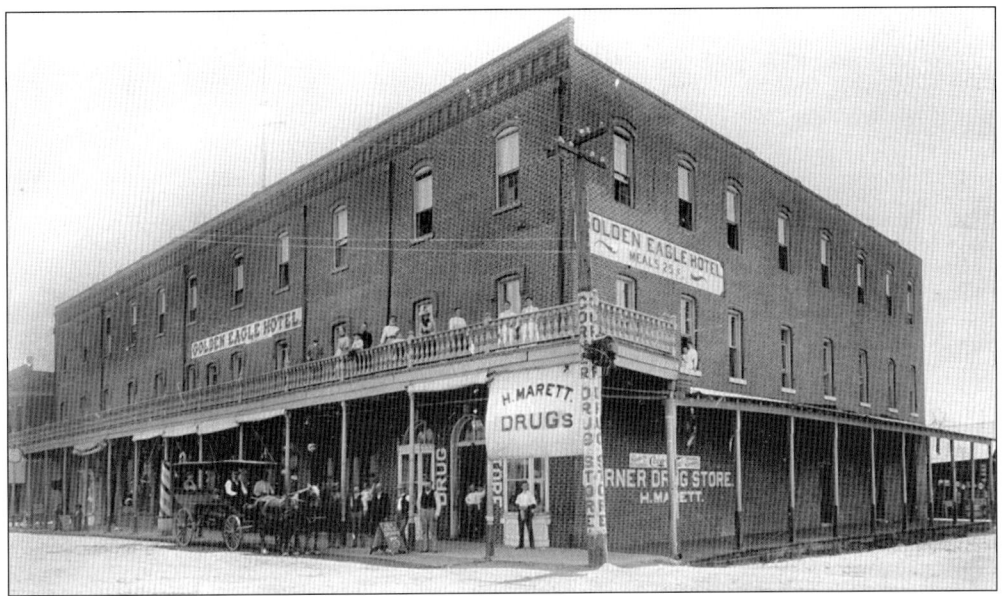

The Golden Eagle Hotel, pictured here c. 1910, was built in 1888 on Yuba and California Streets in Redding. The hotel was purchased by August "Gus" Gronwoldt. With its reputation for first-class service, the business prospered and became one of the best-known hotels on the West Coast. It was destroyed by fire on September 22, 1962.

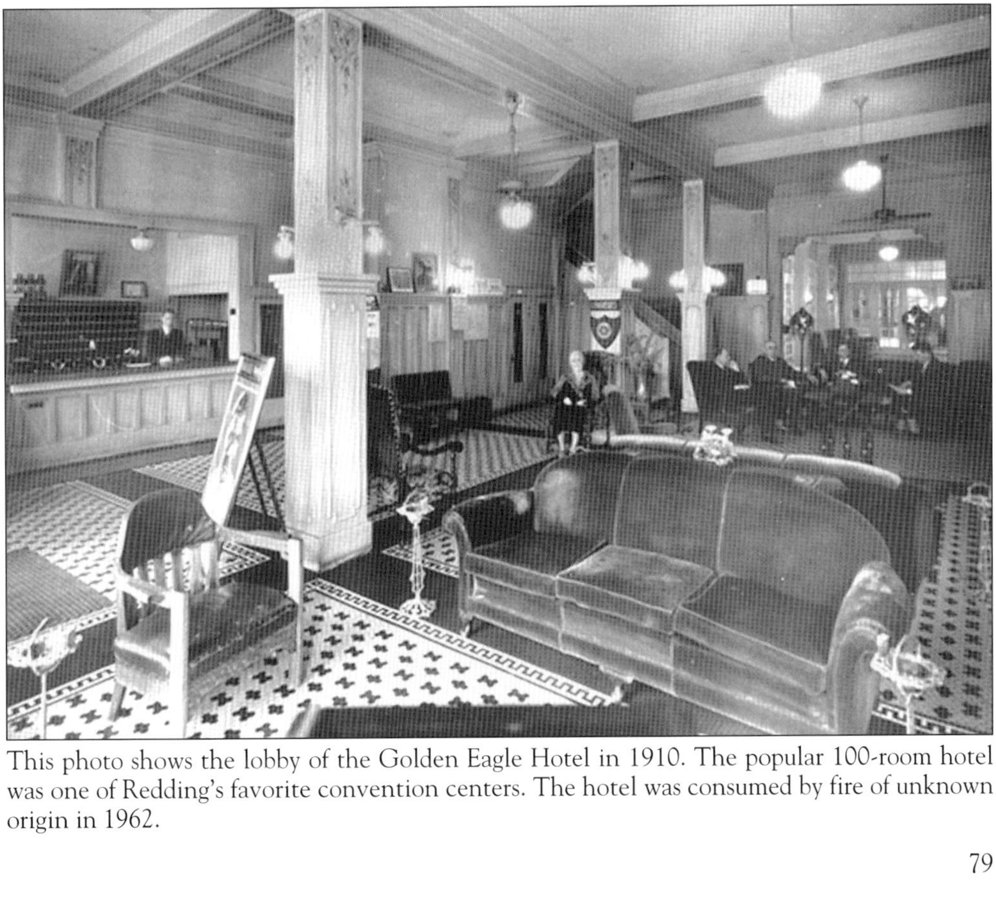

This photo shows the lobby of the Golden Eagle Hotel in 1910. The popular 100-room hotel was one of Redding's favorite convention centers. The hotel was consumed by fire of unknown origin in 1962.

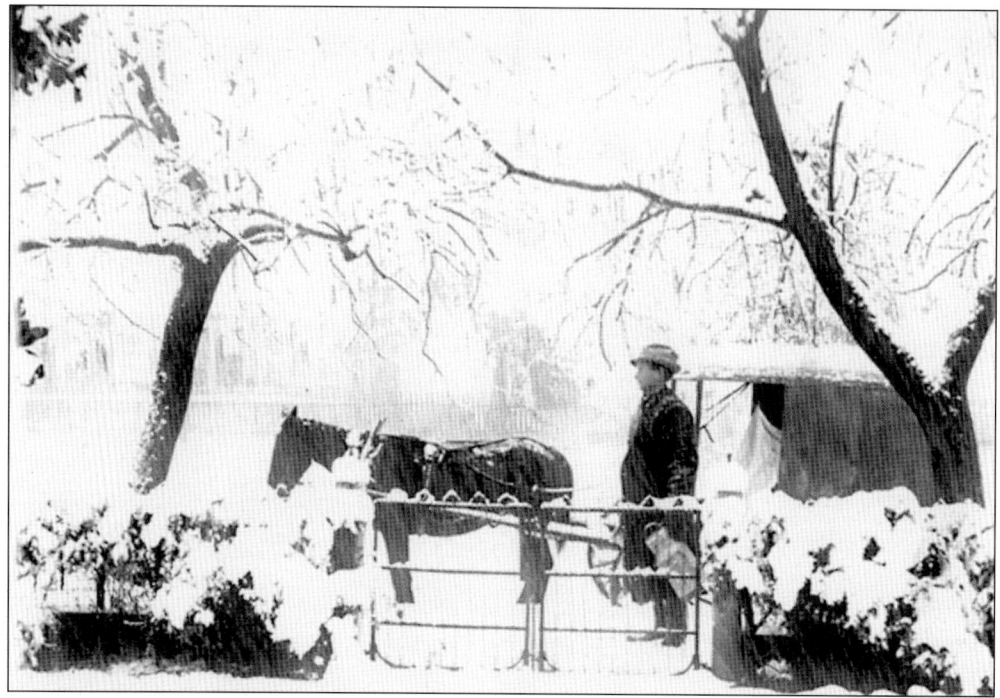

It was a cold, snowy day when this photo was taken in January 1915 as John Granville Kite and his horse made deliveries in Redding.

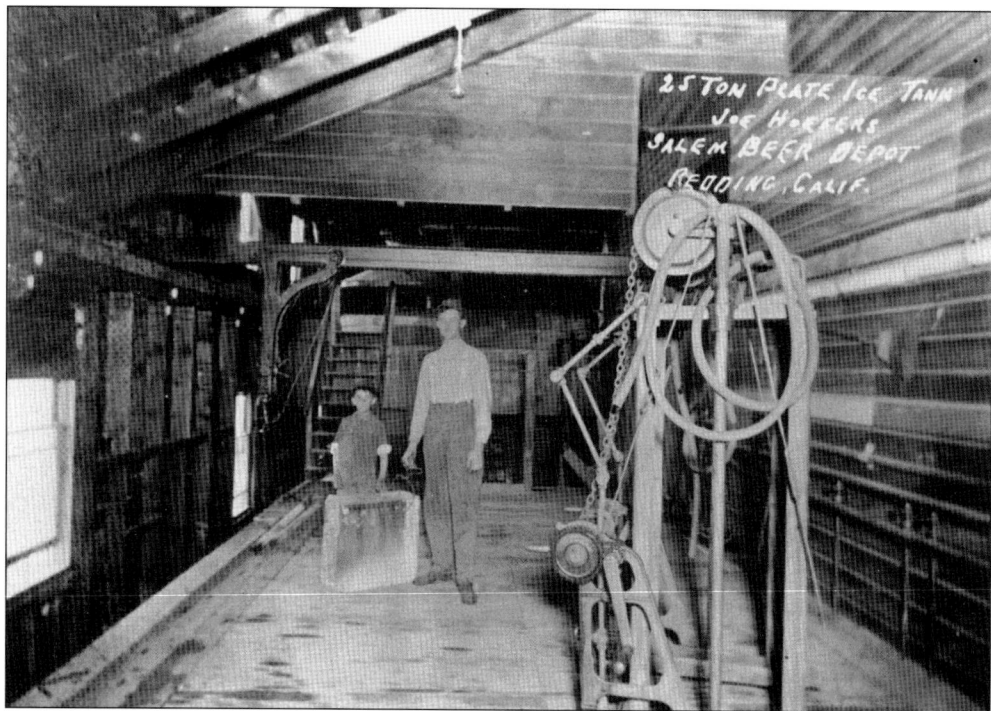

This photo from 1900 shows 100 tons of plate ice in the storeroom of Joe Hoefer's Salem Beer Depot located on the corner of Tehama and California Streets.

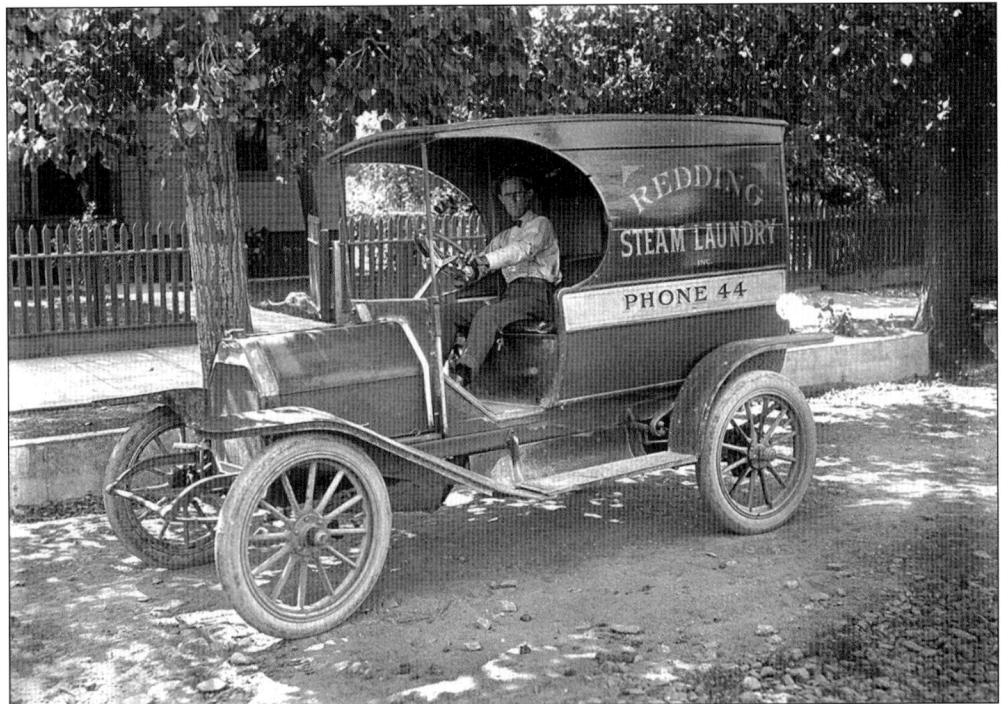

"Commercial and transient work" was the specialty of George and Camille Brouillard, who operated the Redding Steam Laundry at 10 California Street. This c. 1915 photo shows the Redding Steam Laundry delivery truck.

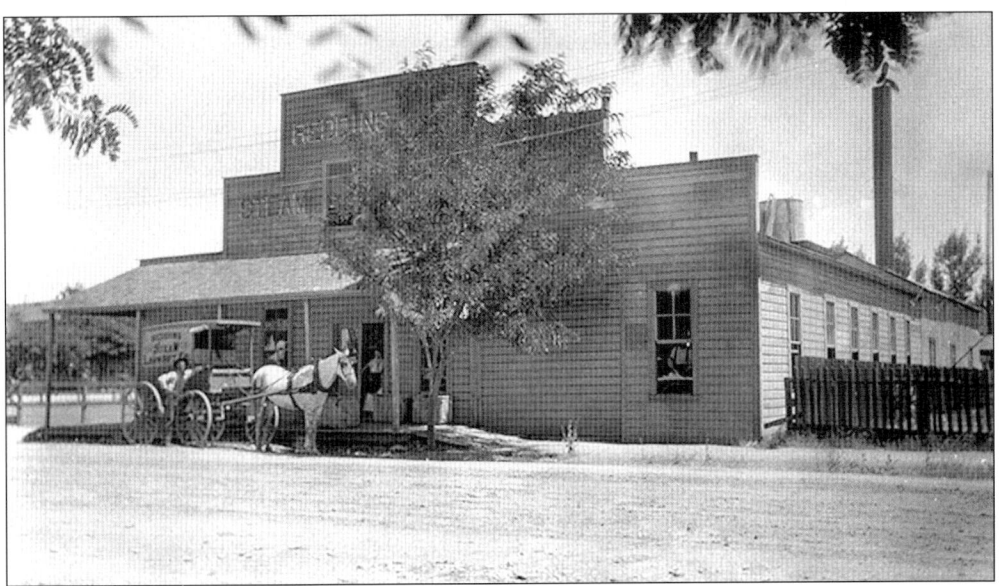

The Redding Steam Laundry was located at the corner of Placer Street and Railroad Avenue, c. 1900. During the 1940s and 1950s, Easter eggs were dyed in the laundry's large vats and then hidden in Caldwell Park for children's events.

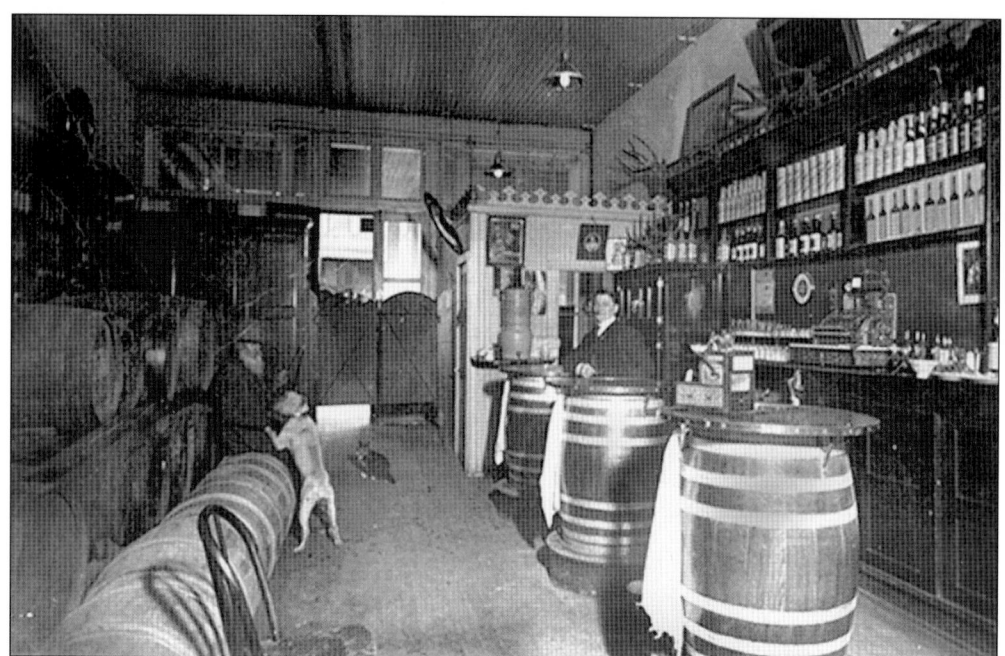

The name of this early saloon is missing but not the intent of the barrel bars that are set up for a serious shot of whiskey.

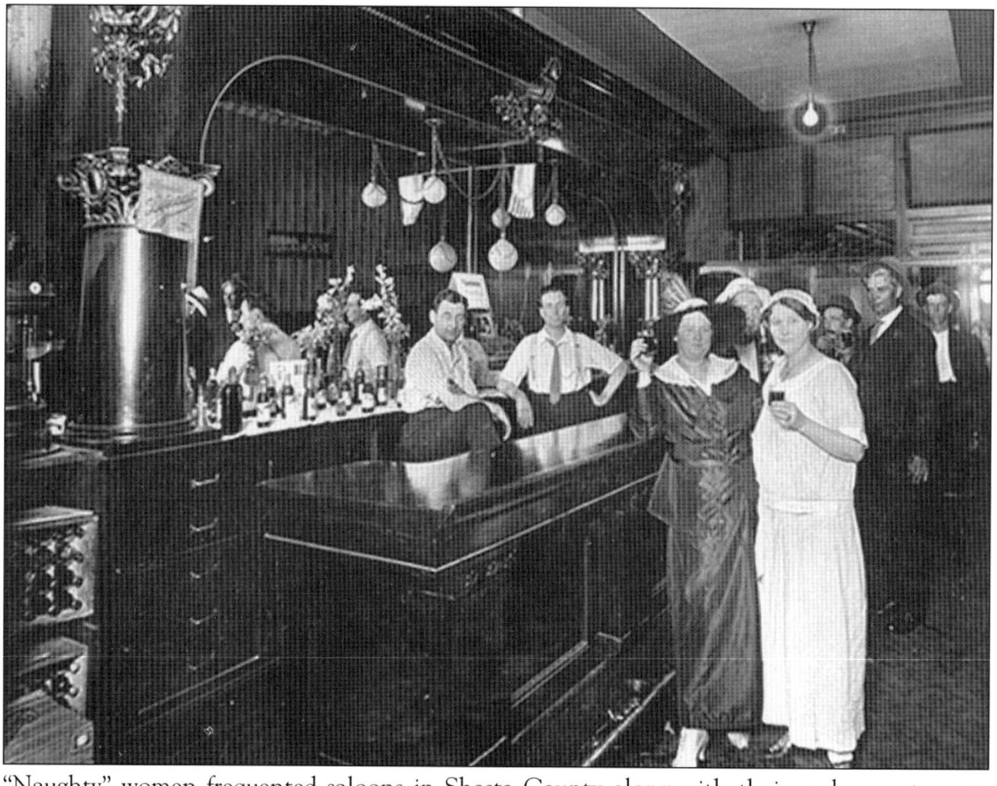

"Naughty" women frequented saloons in Shasta County along with their male counterparts until prohibition went into effect in 1920. This bar was probably located on California Street.

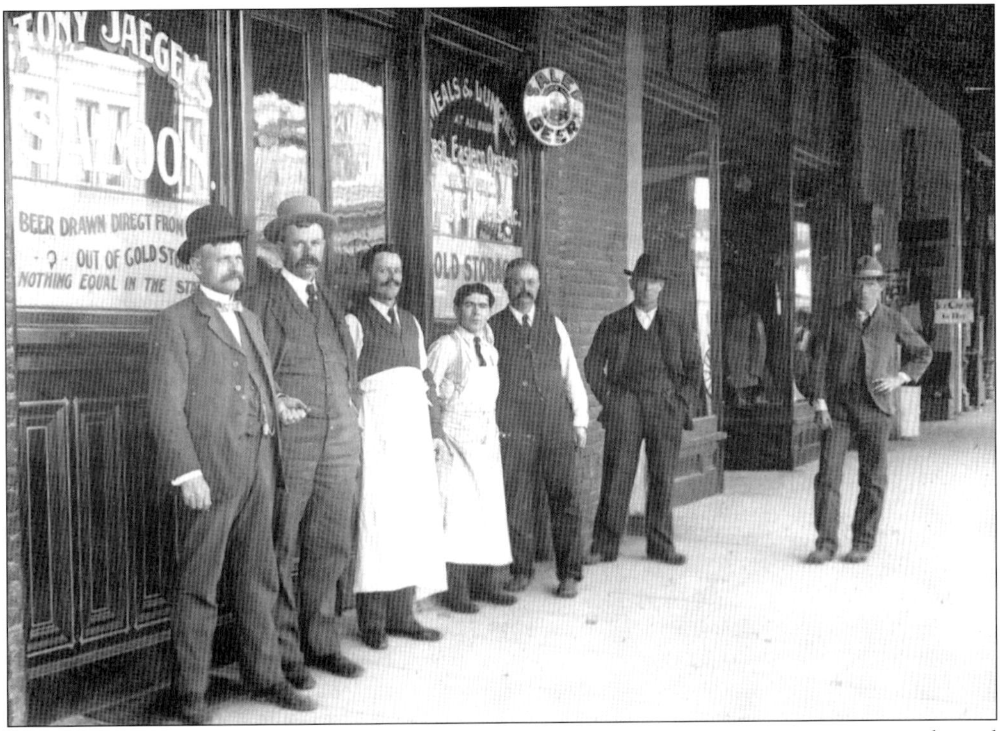

Tony Jaegel's Restaurant and Saloon on Market Street, pictured here in 1927, served good food and drinks. It was later owned by George Lapp, whose mother was a Jaegel. Someone once said, "There was more farming and mining done there than was ever done in the field or in the mines."

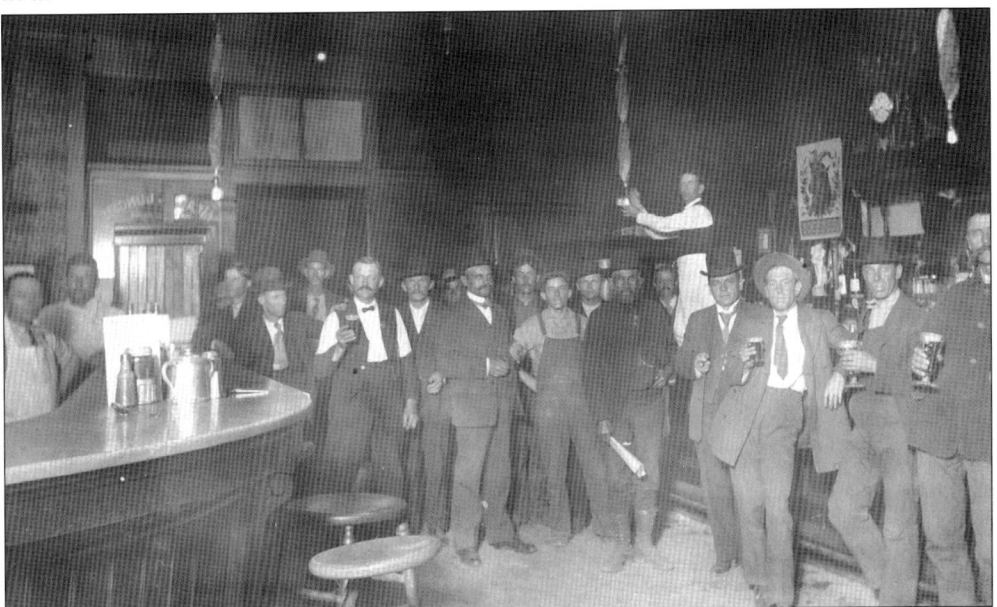

All the cooking at Jaegel's was done behind the counter on a wood stove. The meals were served at the counter except for a couple of tables at the back where the few women who came in were served.

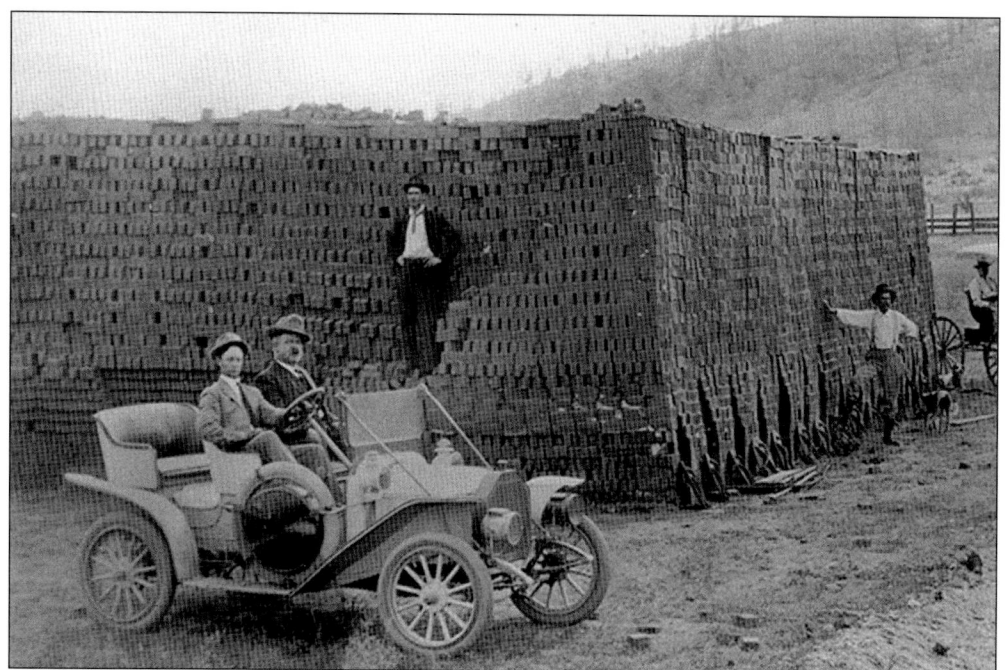

The Holt and Gregg brickyard was located just south of the Redding city boundary on a railway spur. Operations began in 1880 and the company manufactured the materials for nearly every brick building in this part of the state until it closed in 1918. In this 1913 photo a stack of finished bricks awaits shipment.

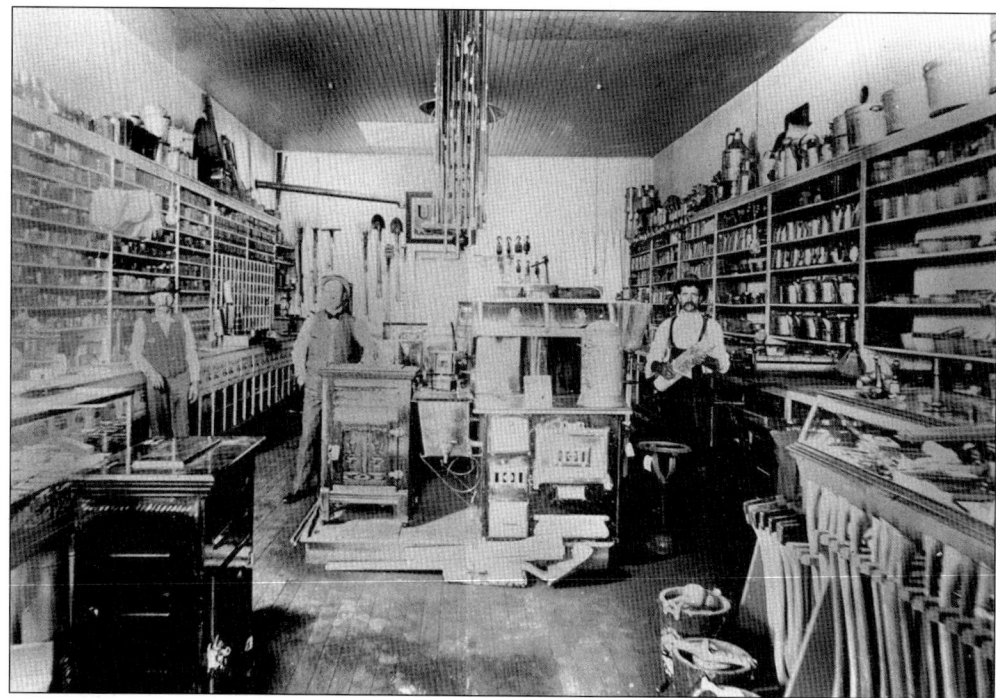

This interior view of the Russell & LeFebvre Hardware store was taken in 1913. The building is now the home of the Shasta Historical Society in the downtown mall.

The dredges, shown here c. 1910, were floating mining machines whose endless chain of steel buckets could reach down into the bedrock under the deeper gravel beds where gold could be found. Waste was pumped out of the rear as tailings. The ban on gold production forced the end of dredging in 1942.

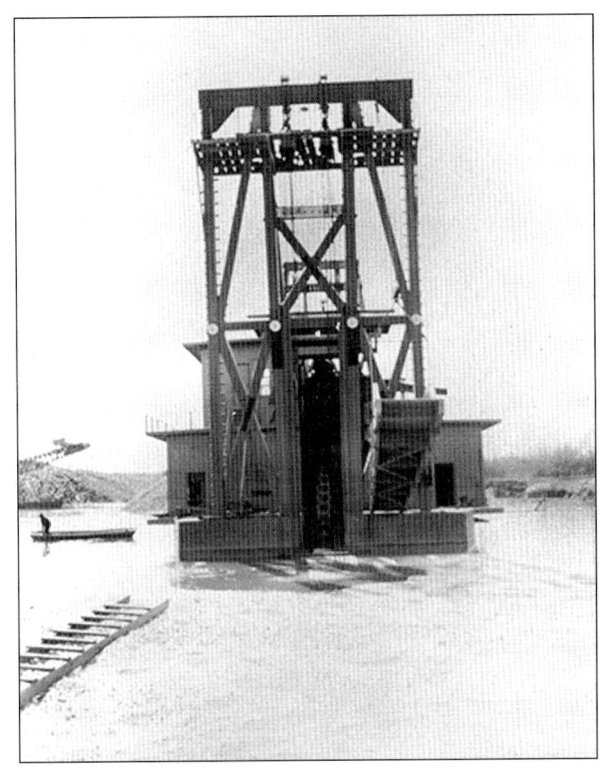

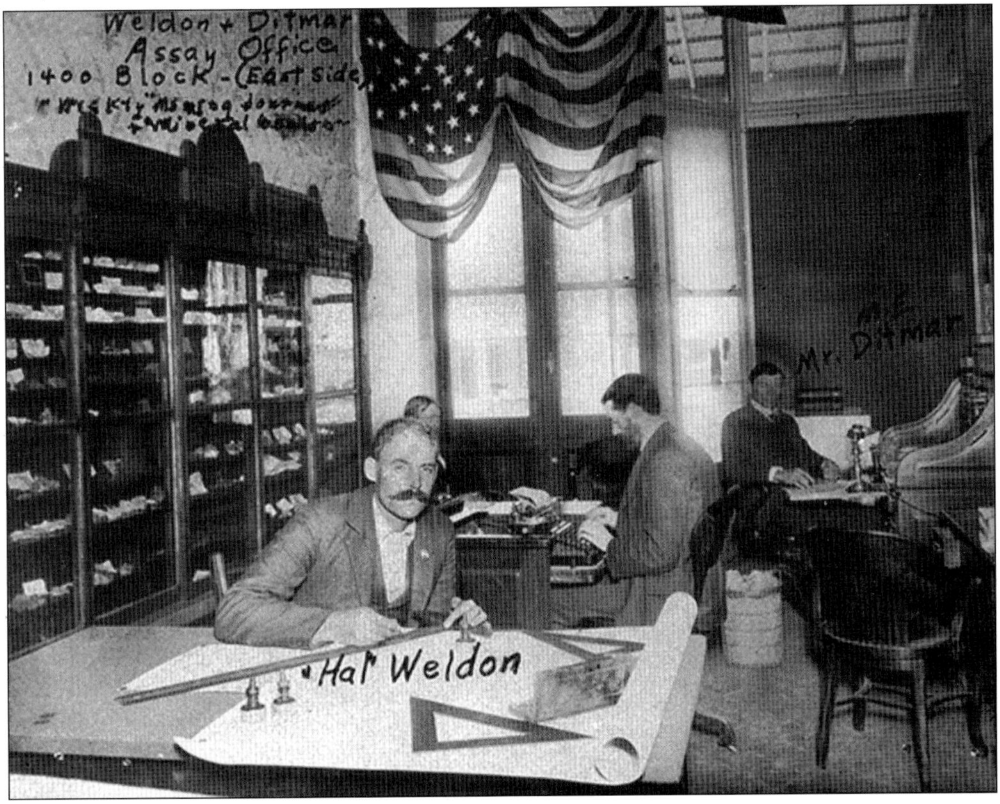

The Weldon and Dittmar Assay Office, shown here c. 1915, was located at 1449 Market Street in Redding. Besides having an assay and drafting business, Hal Weldon and M.E. Dittmar produced a monthly mining journal called *Mineral Wealth*. Weldon invented a simple process for assaying gold and silver ore using a solution that sold for $1 a bottle.

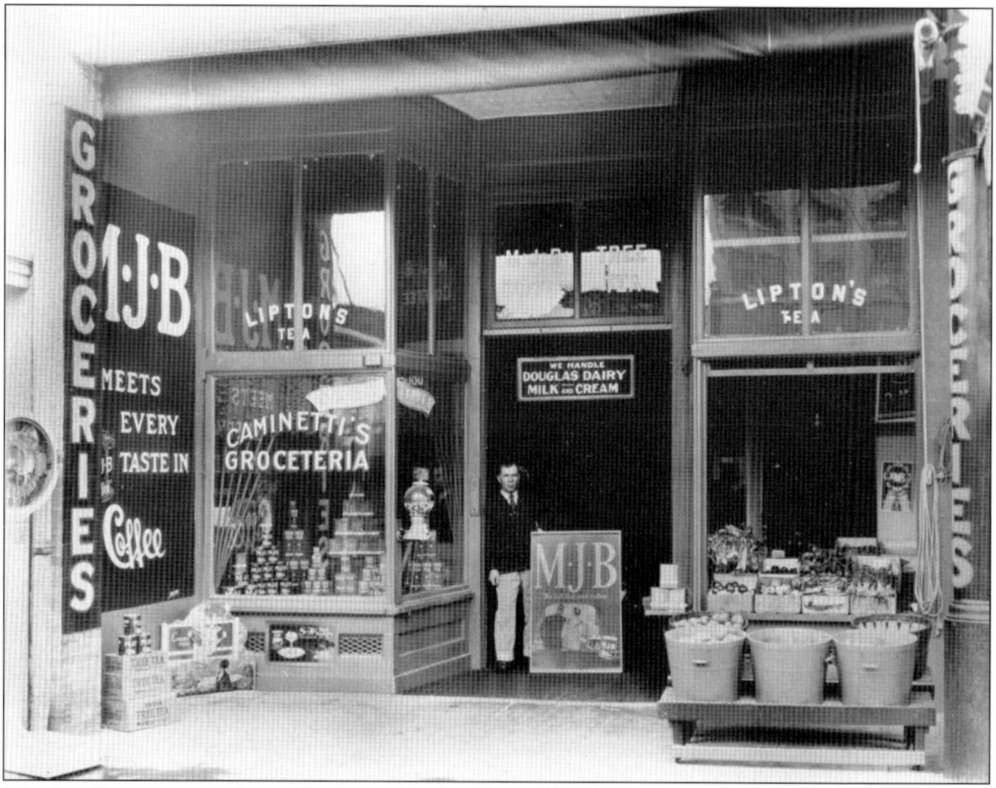

Charles Caminetti is shown here in the doorway of his "Groceteria" on Market Street in the 1930s. In the days before supermarkets, stores offered home delivery, credit, and gossip.

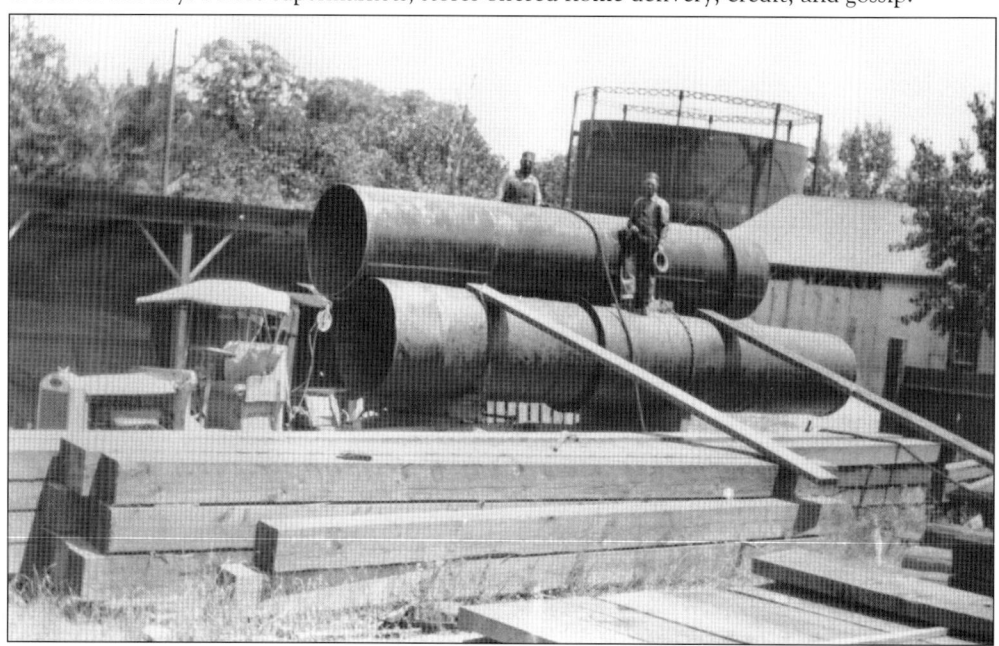

Gerlinger's Iron Works on Placer Street distributed industrial supplies, equipment, steel cable, pumps, and bolts. They are still in operation.

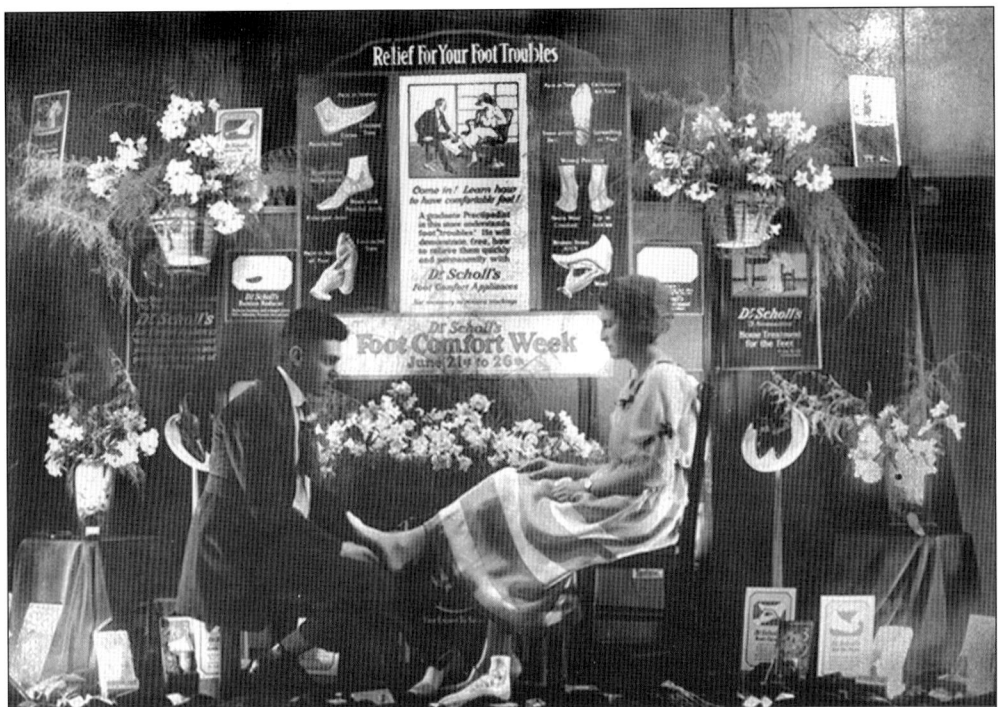
Evelyn Hiatt Blandin samples the wares with the help of an unidentified clerk at the McCormick-Saeltzer store during "Dr. Scholl's Foot Comfort Week," June 21–26, 1920.

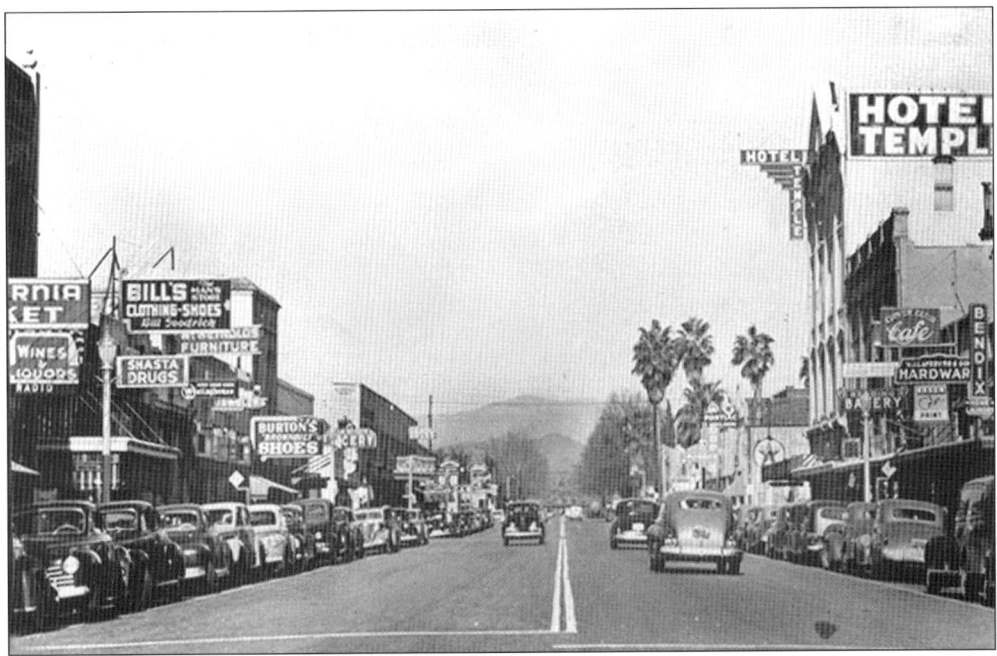
This view shows the 1400 block of Market Street (Highway 99) in the 1930s. In the decade between 1930 and 1940, with the building of Highway 99 and the deterioration of the business district on California Street, Market Street began to grow.

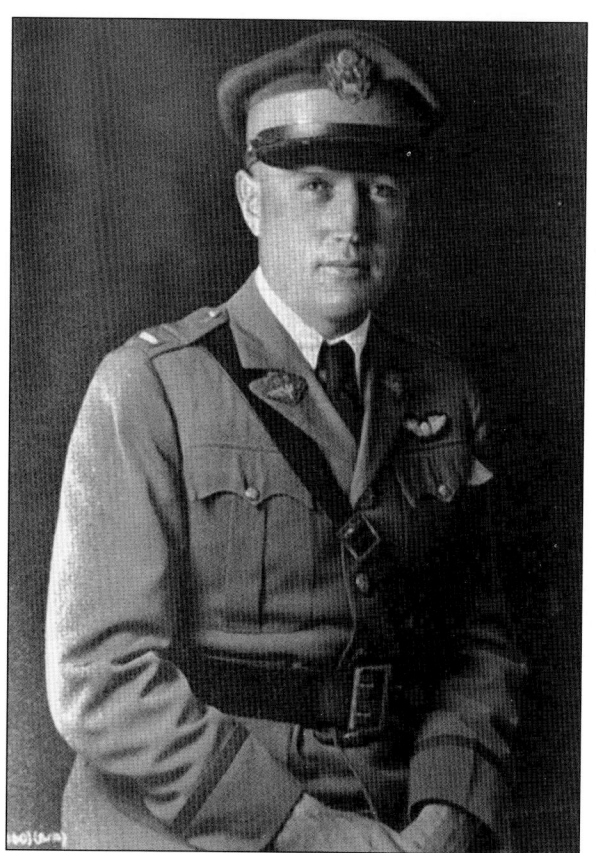

Lt. John Benton, a member of a pioneer family, was killed in Buenos Aires while flying in the Pan-American Good Will Flight of 1927. Benton Airfield was dedicated to him during Fourth of July weekend in 1929. This photo of Lieutenant Benton was taken around two years before his death.

The Benton Airport U.S. Weather Bureau building was first known as Johnson Hill. Established in 1927 on 451 acres adjacent to Placer Road, it served the occasional aviator who, if he planned to stay overnight, used a manzanita bush as a tie-down for his aircraft.

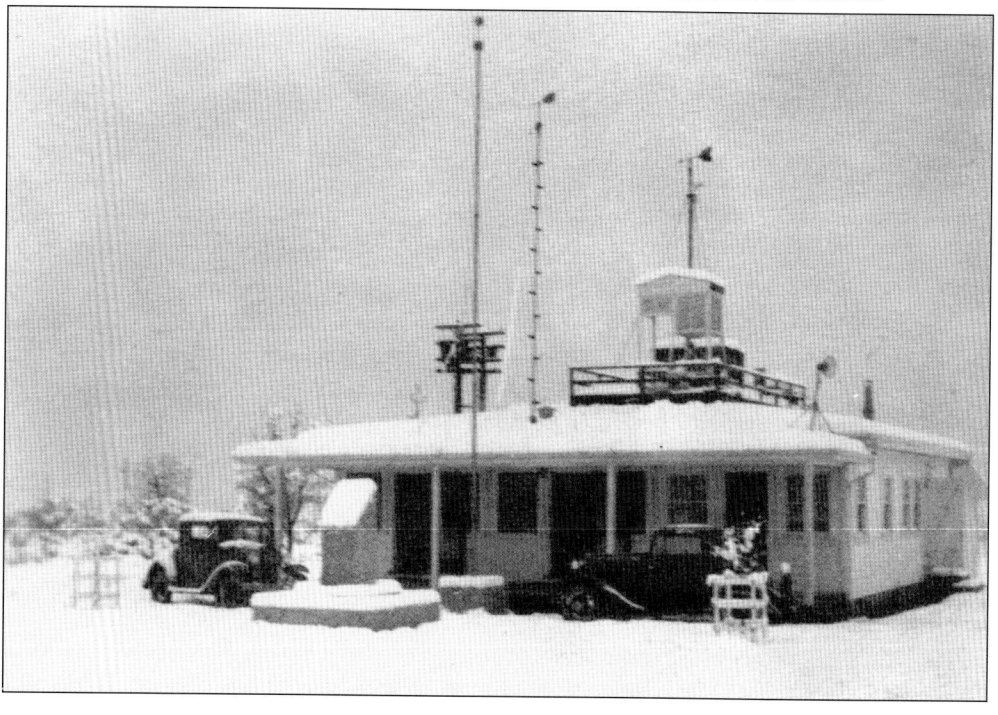

Four

SPORTS AND ENTERTAINMENT 1900–1920

Like most Americans living in the early 1900s, the citizens of Redding wanted to relax and enjoy sports and entertainment on the weekends and on holidays. Among the most popular forms of entertainment for the entire family were the many vaudeville shows that toured the West Coast. The Armory Hall Building in Redding was home to a number of these fun and intriguing shows. During much of this time, the armory hall's proprietor was George W. Bush, who worked hard to bring "class acts" to Redding. Traveling shows were particularly popular in the late fall and winter months when it was difficult to enjoy the area's natural recreational activities. In January 1909 Bush secured the "Jerry from Kerry" show, a "roaring farce comedy and vaudeville attraction" starring two well-known national actors and a "superior uniformed concert band and orchestra." Typically, the actors and stagehands would promote the act days before by handing out show bills all around town. The day before the opening show, they would display some of their costumes and music at a street parade, enticing townspeople to spend the 50¢ to see the full act. Usually a full review of the performance would be written up in the Redding *Searchlight* newspaper, providing details of the acts and actors. For example, in the "Jerry from Kerry" show, the following account appeared two days before the opening:

> *The next attraction at the Armory will be Patten & Perry's funny musical farce comedy and vaudeville show. This company has been playing with unprecedented success, and is beyond a doubt the brightest and most refined amusement on the road. Among the many special features with this company are Campbell and Fletcher, the comedy acrobats; the famous Gibbs children, in the great juvenile act; Professor Cailloute, the king of the wire; and many other high class specialties. This company also carries its own special uniformed band and orchestra.*

All sorts of oddball shows came through Redding in those early years. Traveling magicians and fortune-tellers were among the popular entertainers on the circuit, as were clairvoyants and psychics. Known as "The Temple," one New York palmist made a big splash in Redding when he arrived in town claiming, "I positively tell just what you wish to know. I have hundreds of letters to prove it." He claimed to have special clairvoyance for providing helpful information on mining prospects, business, and law investments, and "wonderful news on love and marriage." He set up shop in the lobby of the Golden Eagle Hotel, posted office hours for individual consultations, and special show-time performances for the non-believers. One of his ads ran this message for the untrusting: "Realizing that a personal visit will do more to advertise him than columns of self-praise, The Great Temple invites you to call, and unless you are thoroughly satisfied, he will accept no fee."

Redding residents became excited when they learned that Professor Fait, a self-proclaimed "world-renowned hypnotist" scheduled a multi-day performance in town. The "professor" traveled with an assortment of assistants who helped solicit questions from the audience. These questions were written down on paper and submitted to Fait during the performance. He would then proceed to "answer" the questions correctly while the unbelieving audience broke loose with thunderous applause. His ads claimed that he was so good that he must surely be "in league with supernatural forces." Of course, the "professor" could only take a limited number of sealed questions from the audience and one was never sure of the source of each question. The final part of the show had "selected customers" brought up on stage, hypnotized, and made to do amusing stunts. The ad for this show promised that Professor Fait would "change the program every night," and it encouraged patrons to come back with someone new and see another show. Show prices ran from 15¢ for the back seats to 35¢ for the front "Loge seats." "The Psychic Wonder" performed for a full two hours with "roaring fun" guaranteed.

Music was a very important part of the lives of all Redding residents, men and women, young and old. Local concerts by high school bands and private orchestras led the way with regular performances in hotels, at the armory and in the high school auditorium. The radio was a must for all families and hours were spent with the family clustered around the radio listening to musical programs such as John Phillip Sousa's rousing marches and pop tunes. Weekly comedy and drama programs were particularly engrossing and families regularly tuned in for their favorite radio show. The phonograph, invented by Thomas Edison in the 1880s, was another popular device that brought favorite music into the privacy of the home and could be listened to time and time again. Edison's Amberol records, an improvement on the original records, sold for 50¢ and could be obtained in Redding at several stores. By 1910 a lucrative mail-order business sprouted up with residents able to order their favorite tunes from a San Francisco-based firm. Pianos, too, were very popular, despite their high price.

Baseball was big in Redding, beginning in the late 1880s and continuing into the first decades of the 20th century. Local high school leagues planned schedules for boys and girls, with competition tough among the area's secondary schools. Games were grand entertainment affairs as well, and the local newspapers played up major contests. Men's leagues grew during this time and on Sundays starting in April baseball offered Redding families an inexpensive afternoon of fun. The Redding Tigers met and conquered most of the area teams throughout 1910–1920. One contest matched the favored Redding team against the Marysville Tigers. While the Tigers were not in "the normal league," the Redding players eagerly accepted the challenge to a Sunday shootout. Both teams fielded eleven players; nine started and played, while one relief pitcher and one player were kept in reserve in case of injury to a teammate. By 1920 baseball scores for local teams and the up and coming professional teams appeared in the newspaper, and local baseball fans followed the game intently. It is interesting to listen to the reporting of the above noted game and the excitement and anticipation that led up to it:

> *The Redding Tigers defeated the Marysville Tigers Sunday afternoon in Recreation Park by the score of 5 to 4. At the end of the ninth inning the score was 4 to 4. Marysville failed to add another tally to their list in the tenth frame. In Redding's frame of the tenth inning Gilbert DeForrest came to the bat when the score was tied and with Casey Bergin on second base. The batsman laced out a clean drive that could well have been a home run, but as Bergin scored the winning run, the game was ended and DeForrest walked calmly to the grandstand amid cheers. Sunday's game between Marysville and Redding Tigers was the best contest ever pulled off in this city.*

Basketball, begun back east in the late 1800s, was another popular game in Redding. Dr. James Naismith, a physical education instructor at the Young Men's Christian Association Training School in Springfield, Massachusetts, invented this indoor game in 1891. By 1905 it had swept the country, including the North State. In these early years of the game, it was not uncommon to see a wide range of rules enforced, including allowing up to 15 players on the court at any one time.

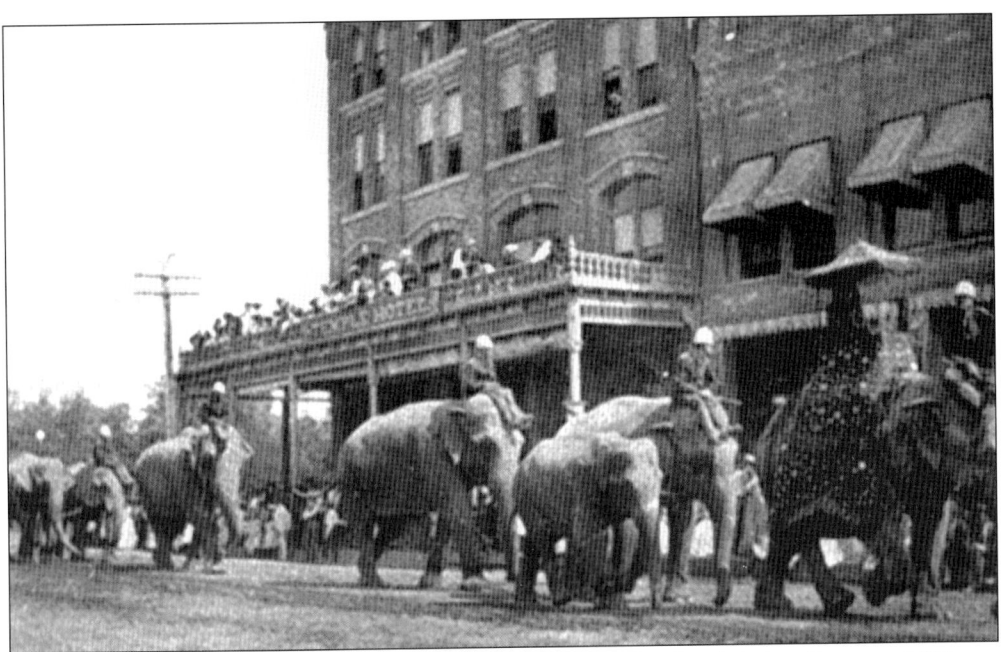

A parade of circus elephants passes in front of the Temple Hotel on Market Street, c. 1900.

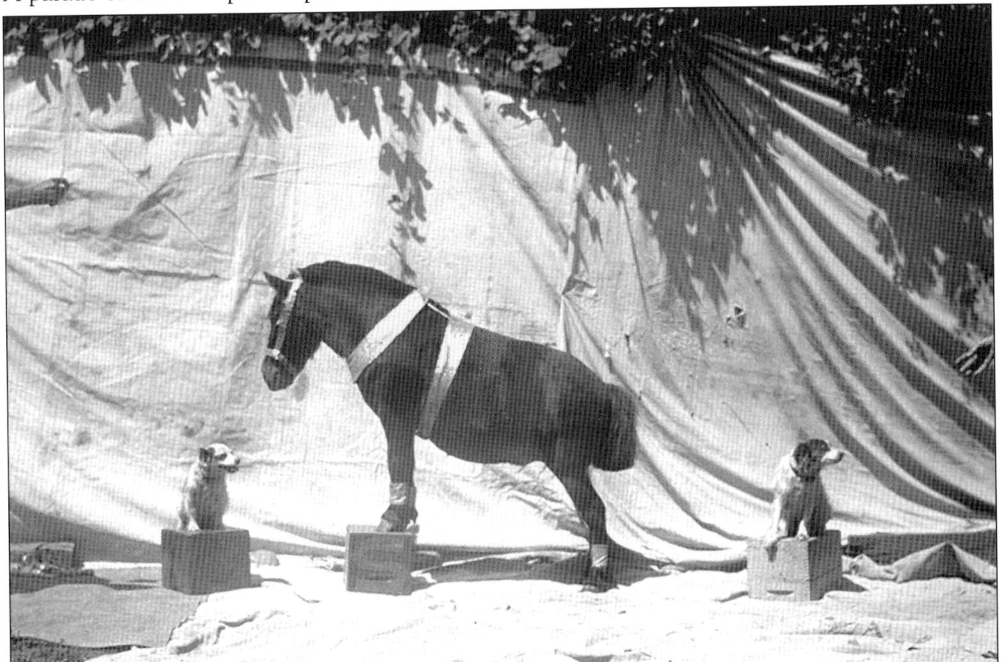

For 20 years, until 1931, Mark and Ada Merrill had a traveling tent show featuring two bears, two ponies, sheep, monkeys, and dogs. At first they traveled by team and wagon and later by truck. In the spring the show traveled for four months throughout Northern California, Nevada, and eastern Oregon. Mark was also in charge of the armory hall and was stage manager for a vaudeville theater in Redding.

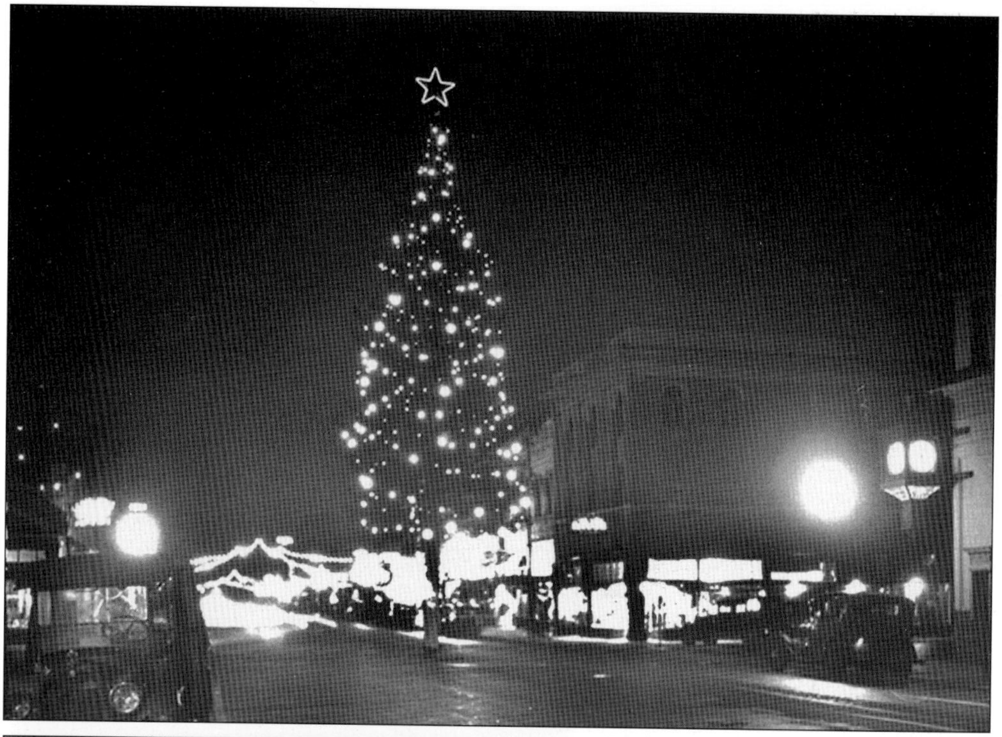

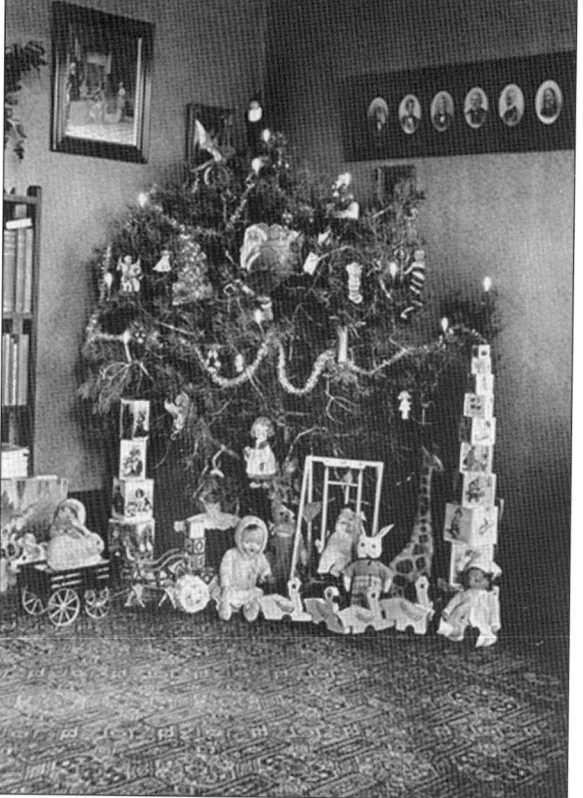

In this photo, Redding residents celebrate the holiday season around the city's Christmas tree, located in the middle of the intersection of Market and Yuba Streets, c. 1920. Students were treated to a free movie at the Redding Theatre, and Santa Claus passed out bags of candy, nuts, oranges, and apples.

Santa brought these toys for a lucky little girl one night before Christmas in 1920. A Shasta County family decorated the tree with candles and a variety of ornaments.

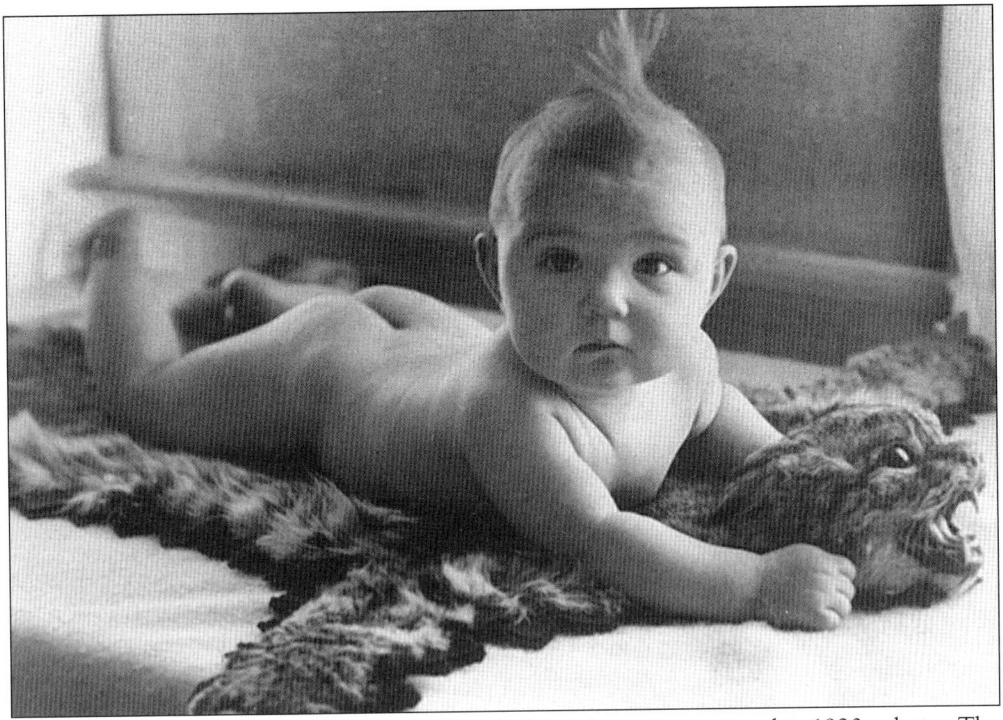

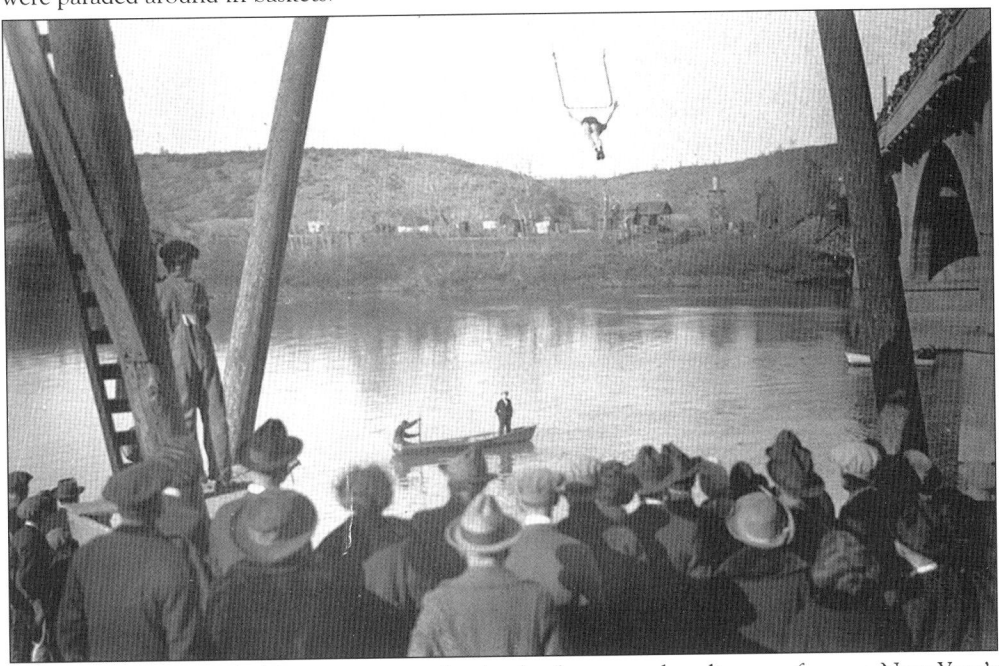

A Shasta County infant doesn't seem excited about the new year in this 1920s photo. The tradition of using a baby to signify the New Year began in Greece about 600 B.C. when babies were paraded around in baskets.

From a swing suspended between two poles in the foreground, a diver performs a New Year's Day high dive into the Sacramento River in Redding in 1918. The Benton farm is on the north side of the river.

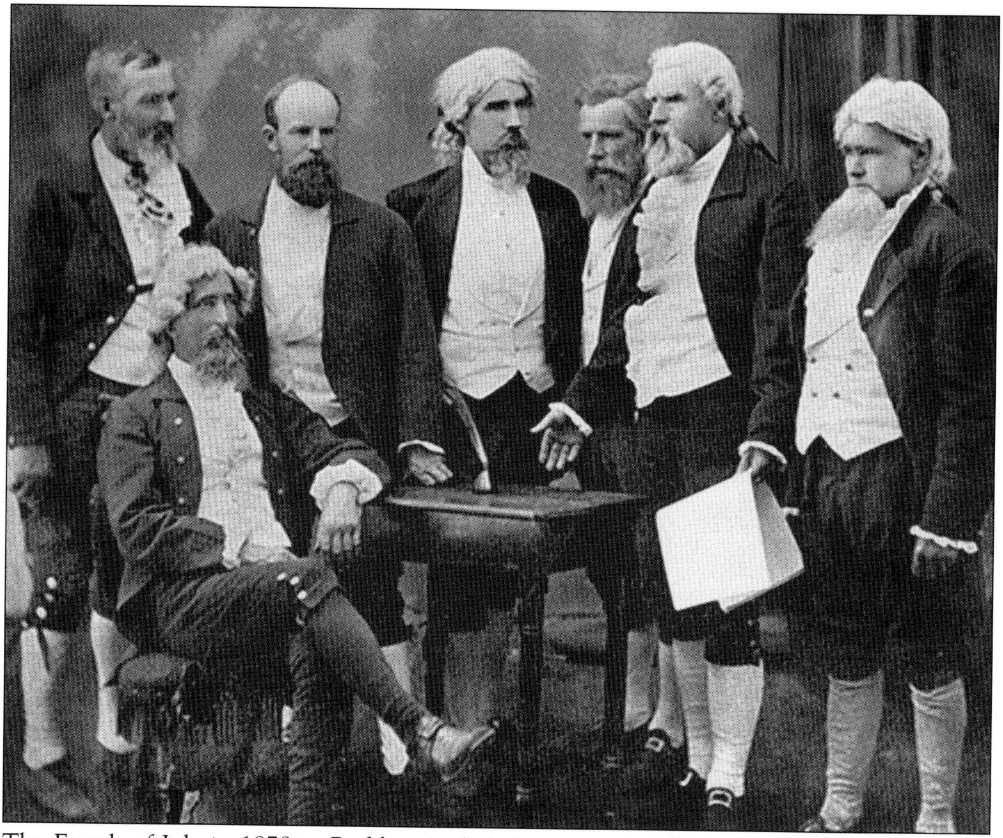

The Fourth of July in 1878 in Redding included a procession featuring historic vignettes re-enacted by a number of costumed residents. According to a newspaper report of the festivities, this scene related to the signing of the Declaration of Independence and was titled "Iron Sons of '76."

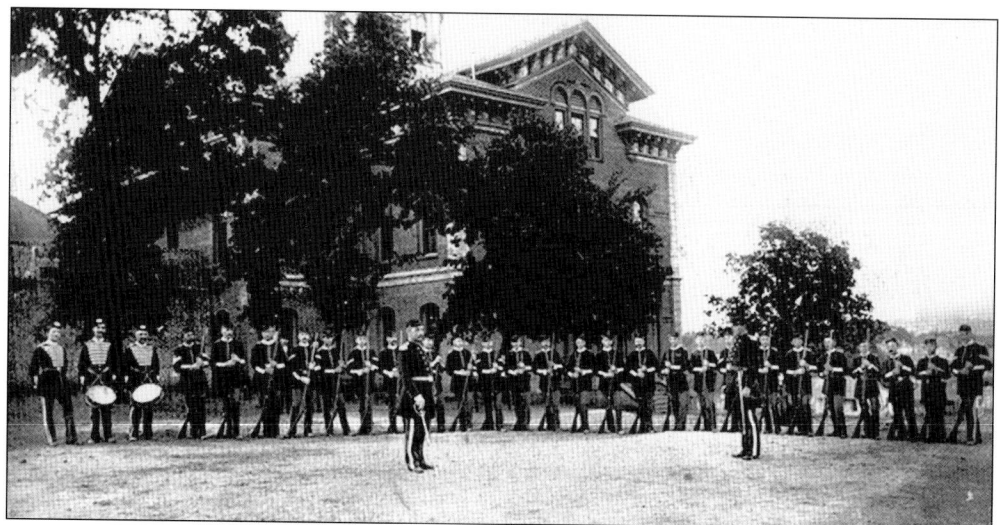

"Pop" William Smith, who later became police chief, stands with the state militia in front of the courthouse.

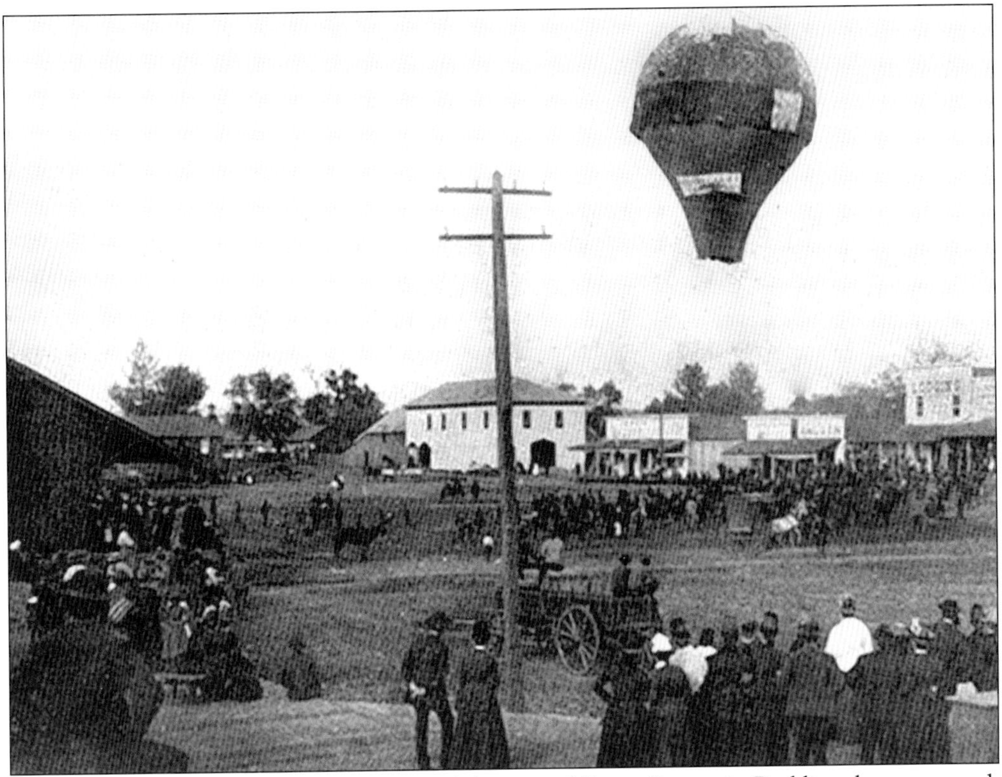

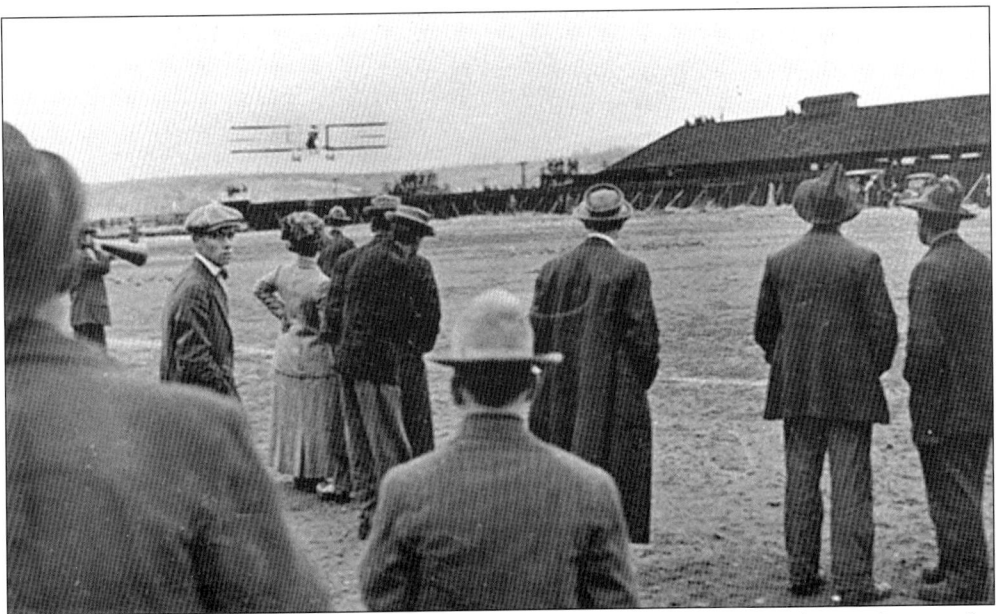

A balloon ascension near the corner of California and Butte Streets in Redding draws a crowd, c. 1900. The vacant field was the site of many events. At one time California Street, visible in the background, was the main thoroughfare of Redding because of its proximity to the railroad.

The first plane to land in Redding in 1909, a Curtis biplane, arrives for the air show at the fairground at the north end of Court Street.

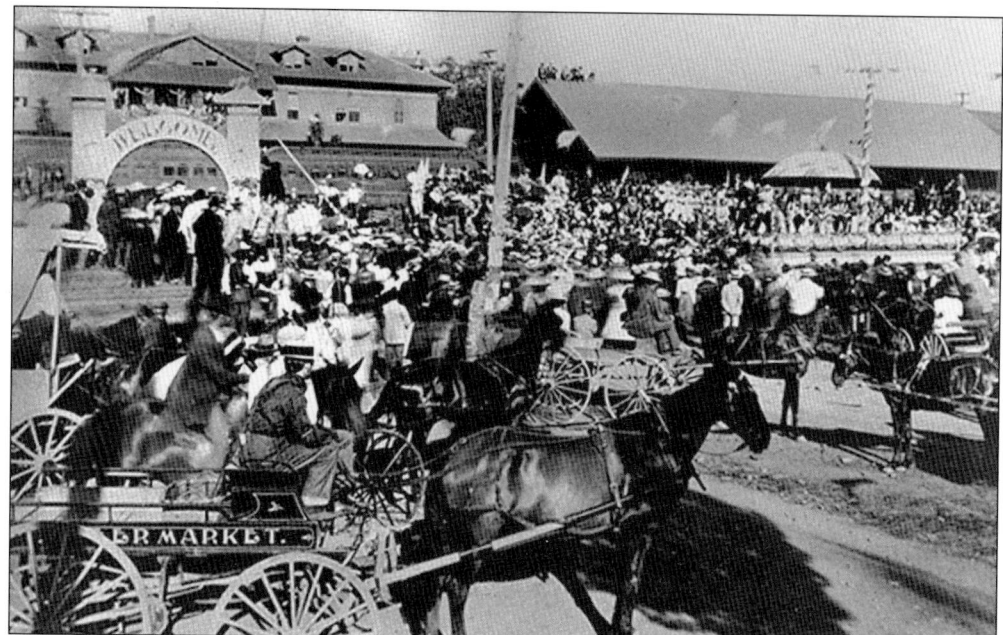

William Jennings Bryan visited the train station in Redding around 1896. He was running for president and decided the best strategy was to take his message to the people by speaking around the nation. Bryan, a Populist candidate, supported free silver. He lost to William McKinley who ran on a single gold standard platform. In 1925 Bryan faced off in a courtroom battle against Clarence Darrow in the famous "Scopes Trial," which argued whether evolution could be taught in schools. Bryan, who represented creationists, died a week after the trial.

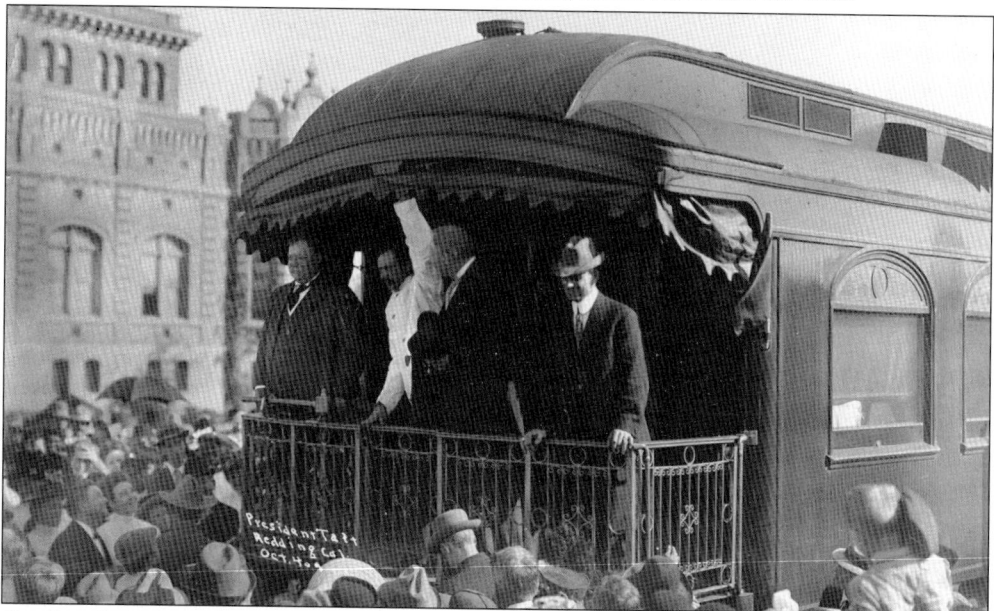

On October 4, 1909, President Taft visited Redding and was greeted by 2,000 people who listened to an address by the portly chief executive. Apparently at a loss for words, he generalized on Redding's "sturdy upright men and chubby-legged babies." Taft then sank back in his easy chair and waved the train on.

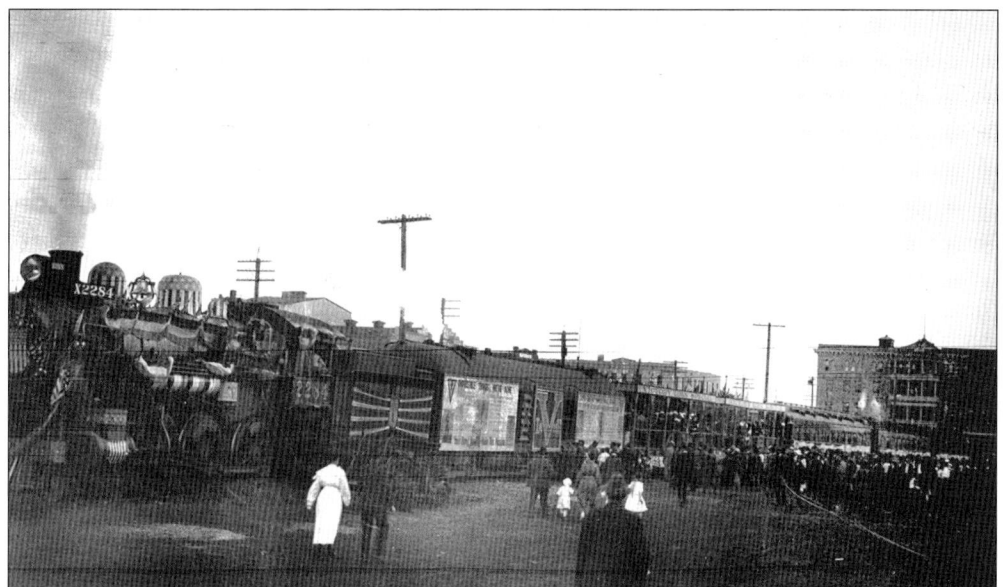

On November 11, 1918, the World War I Victory Train passed through Redding. The signs say "Impossible Things We've Done," and "Let's Do the Impossible Again." The white hats of sailors can be seen in the open car.

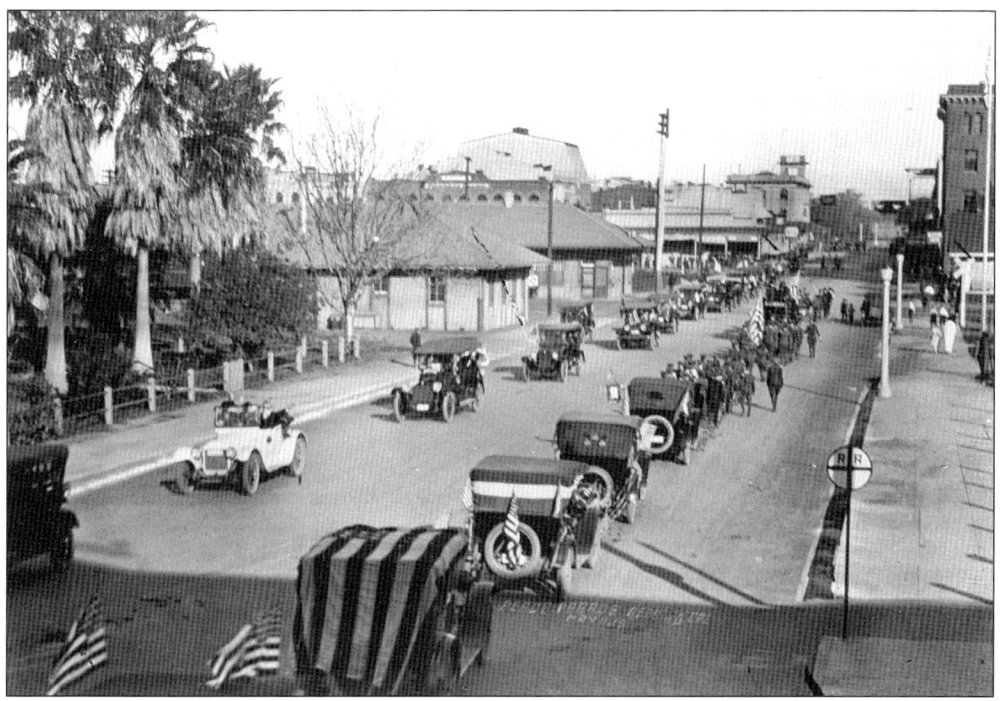

World War I ended on the 11th hour of the 11th day of the 11th month. Many people are wearing flu masks in this photo, taken during the Peace Parade on November 11, 1918. From 1918 to 1919 an epidemic spread from the Western Front, killing an estimated 500,000 people in the United States.

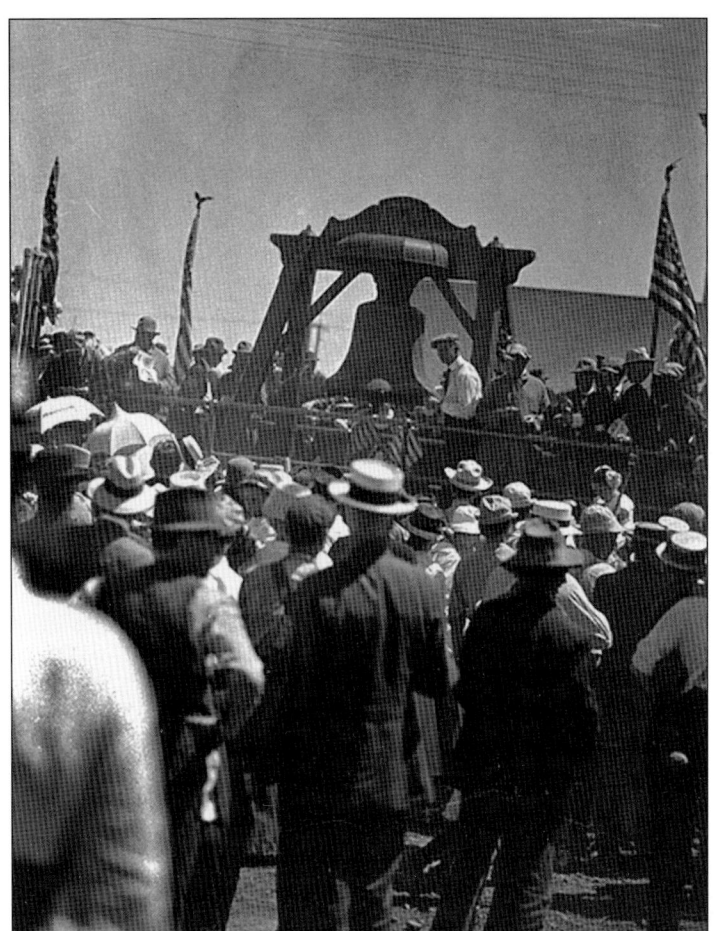

The Liberty Bell arrived in Redding on July 15, 1915, en route to the Panama-Pacific Exposition in San Francisco. The bell traveled over 10,000 miles on the trip, stopping in many towns and cities along the way.

In this photo from 1918, a parade of Native Sons of the Golden West and Native Daughters of the Golden West passes by the Golden Eagle Hotel.

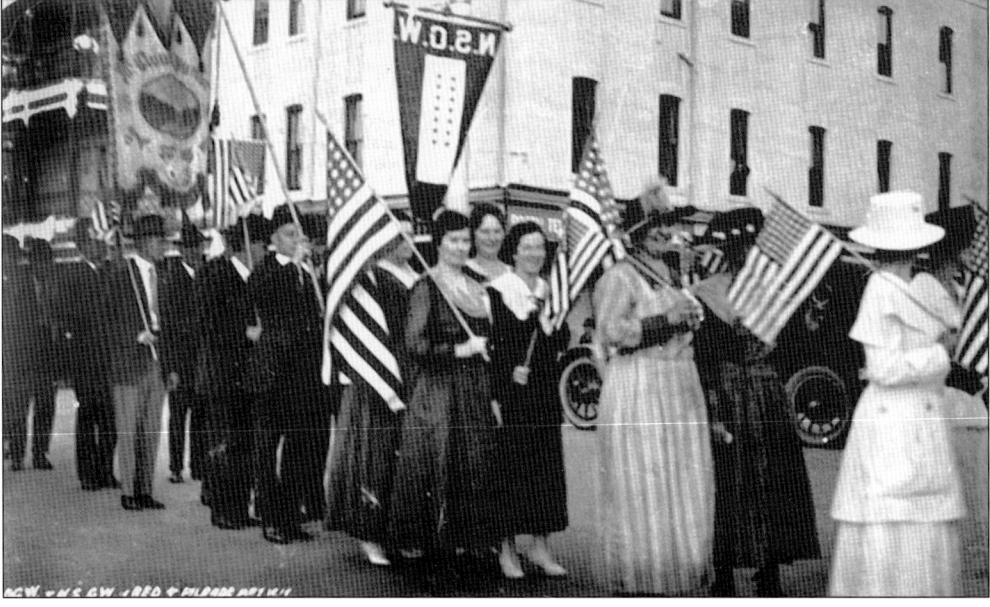

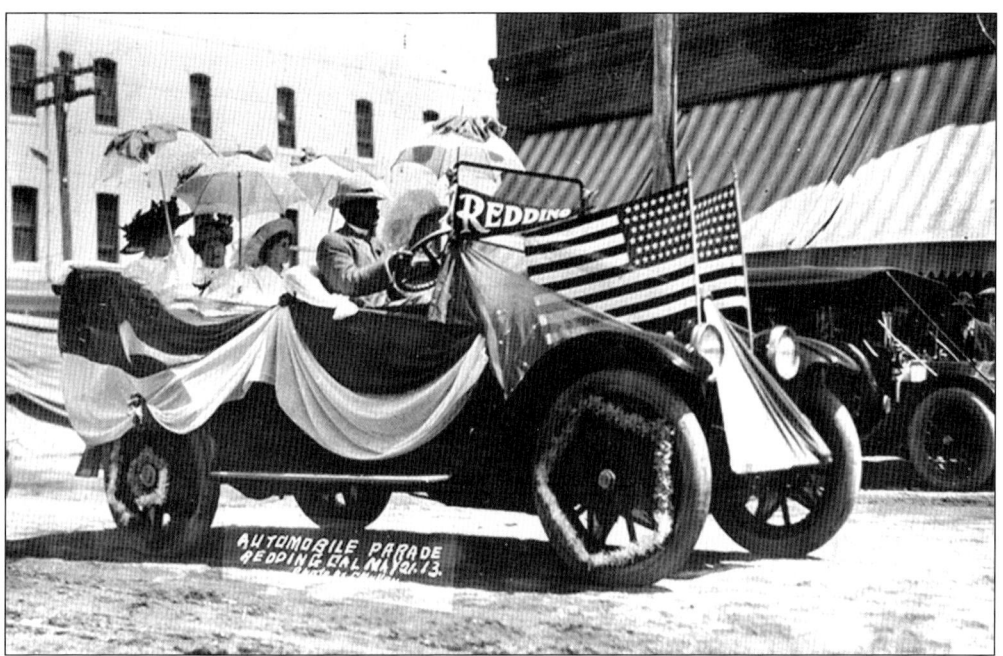
An automobile parade passes down Market Street on May Day in 1913.

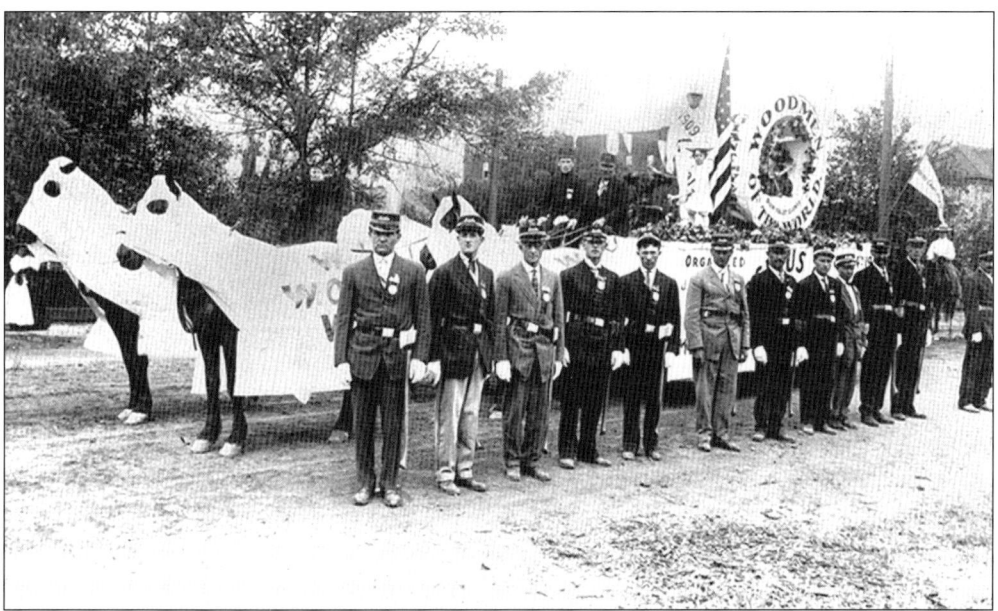
This Woodmen of the World float participates in the Fourth of July parade in 1909. Woodman of the World was one of the first fraternal benefit societies in the United States. It was founded in 1883 by Joseph Root of Iowa, who dreamed of a fraternal benefit society designed to provide financial security to families from all walks of life. The society had its own semi-military "Uniform Rank" and is still in operation today with 825,000 members.

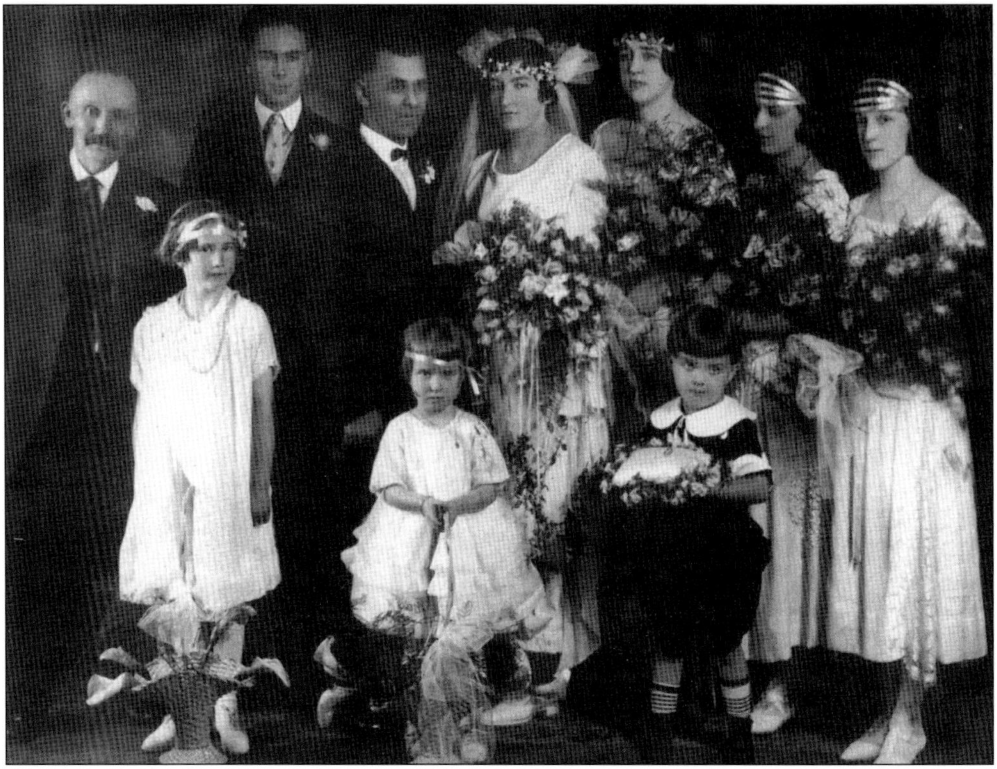

Albert and Myra Scragg Grigarick of Redding were wed March 2, 1924. John Scragg, father of the bride and owner of the Redding Florist, is on the far left. The flower girl (center) is Sara Fraser Magnussen, and Aurelis Shuffelton is on the far right. The wedding was held in the Methodist church located on Market and Sacramento Streets. Arthur E. Hoyt performed the ceremony.

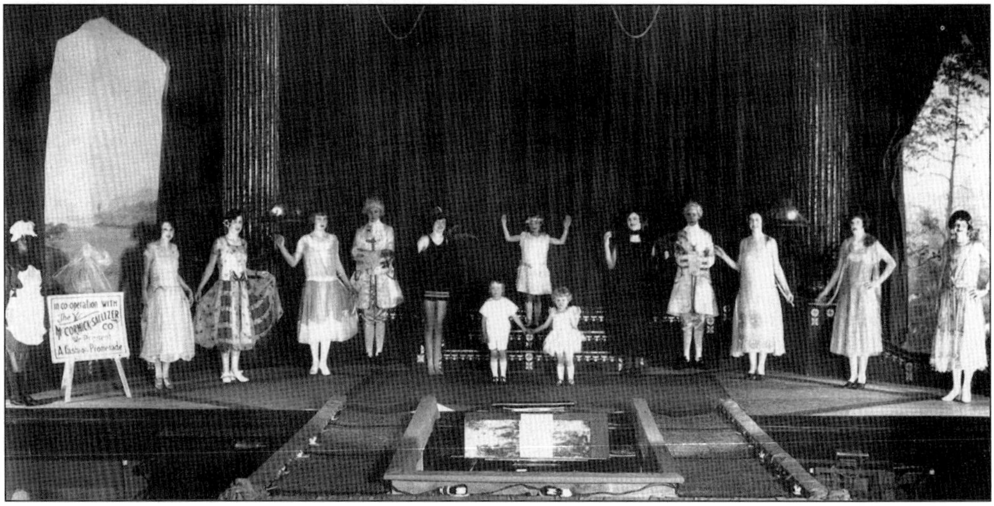

A McCormick-Saeltzer style show was held at the Redding Theatre in 1925. Participants, from left to right, included Willie May Strickland, Wanda Alward, Lois Williams, Dorothy Aberg, unidentified, Helen Thurston, unidentified, La Diem Cordi, Dorothy Cordi, Nelda Hunt, unknown, Virginia Webb, Verna Platz, and Edith Spangler.

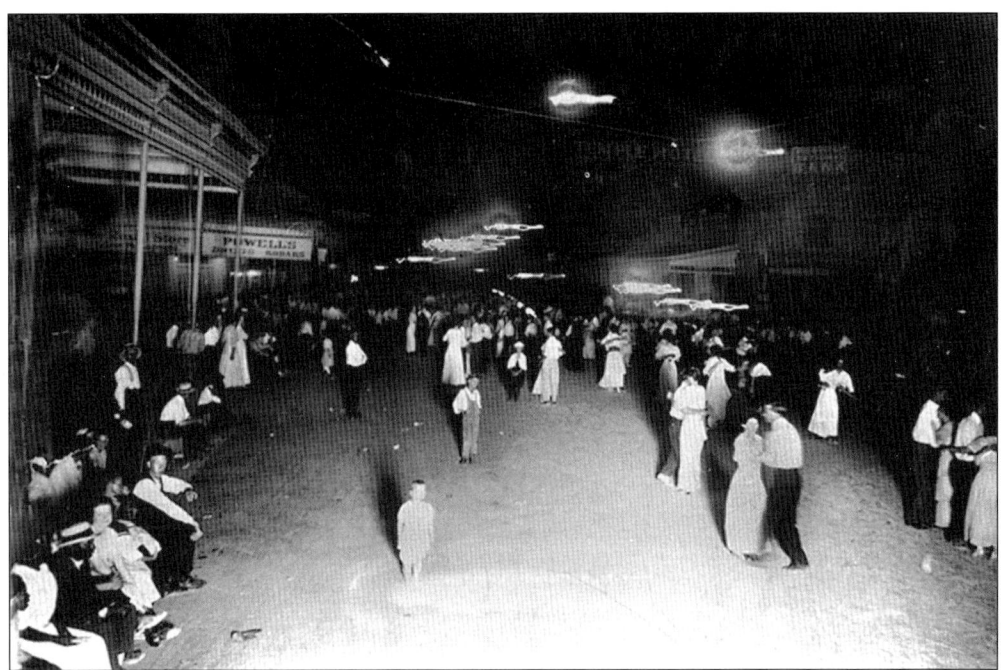
This 1916 street dance was held on Market Street between Yuba and Butte Streets.

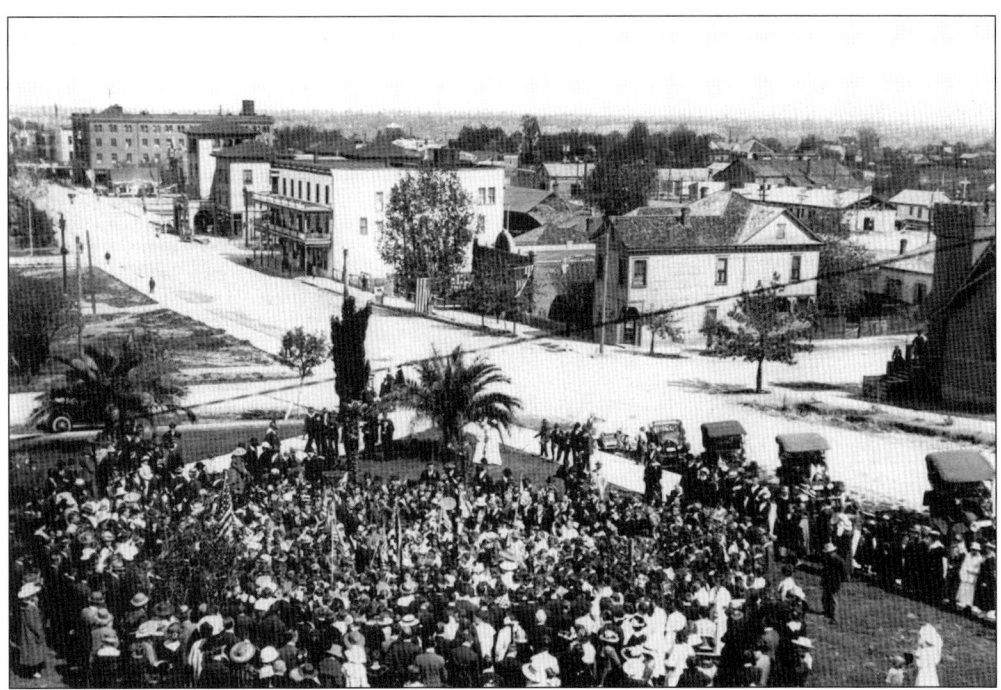
A tree planting ceremony was held by the Native Sons at the courthouse at Yuba and Court Streets in April 1917. The marker and a sycamore tree are still there. In the background is the Western Hotel with its balcony, and at the far left, the chamber of commerce, Carnegie Library, and Lorenz Hotel can be seen. The church is All Saints Episcopal.

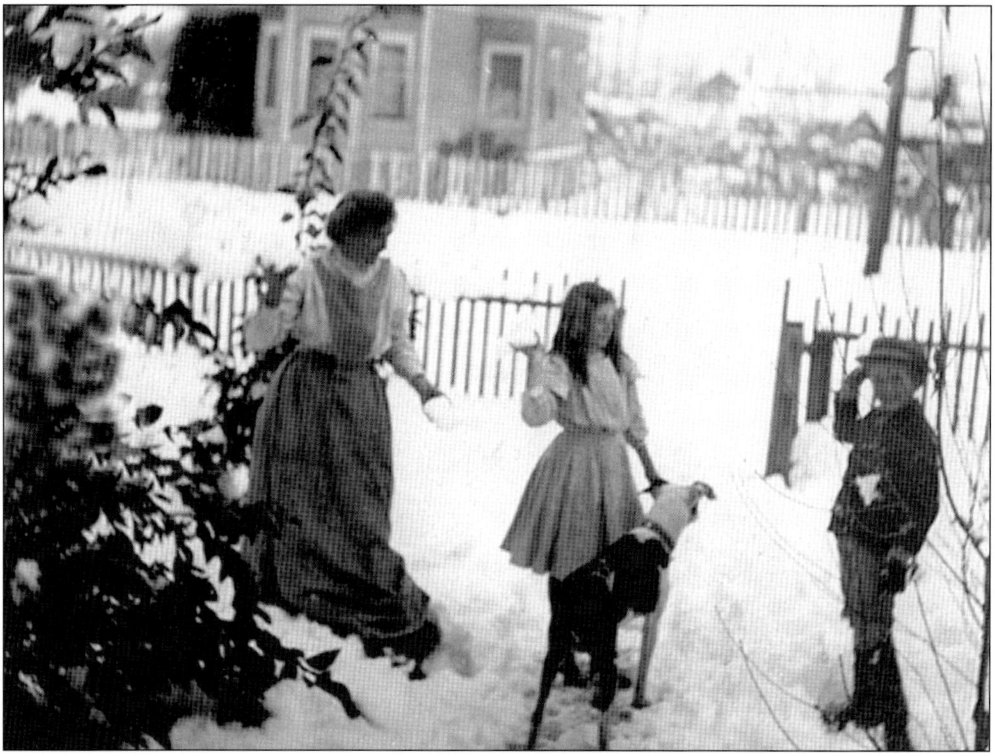

Shown here, from left to right, are Irene Bidwell, Thelma Richardson, and Babe Bystle having some fun in the snow at the Adolph Bystle residence on West Street, c. 1900.

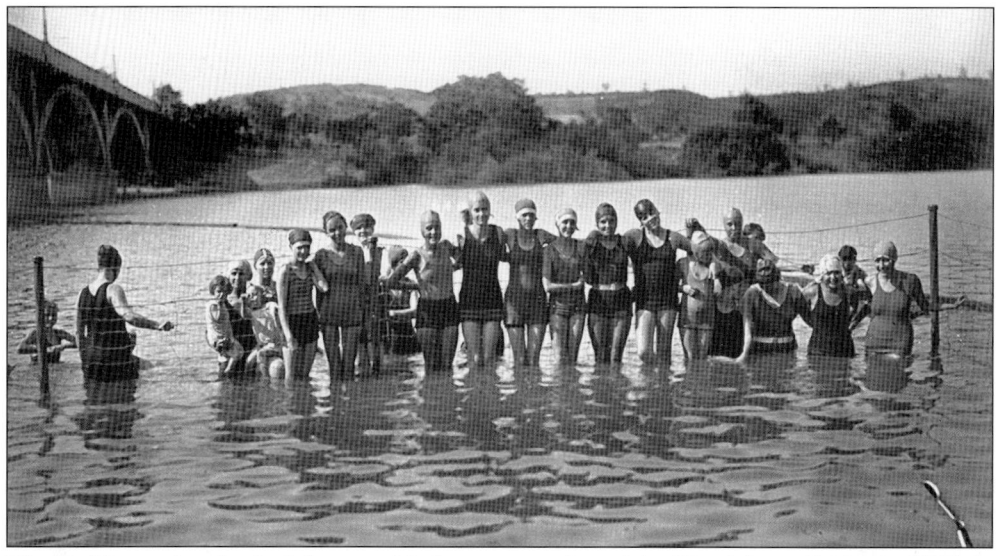

The Redding swimming hole began with the construction of the Diestlehorst Bridge in 1915. In 1923 the city hired Mrs. Walter Dimmick as a supervisor for the swimming season at $75 per month and Robert Hill as a lifeguard. Later, concrete steps and a kiddie pen were built. Mrs. Dimmick became the city's summertime babysitter. As soon as the children learned to swim their parents would bring them to the swimming hole for the entire afternoon, picking them up in time for dinner.

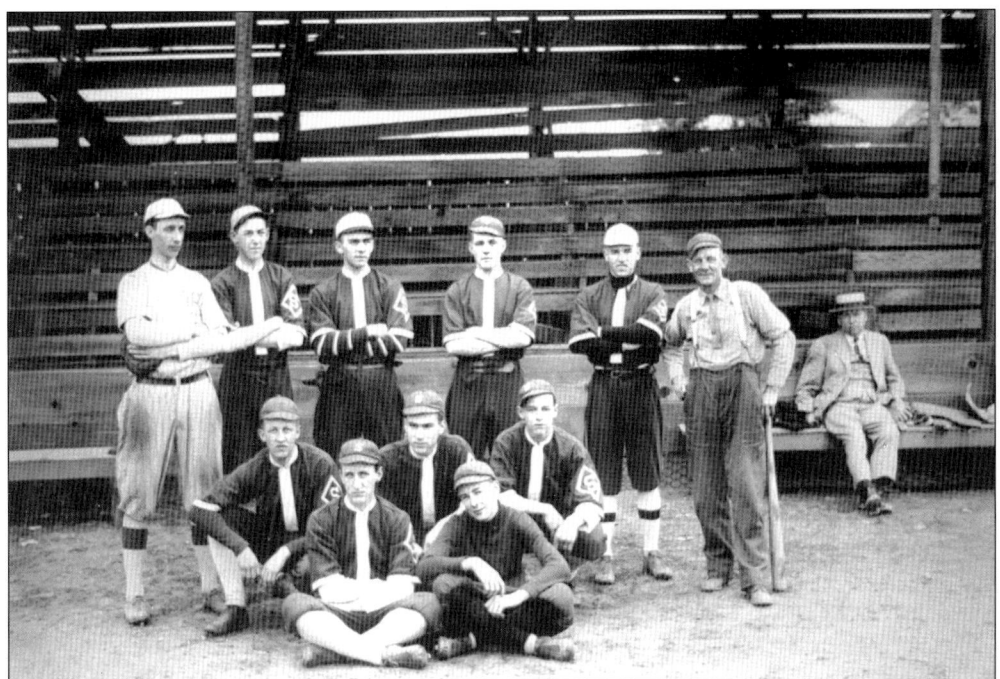

The 1911 Redding Tigers baseball team included Russell DeForest (back row, left), Emil Wickert (back row, fifth from the left), Jack Giblin (back row, right), and Earl Scholes (middle row, left). Seated on the bench is the business manager Jack Gardner. Russ DeForest signed with the Sacramento Senators (Salons) Pacific Coast League in 1935.

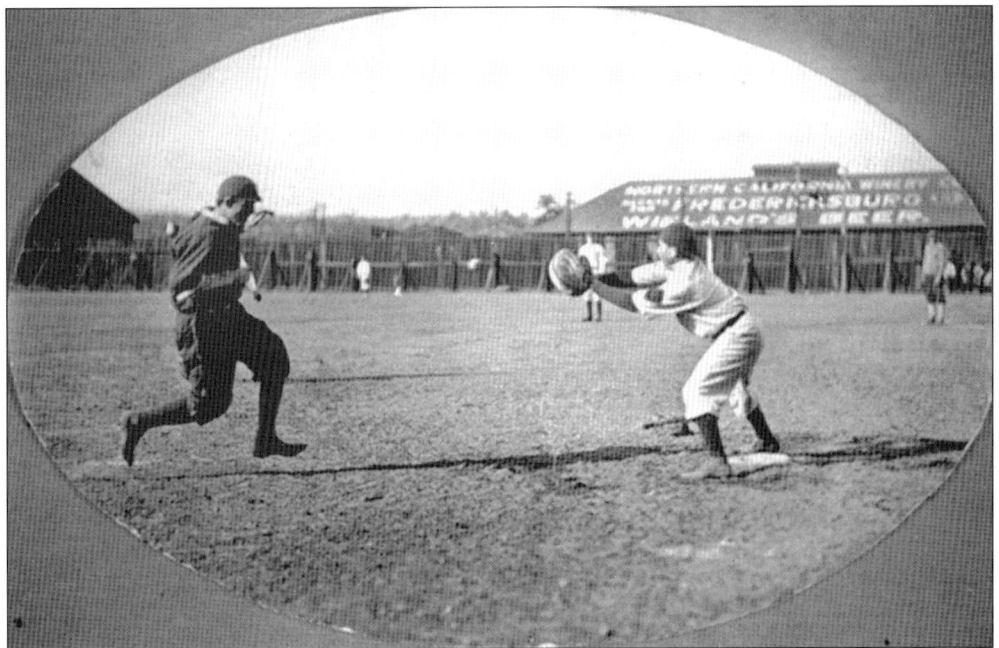

Gil DeForest scores a run for his Redding Tigers baseball team in 1915.

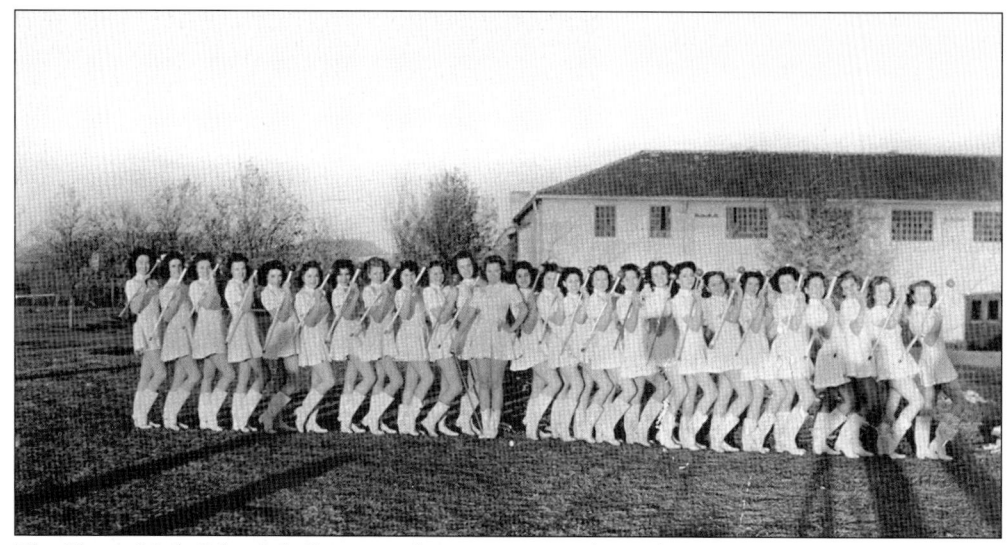

The Shasta High School drill team and majorettes are shown here in 1940.

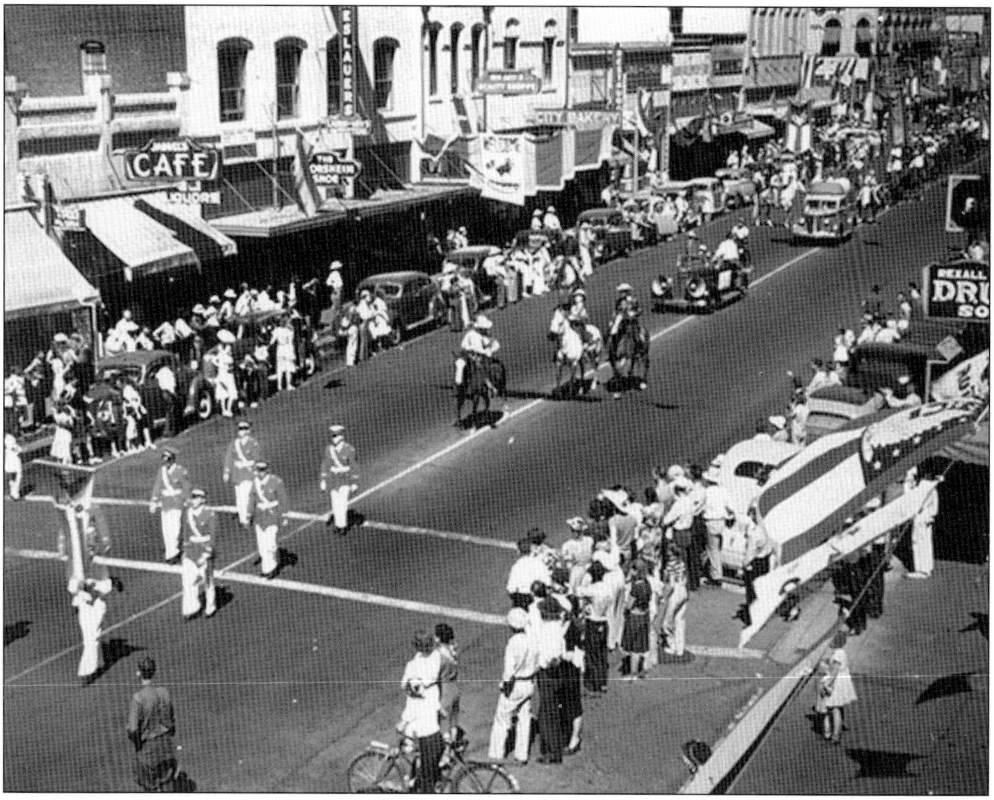

This 1930s photo of a rodeo parade down Market Street also shows Jaegle's Cafe, Breslauer's, City Bakery, and Rexall Drug Store in the background.

Lassen Peak erupts in this October 6, 1915 photo by Chester Mullen. Determined to get pictures of the volcano in action, Mullen visited the area several times, traveling by auto, motorcycle, and horse and buggy. He set up camp at Reflection Lake for a week or more at a stretch, and his vigilance finally paid off with this picture.

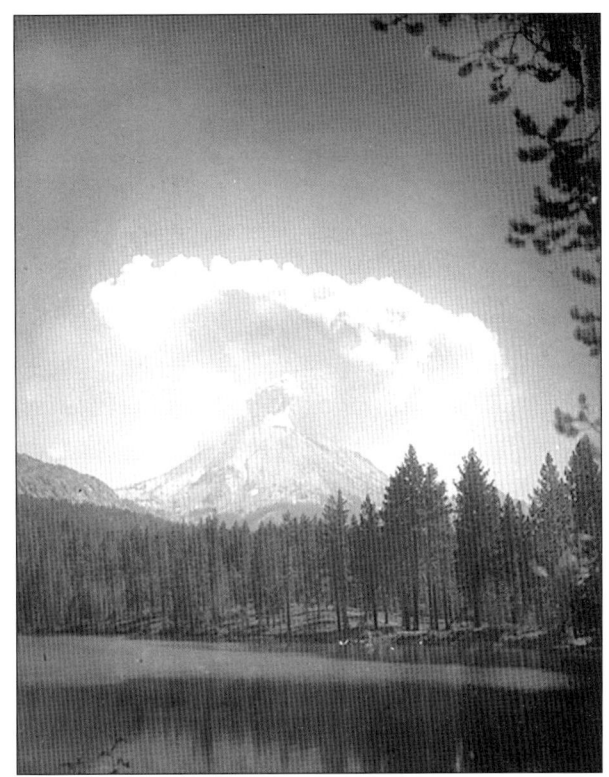

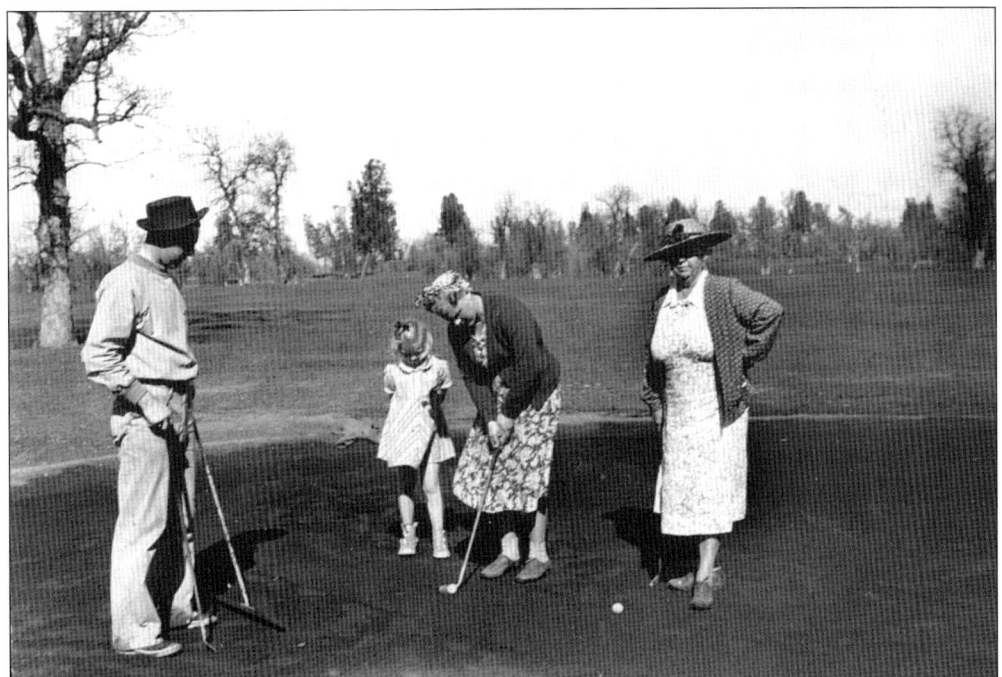

This 1930 photo of the Redding Golf and Country Club shows Jimmy and Laura Wright waiting while Mrs. Bill Anderson and her daughter Laura Wright putt on the ninth hole. The club was abandoned after World War II and is now the site of Lawncrest Cemetery.

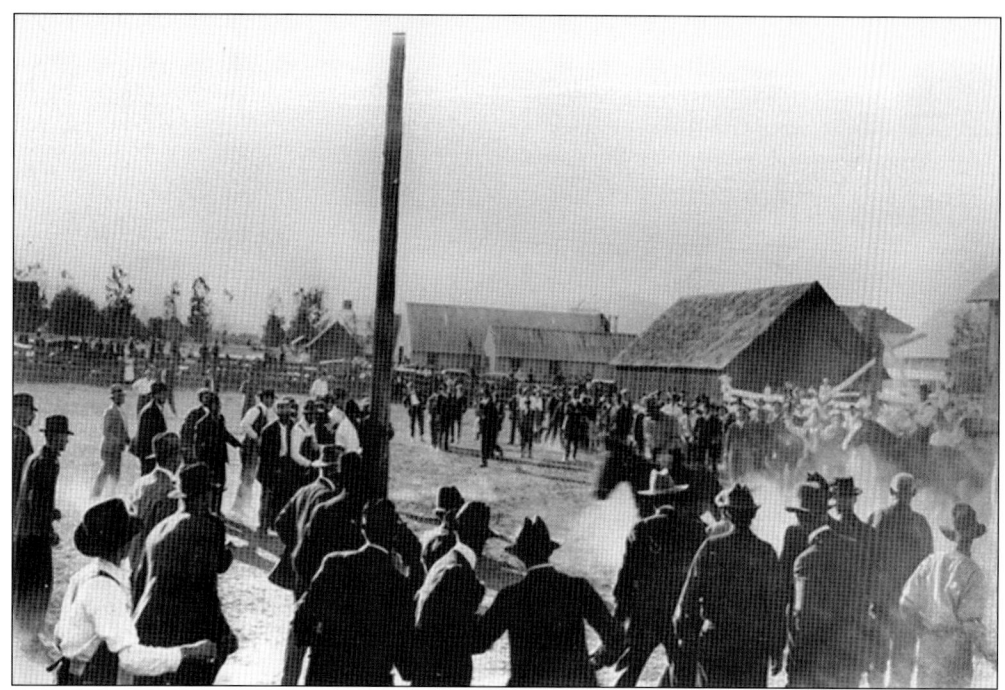
This c. 1900 impromptu rodeo brings out the town's men.

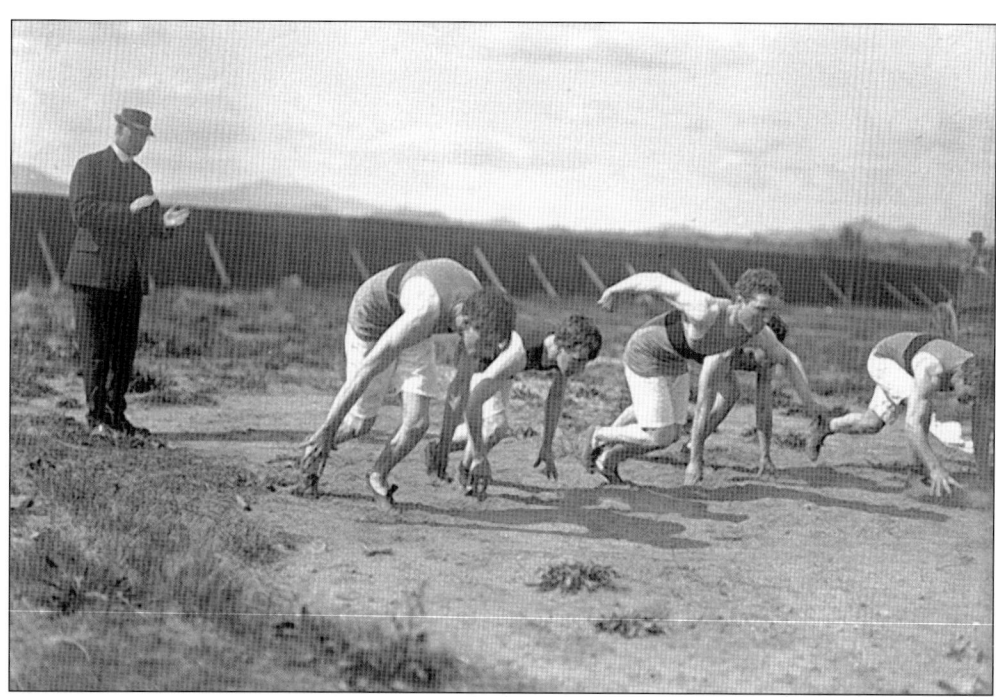
Potential Olympic champions? Chester Mullen took this photo at an athletic field on North Court Street around 1915. The gentleman on the left, starting the race, is J.O. Osborn, principal of Shasta High School.

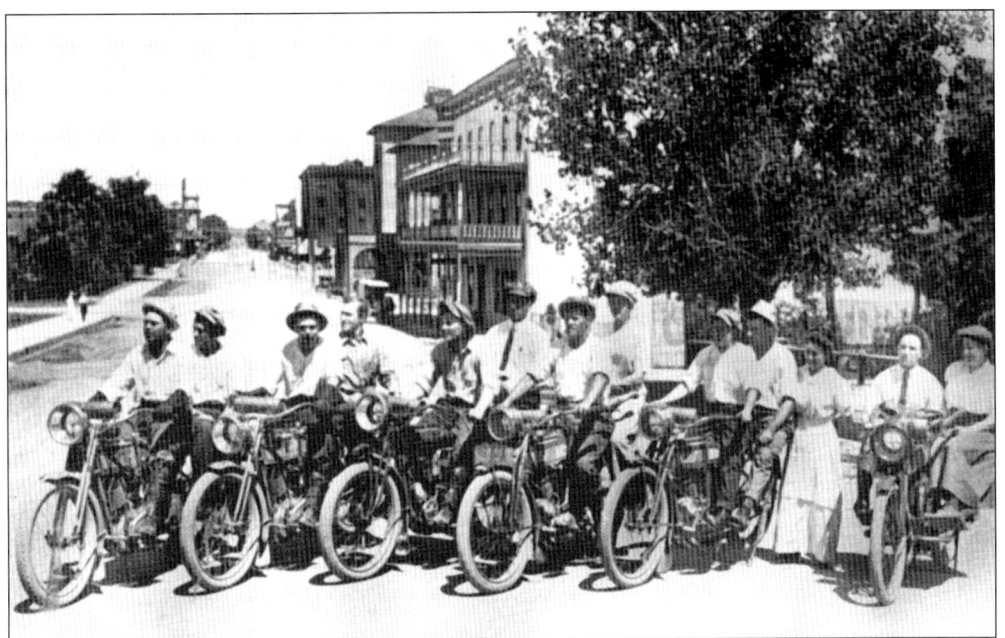

Ready for a motorcycle outing are some of Ma Wood's boarders. Pictured in front of her house on Court and Yuba Street, from left to right, are Ross Huston, Frank Vogt, Ed Hilbey, Carl Kerlin, Elmer Thompson, Stanford Scott, Jess Moore, Mae Wood, Charlie Neissey, Harold Wallace, Ma Wood, and Vincent and Viloa Dobrowsky.

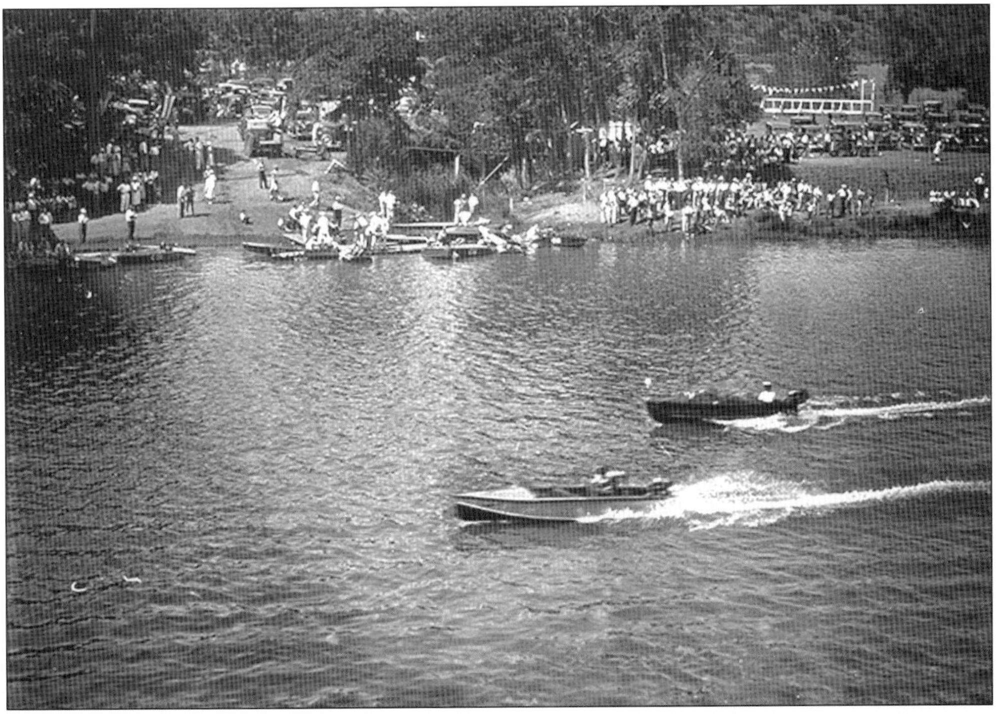

This 1930 boat race took place at Lake Redding on the north side of the Sacramento River.

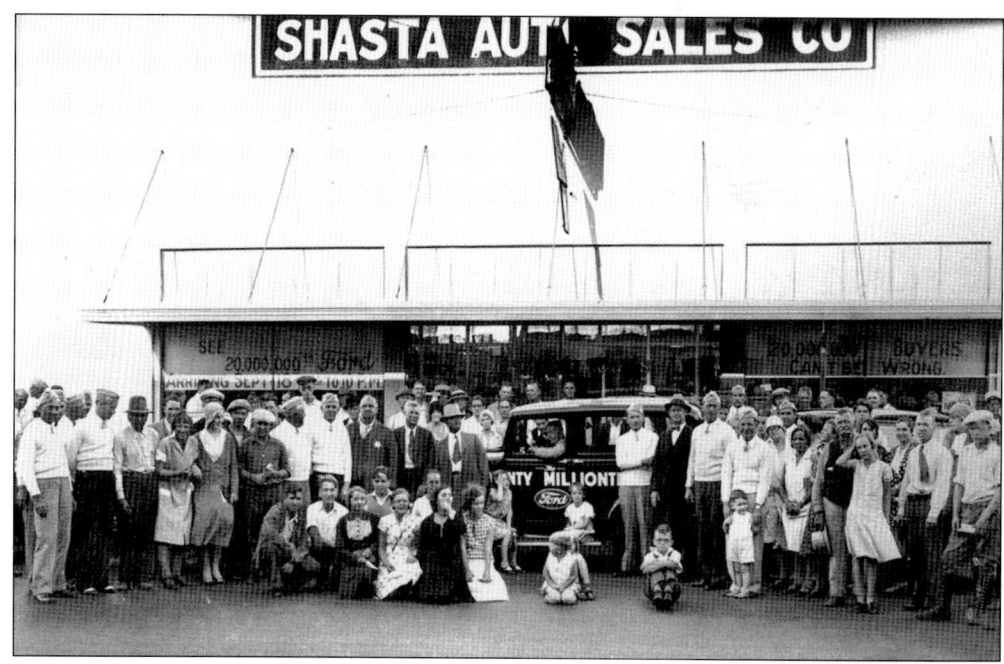

In 1929 the Shasta Auto Sales group gathered around Ford's 20 millionth automobile. In the early days, automobile dealerships were open 24 hours a day, and the new customer was often taught how to drive. Goods and services were bartered in exchange for animals, meat, grain, and labor.

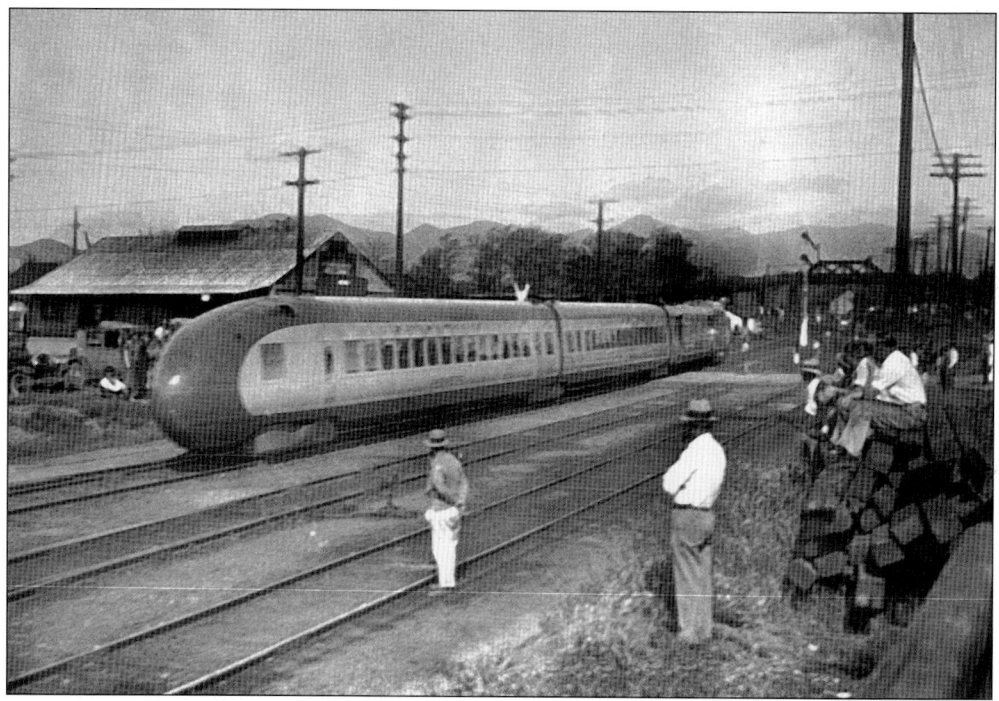

This photo shows a crowd waiting for the Silver Streamliner in 1933. School was let out early so students could see the "wave of the future."

Five

DEPRESSION, SHASTA DAM, AND THE POST-WAR BOOM

Redding residents, already reeling from poor economic conditions during the 1920s, barely reacted to the stock market crash of October 1929. However, as the winter months of 1930 melted into the hot summer of 1931, business owners noted a significant decrease in tourist business and, therefore, profits. Auto traffic still rolled along, heading north and south on the Pacific Highway, but most vehicles were commercial trucks, only stopping for a quick gasoline fill-up and some food. Pleasure driving declined dramatically the next year while the country waited for its newly elected president, Franklin D. Roosevelt, to turn the economy around.

For years, area politicians and Redding civic leaders argued with state and federal water officials for the construction of a major concrete dam in Shasta County. State Senator John McColl and County Judge Francis B. Carr lobbied Congress and the United States Bureau of Reclamation officials with a barrage of letters and visits to Washington for federal funding to start the project. The logical site appeared to be in Shasta County, at a location below the confluence of the Sacramento and Pitt Rivers. Finally, in 1937, the commissioner of the Bureau of Reclamation announced that monies had been approved to begin work. By that summer, scores of Reclamation engineers arrived in Redding and set up temporary headquarters.

Bureau officials soon realized that Redding was too distant to serve as the functioning headquarters for the day-to-day administration of the work force and materials. They opted instead for a new "town" on level ground only one-and-a-half miles from the dam site. Situated among the manzanita brush and just off the newly graded access road, named Shasta Dam Boulevard, the "town" became known as Toyon. But it wasn't really a town—it was the administrative center containing offices, warehouses, and lodging for Bureau of Reclamation inspectors. No stores or restaurants were allowed.

All major national newspapers and radio news programs carried the announcement that work was beginning at Shasta Dam. With the Depression still taking its toll on the national economy, hundreds, then thousands of unemployed men and their families streamed into Redding. City residents pressured city council members, who then called Reclamation officials about the growing influx of out-of-work migrants. Housing was desperately needed close to the work site. Before long three new "dam boomtowns" thrived: Central Valley, Project City, and Summit City.

Down at the dam site, the contracting company that won the bid to build Shasta Dam erected their own lodgings, known as "Contractor's Camp" or Shasta Dam Village. The "camp" contained a complete-care hospital, a huge 2,000-man capacity mess hall, and a fully-equipped recreational hall. Even the main hiring operations moved from Redding to the dam site. But off-duty workers poured in droves into Redding to have a good time in the growing entertainment houses—saloons, dance halls, restaurants, theaters, and gambling establishments. Most of the "action" occurred along California and Market Streets.

Like the rest of the country, news of the Japanese attack on Pearl Harbor shocked local families. Young men, aged 18 to 25, rushed to enlist in the army, navy, marines or Army Air Corp, while young women volunteered for the WACS, WAVES or served in the American Red Cross. In the weeks and months following the outbreak of hostilities Civil Defense volunteers patrolled the streets of Redding with hard hats, flashlights, and their CD badges proudly displayed on their jackets. All residents complied with the "no lights after dark" regulations. This required homeowners to hang dark, light-blocking curtains and drapes. Almost everyone proudly displayed an American flag, large or small, paper or cloth, from their porches or windows. Families that had loved ones in the military placed pictures and "service stars" on fireplace mantels or specially arranged end tables.

Out at the dam site, security that was already strict was ramped up to ultra-high levels. Armed guards carrying rifles with live ammunition stood posted at all key road intersections leading into the work site. Everyone carried identification cards and site restrictions were placed on the public. In droves, patriotic dam workers quit their construction jobs at the dam and enlisted. With this exodus, a labor shortage appeared and, to help fill the gap, high school students worked part-time at selected "non-hazardous" jobs. Also, women like Opal Foxx hired on to do more of the cooking or administrative secretarial chores.

Food and gas rationing became a reality during most of the war years, limiting economic growth. The federal Office of Price Administration regulated prices and supplies in an effort to place America on a wartime footing. Recycling drives were common and the Redding Boy and Girl Scouts gathered heaps of tin and piles of rubber—both critical to the war effort. Paper, too, was in short supply and mounds of used newspapers sat ready for recycling at several locations in the city.

Jubilation broke out in Redding, like the rest of the country, with the news of V-E (Victory in Europe) and V-J (Victory over Japan) Day. The most terrible war in human history came to a close and exhausted servicemen and women eagerly looked forward to returning home, securing jobs, and getting on with their lives. The big question facing returning veterans was Redding's economy. Would Redding and Shasta County still have a pre-war depressed job market or would a successful transition to a post-war consumer-oriented economy occur? Fortunately, the latter scenario emerged, thanks to transportation availability and a national demand for lumber products. Redding was well situated to take full advantage of both factors.

Automobile production for the civilian market exploded in late 1945, as Ford Motor Company, General Motors, and other auto producers re-tooled from building tanks and jeeps to building sleek-looking coupes and sedans. A new road building boom accompanied automobile production and in Shasta County this meant the widening and repaving of city streets. Highway 99 was also widened while Highway 299 to the coast, which had been paved during the war, was widened and straightened. Likewise, new roads ran to Shingletown and Burney, and other foothill and mountain communities. This meant that reliable, relatively quick and comfortable access was now available to all parts of the county.

During the war, lumber was in high demand, and that demand increased after the war. Domestic lumber needs were staggering, as hundreds of thousands of returning veterans wanted homes, furniture, and other wood products. Redding, with its railroad and automobile connections, assured its regional role in transporting lumber to markets farther south.

Shasta Dam was completed at the conclusion of World War II, and the Bureau of Reclamation pressed on with building Keswick Dam (the afterbay for Shasta) and other small dams, dikes and canals. All of these projects employed Redding men. Lake Shasta, full to capacity in the late 1940s, offered many new recreational and commercial opportunities. Houseboats, ski boats, fishing boats—Shasta Lake had them all. Word quickly spread to points south and north—particularly Sacramento—that a huge, new lake sat amid unrivaled natural beauty. The best part of this new recreational resource was that most campers and boaters came from the south and they had to pass through Redding to do so. Indeed, Redding soon became the "Gateway to Lake Shasta."

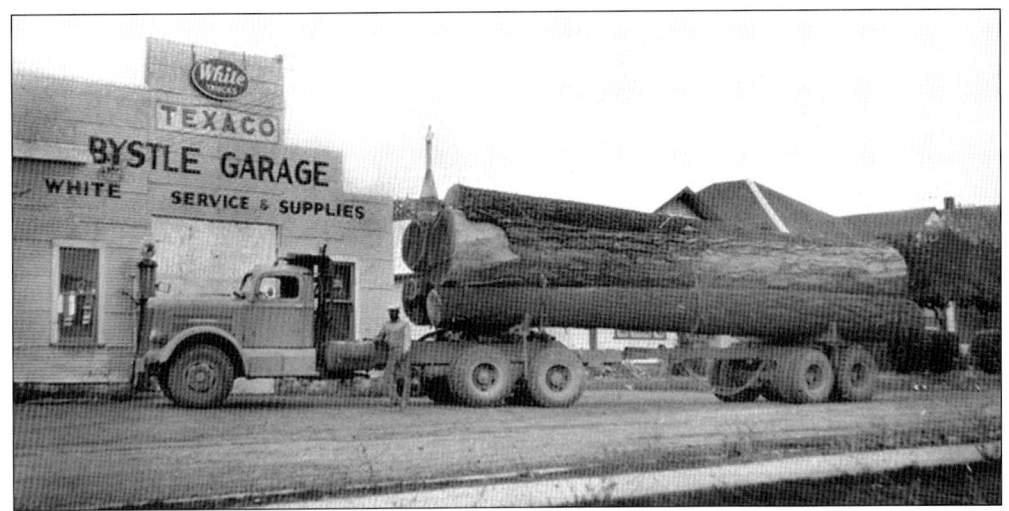

Adolph Bystle and his son William ("Babe") operated the Bystle Garage on West Street until 1939. Logging was a large part of the community's income, and Babe operated a lumber hauling business between Whitmore and Redding.

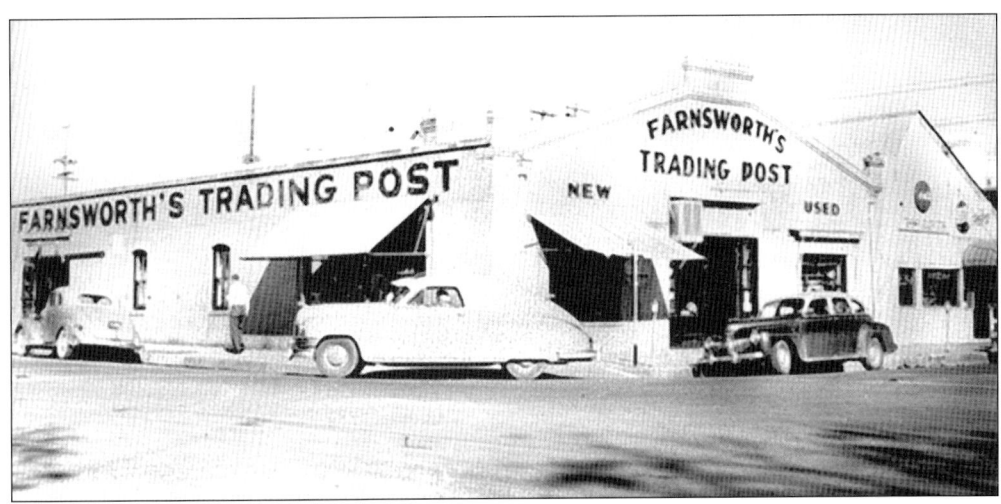

Farnsworth's Trading Post, shown here around 1950, was originally Morrison's New & Used and was started in 1929 by William J. Morrison. It was located on the corner of Tehama and California Streets. In 1935 Richard and Eva Farnsworth purchased the firm and renamed it Farnsworth's Trading Post. The business was later moved to Pine Grove.

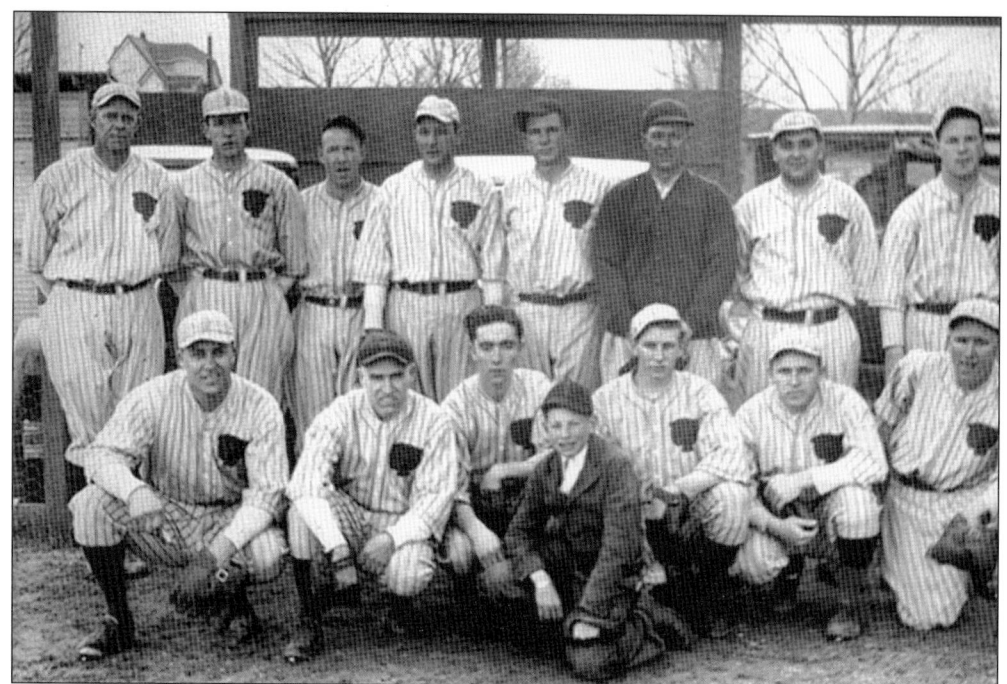

The 1935 Redding Tigers baseball players, from left to right, included (front row) Marion Flowers (OF-P), E. Wickert (OF), Harvey Carmack, Usage Hughes, George Wolfs (2B-SS), Norman Gilbeau (2B-SS), and Billie Wickert; (back row) Art Koehler (mgr-C), Russ DeForest (1B), Stan DeForest (3B-SS), Jas Balma (2B), Spud Murphy (catcher), Chas Douglas (pitcher), Angie Silva (1B-OF), Al Huelsman (C-OF), and Herb Sanders.

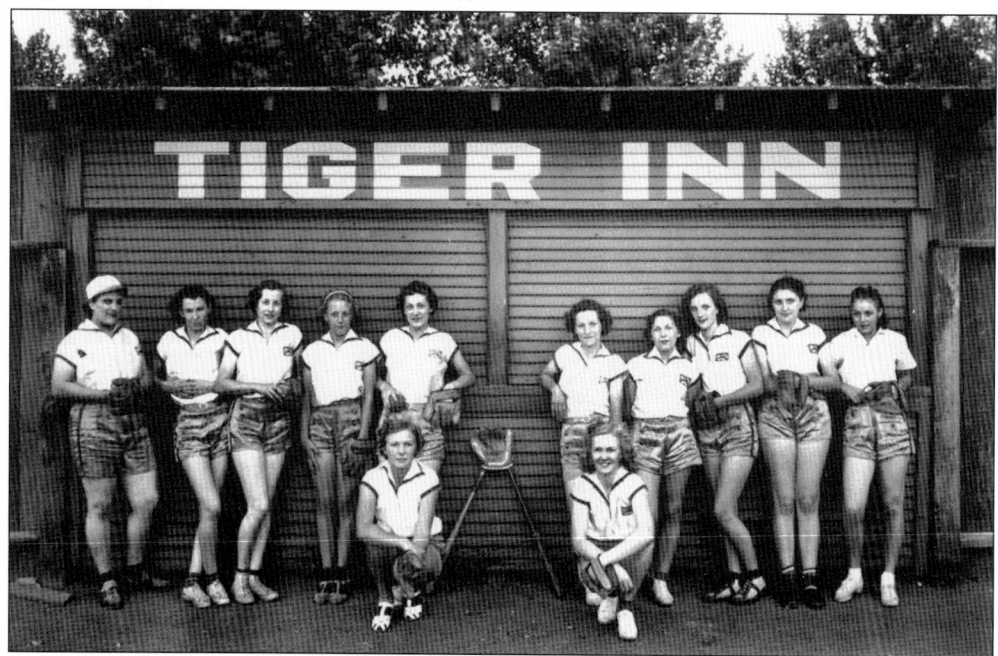

A women's softball team sponsored by the Redding Bottling Works poses for a group picture, c. 1937. Softball was a popular sport in the area with 18 teams competing.

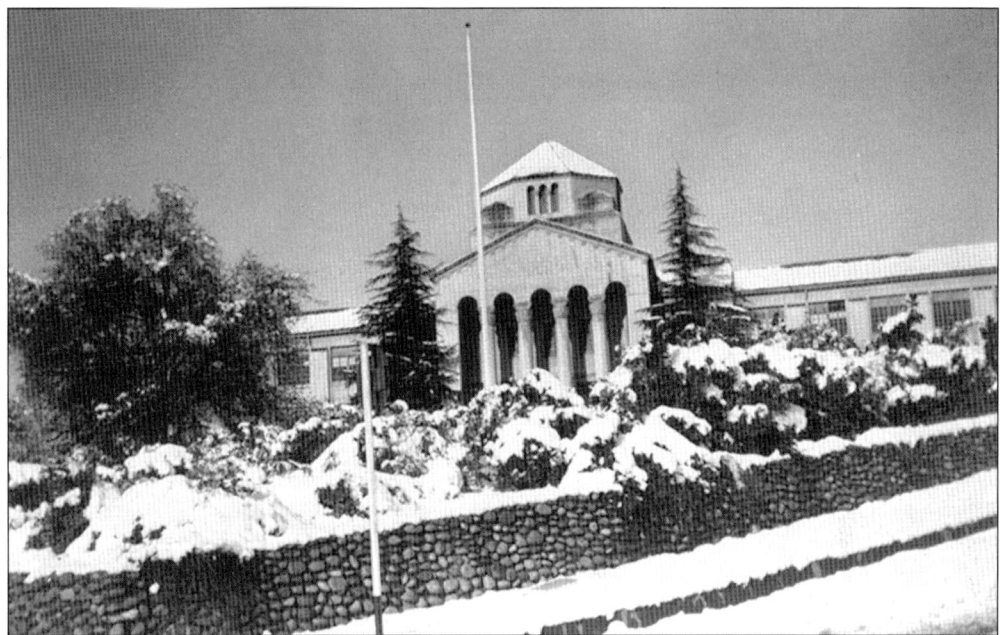

This photo, taken in 1935, shows Shasta Union High School in the snow. Located on Eureka Way, it was considered "too far out of town." In 1967 it became Nova High School for ninth-graders and later became Foothill High School. With the new Foothill school finished in Palo Cedro, the building now houses the Shasta Learning Center.

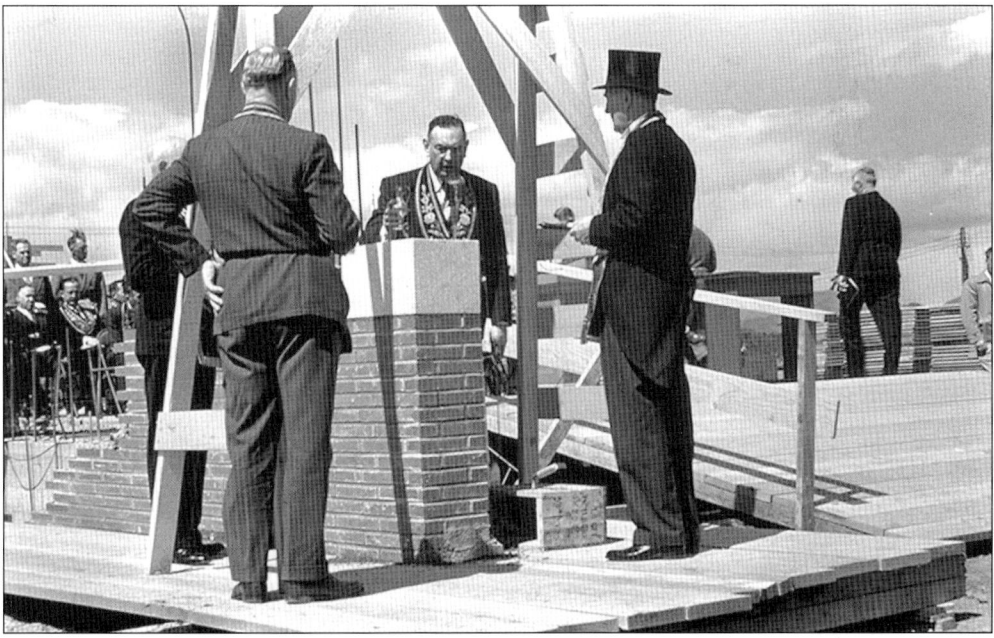

This photo shows the dedication and laying of the cornerstone for Shasta College on Eureka Way in 1951. Strong community support resulted in the passage of a bond to provide funds for the construction. The college, which opened its doors in September 1950 with 275 students, grew rapidly, and a new campus was built in 1967 on 337 acres bordered by Old Oregon Trail and Highway 299 East. The old campus on Eureka Way became Shasta High School.

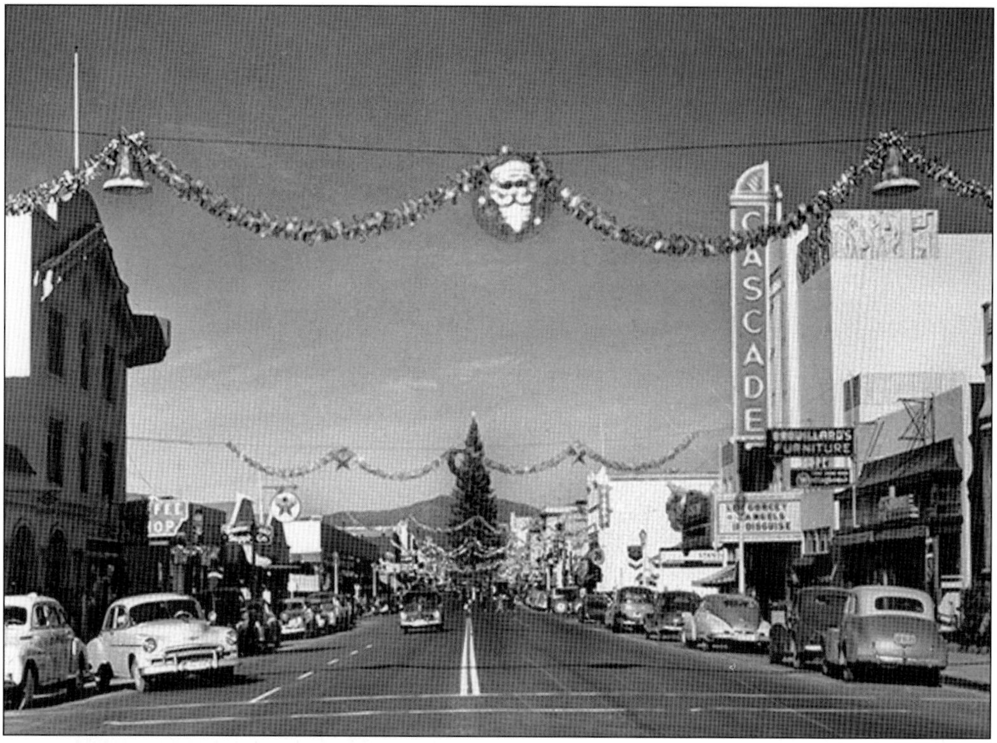

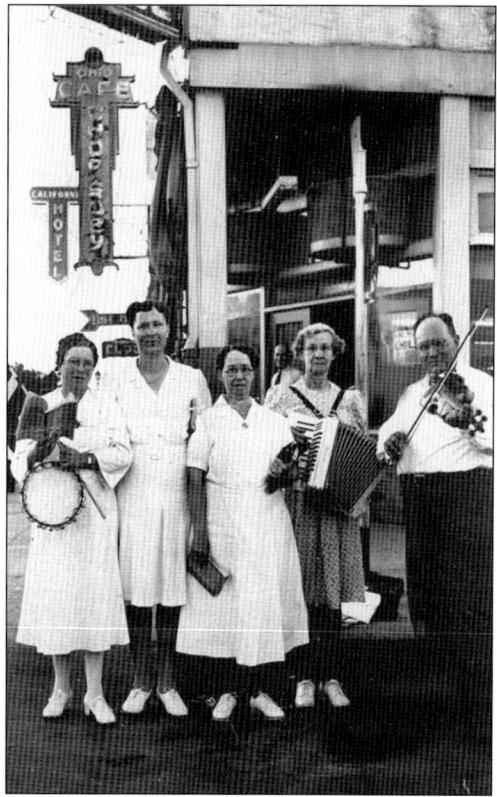

The tradition of Redding's beautiful Christmas tree began in 1919 when volunteers from the city, PG&E, and local businesses installed the tallest tree they could find at the intersection of Market and Yuba Streets. This custom continued until construction of the downtown mall in the early 1970s.

The Redding Rescue Mission began 60 years ago on Easter in 1943, with street meetings conducted twice a week for the next 16 months. The mission received the first permit granted by Redding Police Chief John Balma, overcoming an ordinance forbidding anyone to preach the Gospel on the streets.

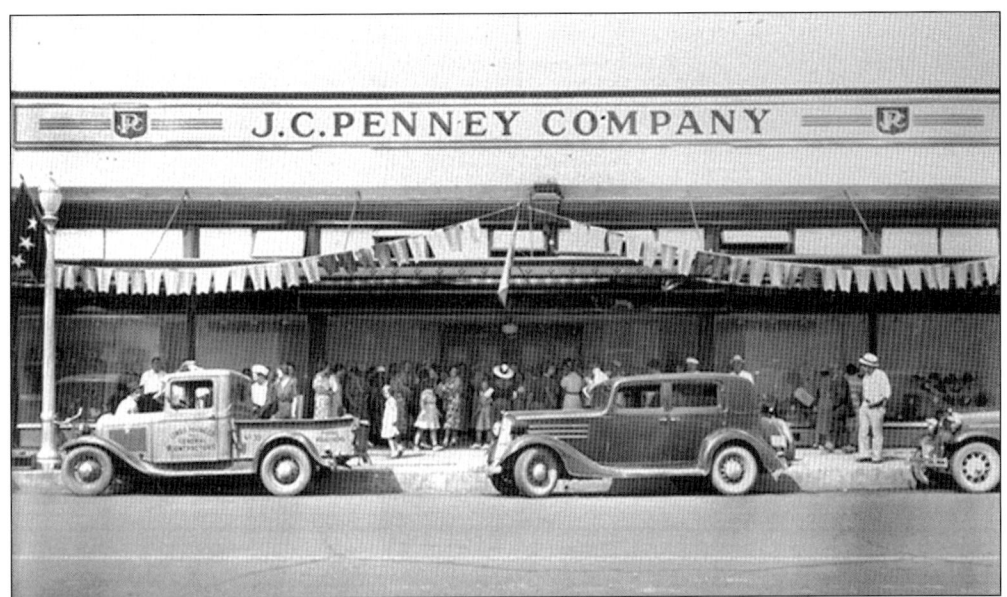

This photograph shows the grand opening of the J.C. Penney Company on Market Street in the 1930s.

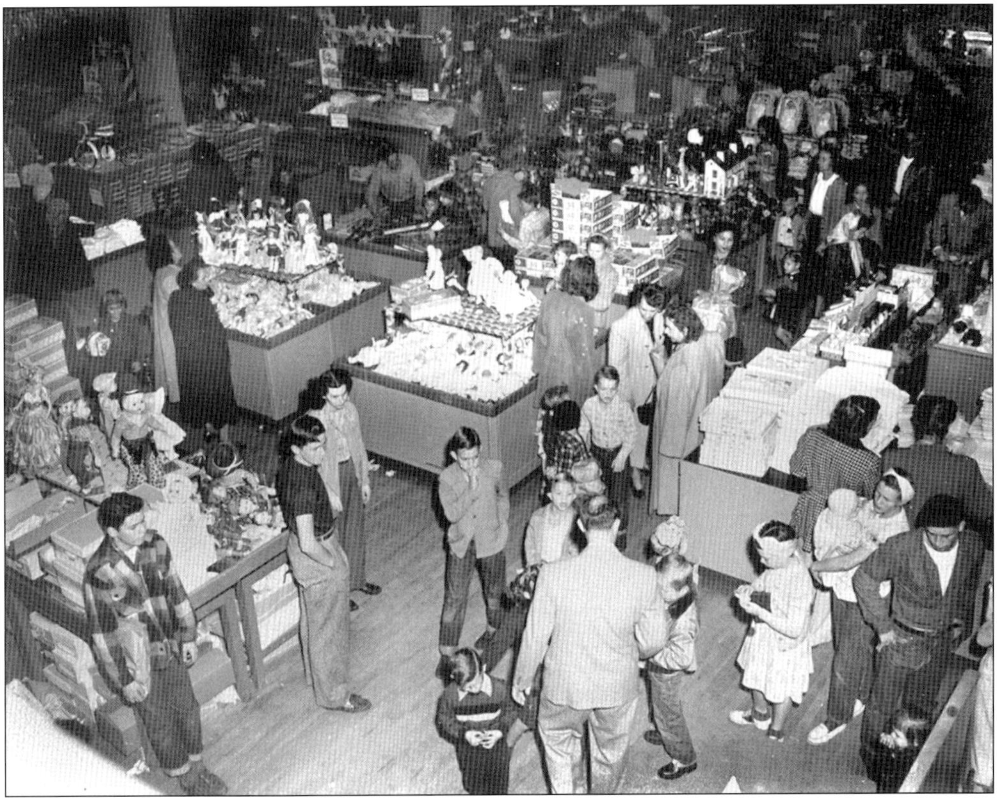

Christmas shopping was a social event at the J.C. Penney store, which was located at 1638 Market Street. The counters are piled high with merchandise in this 1950s photo. J.C. Penney was relocated to the Mount Shasta Mall.

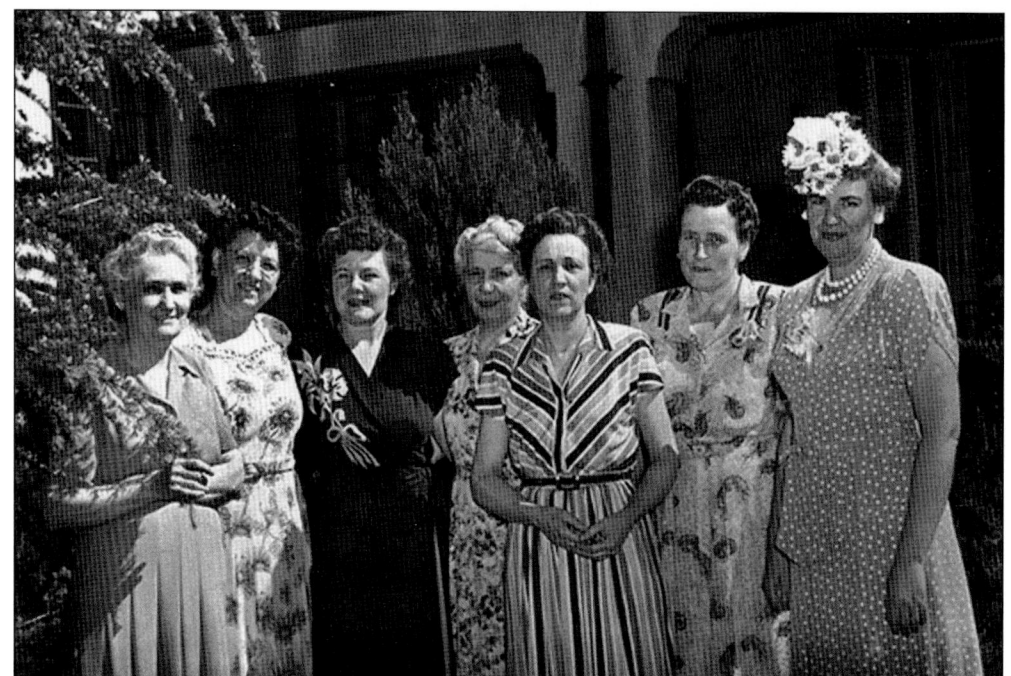

Standing in front of the Women's Improvement Club, c. 1950, from left to right, are Miriam Love, Edna Hazlitt, Georgia Maxim, Norma Mason, Grace Smith, Bertha Johnstone, and an unidentified woman. Established in 1902 and disbanded in 1999, the club worked to beautify and improve the town of Redding. Members paid for concrete walkways and built horse troughs and an iced drinking fountain in the business district. The clubhouse at Tehama and West Streets, completed in 1932, was removed in 2003 to make way for a county parking lot.

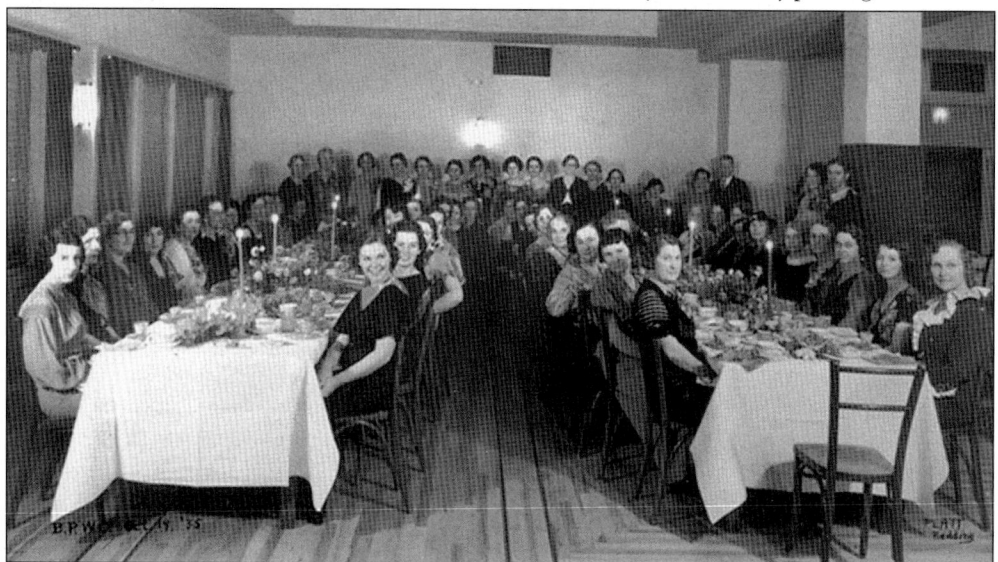

This photo shows the Business and Professional Women's Club luncheon on October 14, 1935. The club was organized with 32 charter members on May 28, 1931. The slogan for the new club was "A High School Education for Every Business Girl," and a program was launched to help girls pursue careers.

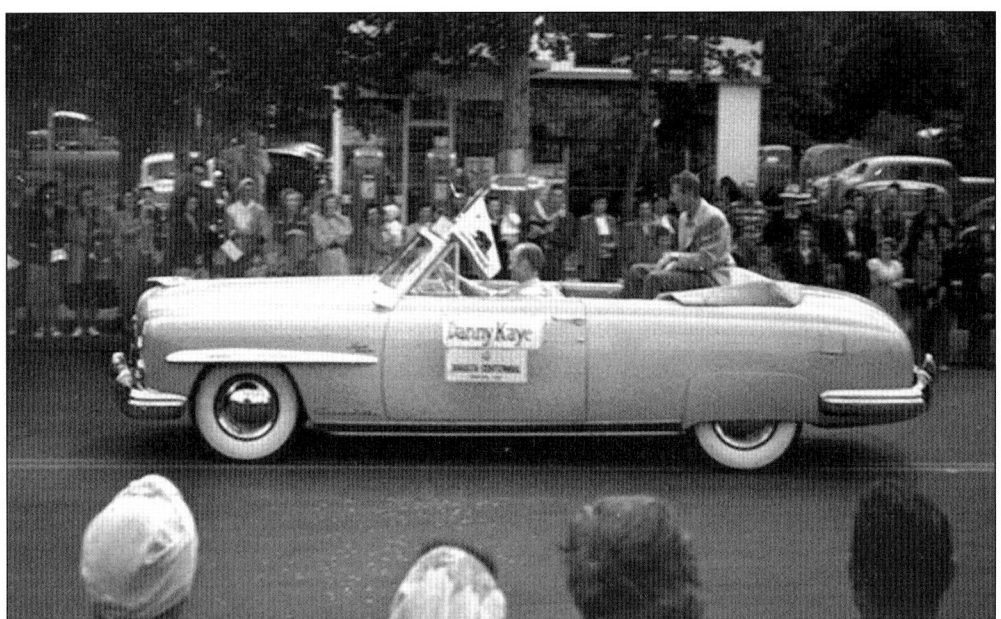

Danny Kaye, in town for the California State Centennial Celebration and Shasta Dam dedication, rides in the lead parade car on June 16, 1950. On the evening of June 17, 15,000 people flocked to Shasta Dam to watch the first release of water over the 487-foot spillway. The water was turned on at a signal from Danny Kaye.

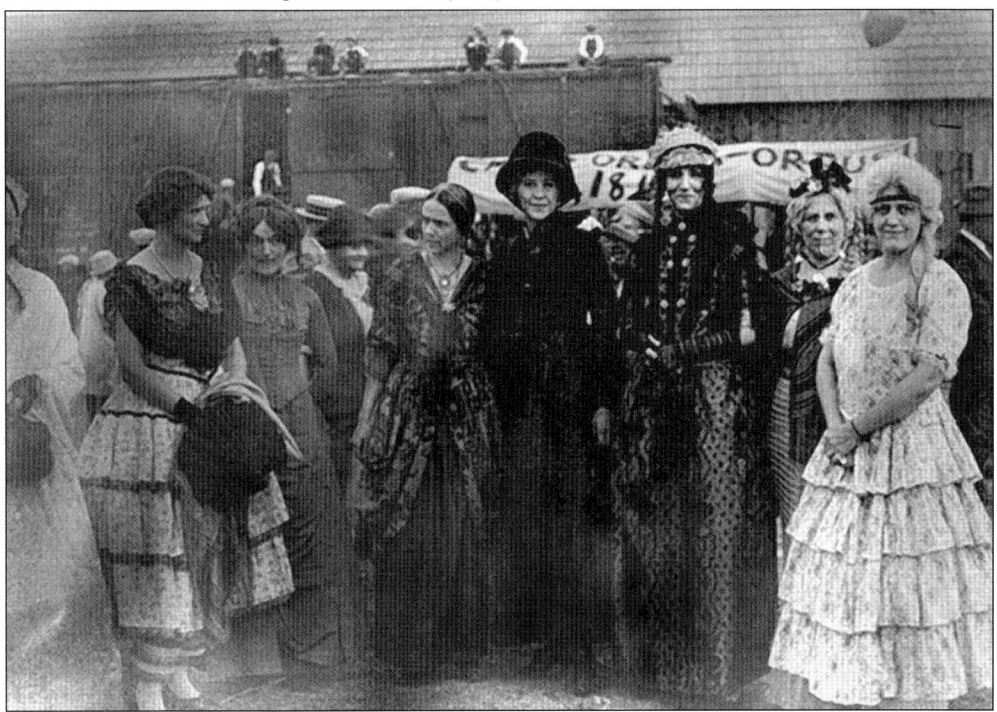

Shasta County celebrated California's Centennial with the "Shasta Cavalcade," June 11–18, 1950. Every aspect of the entire program was researched by locals to make it authentic, using their knowledge, time, costumes, and equipment.

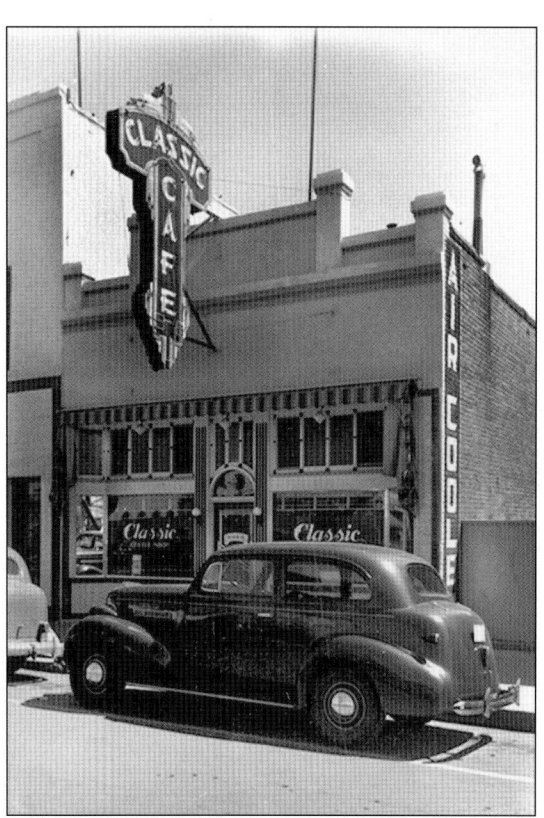

The Classic Cafe at 1617 Market Street is shown here, c. 1940. The automobile parked in front of the cafe was owned by Walter Proebstel.

Jack's Grill, located at 1743 California Street, is shown here around 1950. Built by William Stevens about 1928, the business is still a very popular dining spot.

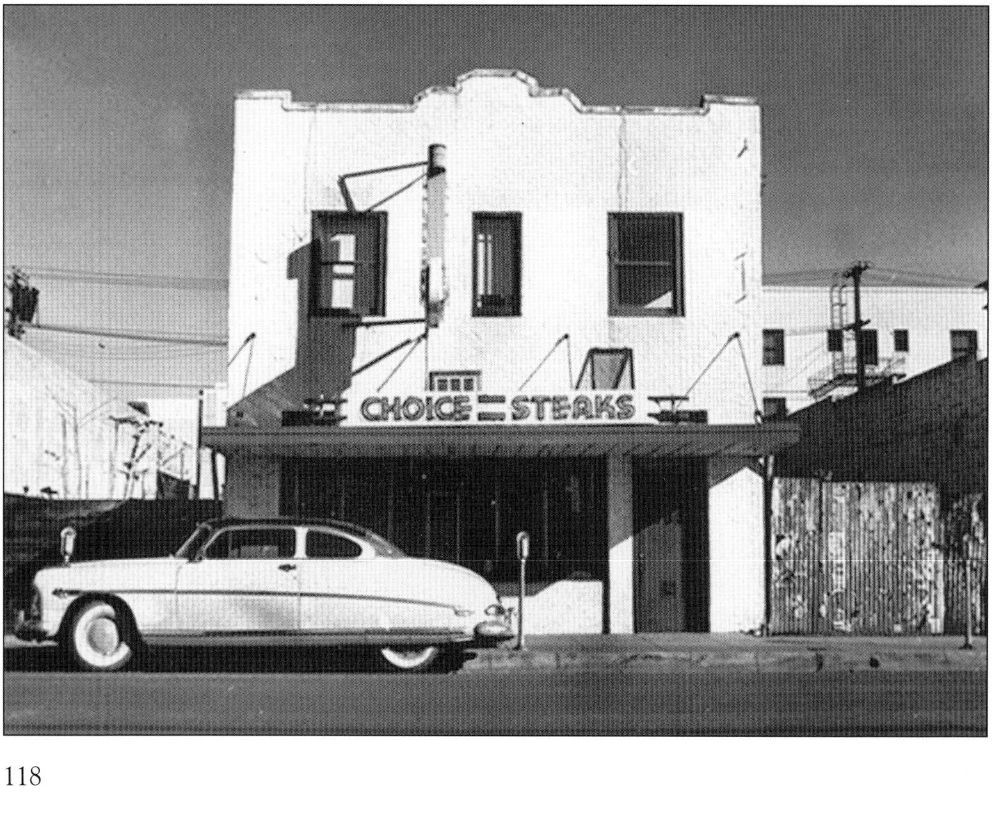

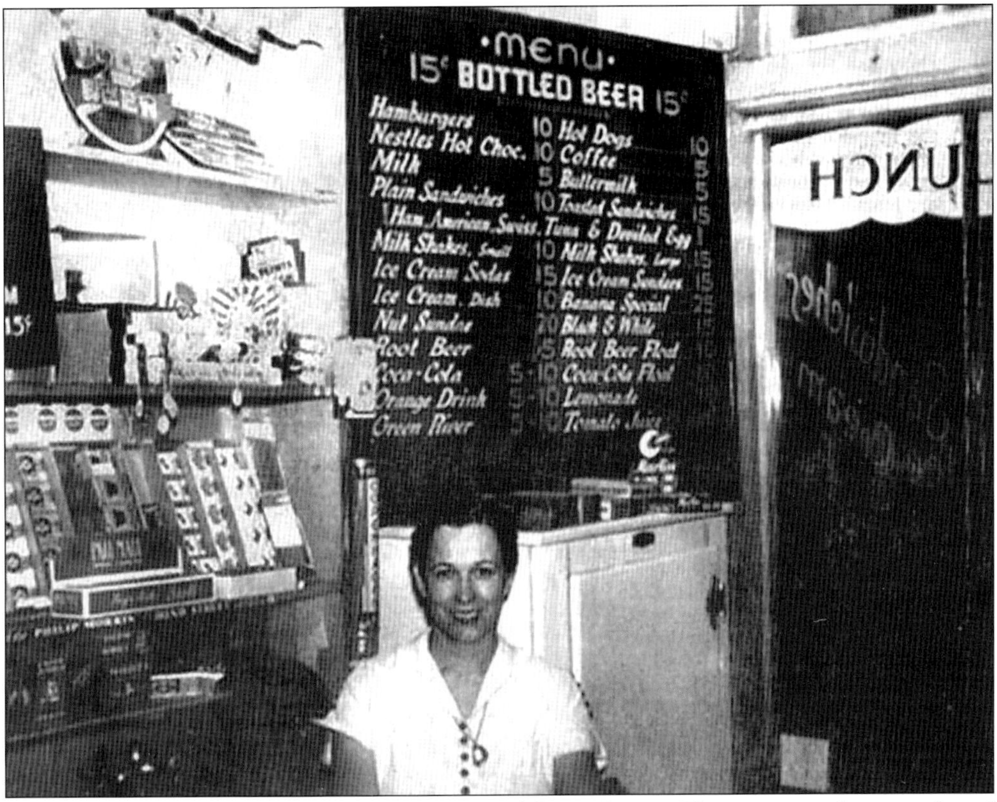

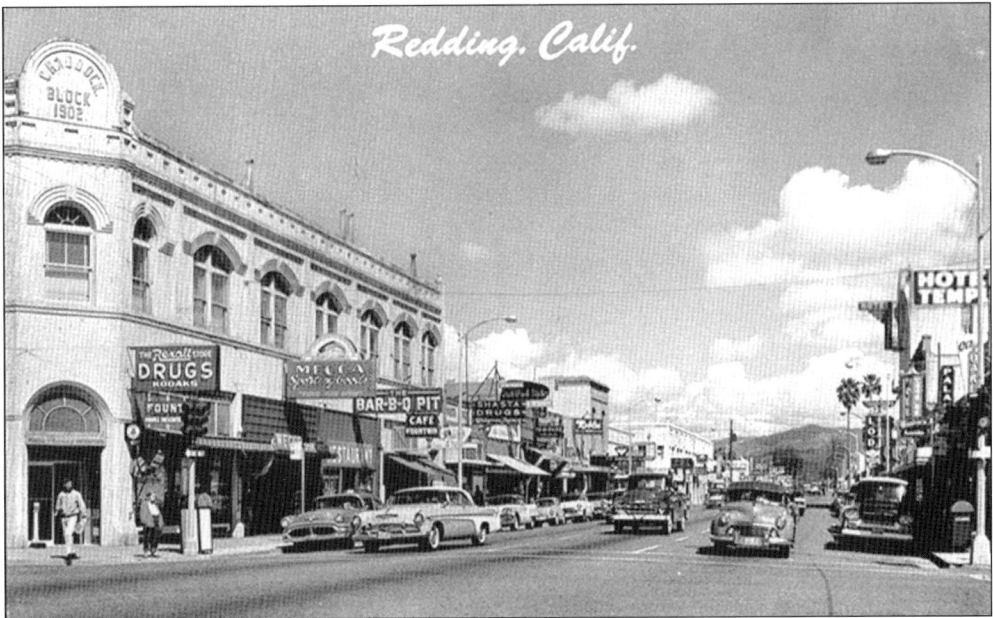

Lillian Bond owned Bond's Fountain at 1411 California Street. The prices on the menu board in this 1940s photo indicate how the value of a dollar has changed since then.

This 1950s photo of Market Street shows Rexall Drugs on the left in the Craddock Building and the Temple Hotel on the right.

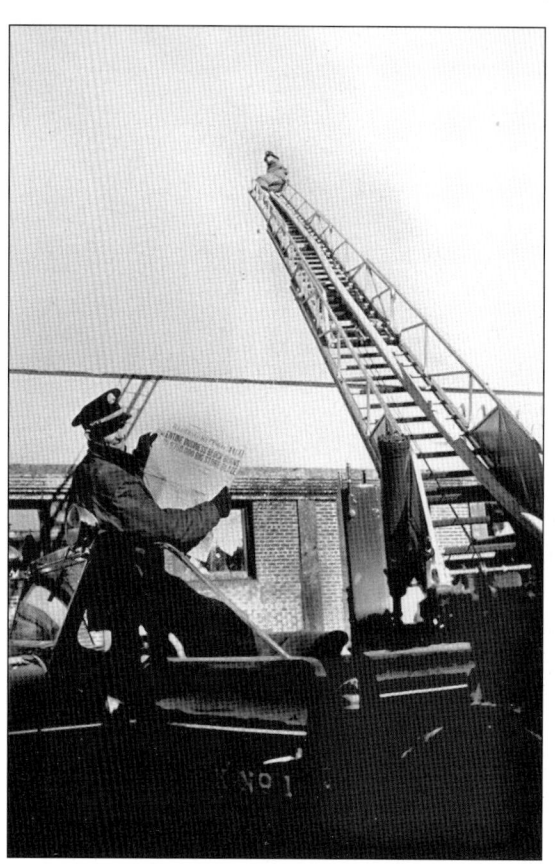

On January 13, 1940, Willburn Grant, assistant fire chief (standing in the fire truck) holds a *Record Searchlight* that reports *"Entire Business Block Burns in $750,000 Big Store Blaze."* The inferno destroyed Maxine's, Classic Coffee Shop, Woolworth's, Redding Printing, J.C. Penney, and McCormick-Saeltzer. Nearly 200 people lost their jobs due to the fire.

This June 12, 1942 photo shows the old Shasta High School on Placer near West Street in flames. At the time, the old school building was being used as county offices.

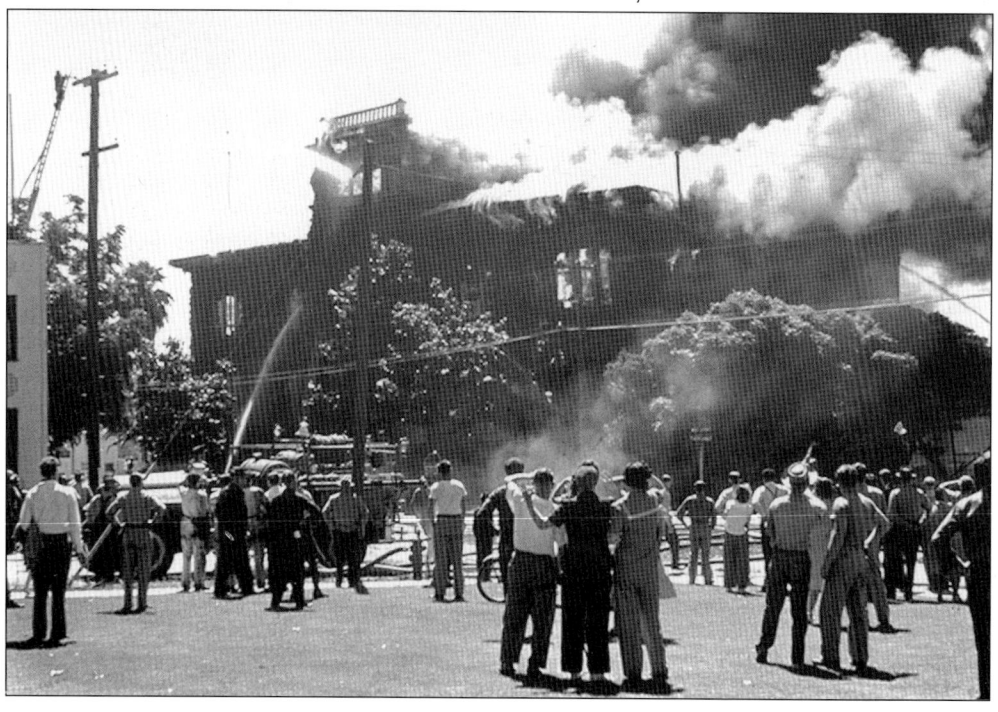

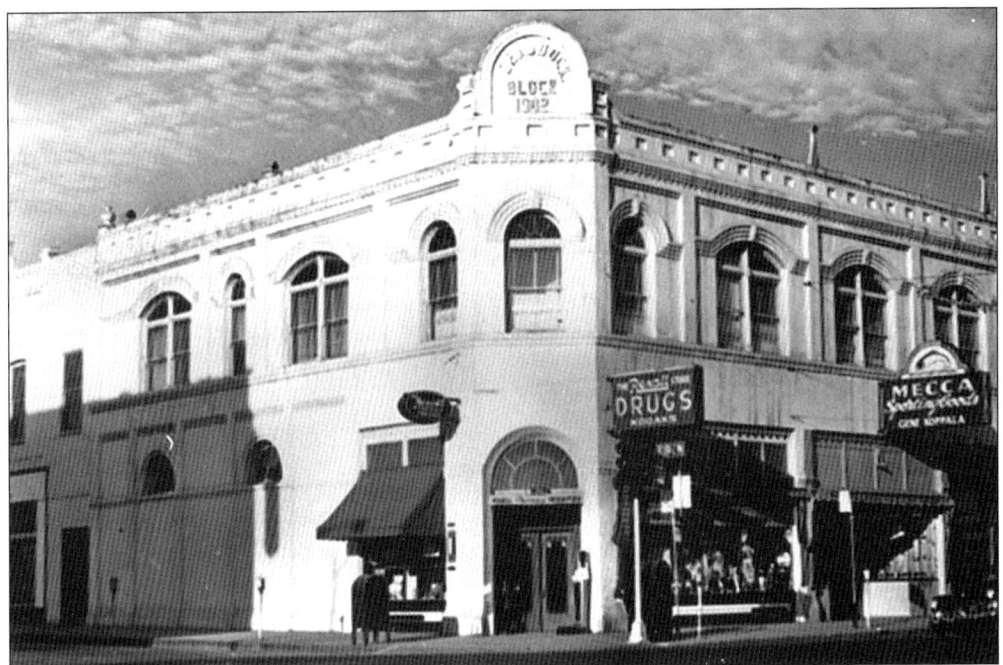

This 1950 photo shows the Craddock Building, which housed Powell's Drugs and Mecca Sporting Goods on Market Street. Built in 1903, the building's lower floor housed storefronts with doctors' offices upstairs. The county's first medical laboratory was established in the building and run by Rose Trautz.

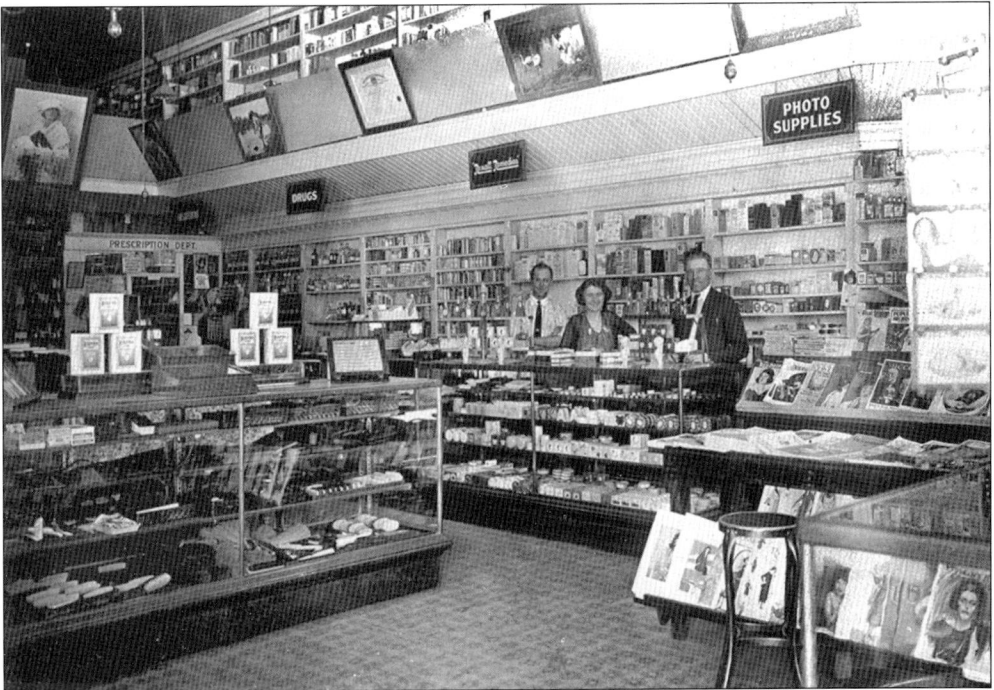

This photo from 1922 shows the interior of Powell's Drug Store when the *Police Gazette* was a popular newsstand item.

John Haner moved to Central Valley in 1939 with his family. His father worked on the Central Valley Project. In 1941 John graduated with the first eighth-grade class from the new Central Valley Grammar School, started Shasta High School that fall, and worked at Shasta Dam during the summer of 1942. In 1944, during his senior year of high school, he enlisted in the U.S. Navy in the V-6 program (Combat Air Crewman). After the war, John returned to Shasta High School and graduated with the class of 1947.

Army Sgt. H.E. Whitlach stands guard in this December 8, 1941 composite photograph at the Kennett Dam, later called Shasta Dam. Military officials, fearing a Japanese sabotage attempt on the dam, ordered soldiers to guard the facility.

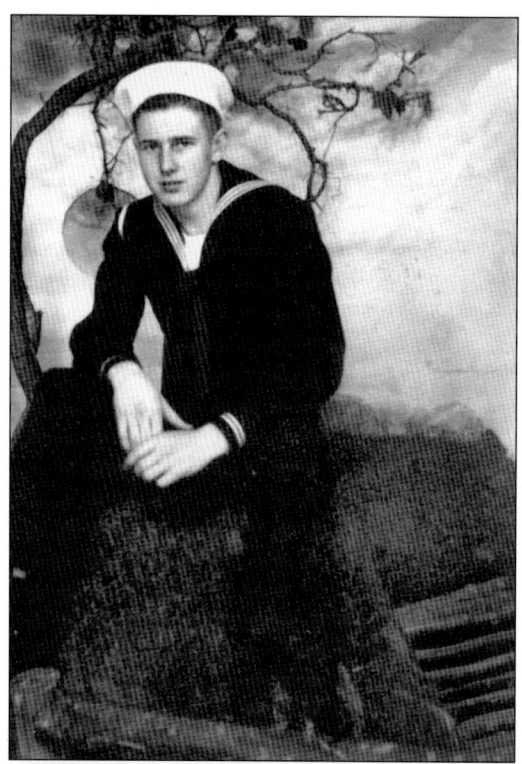

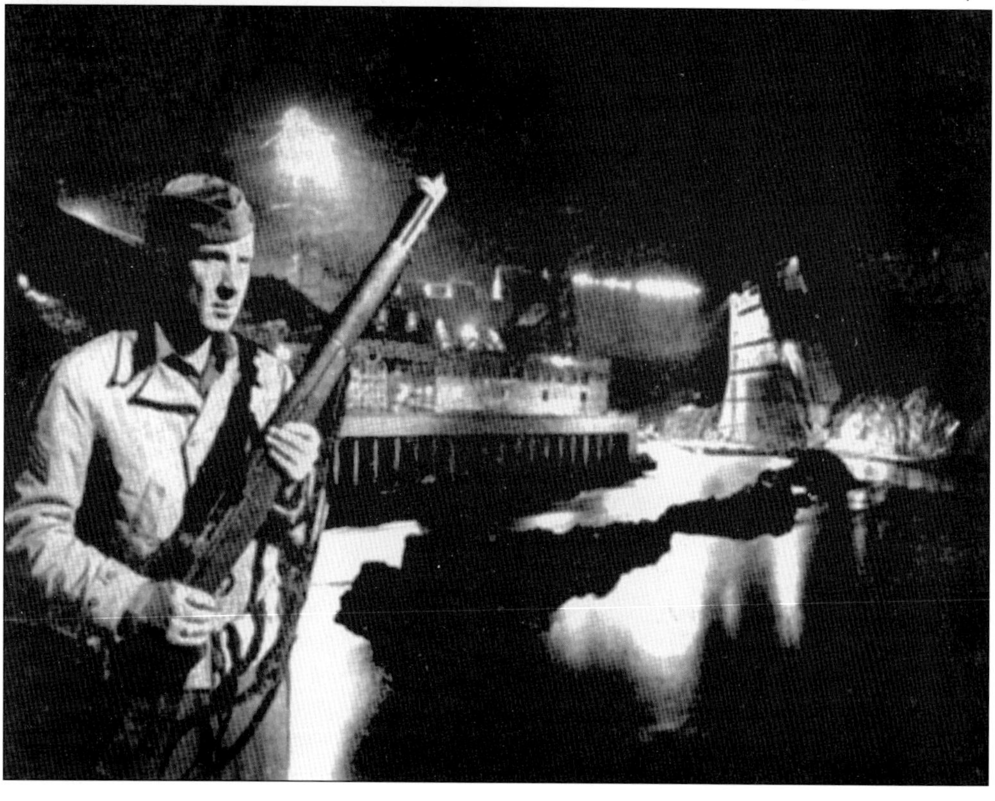

Lulu Morris and Muriel Moravec stand near a military observation tower, c. 1940. The tower, used to watch for enemy planes, was manned 24 hours a day by volunteers in four-hour shifts. It was one of 3,000 observation posts that were established throughout the state.

Several Shasta County residents, pictured in this photo from the 1940s, promoted buying U.S Savings Bonds. The bonds were sold to help the United States during World War II. They sold for $18.75 and were worth $25 when they matured.

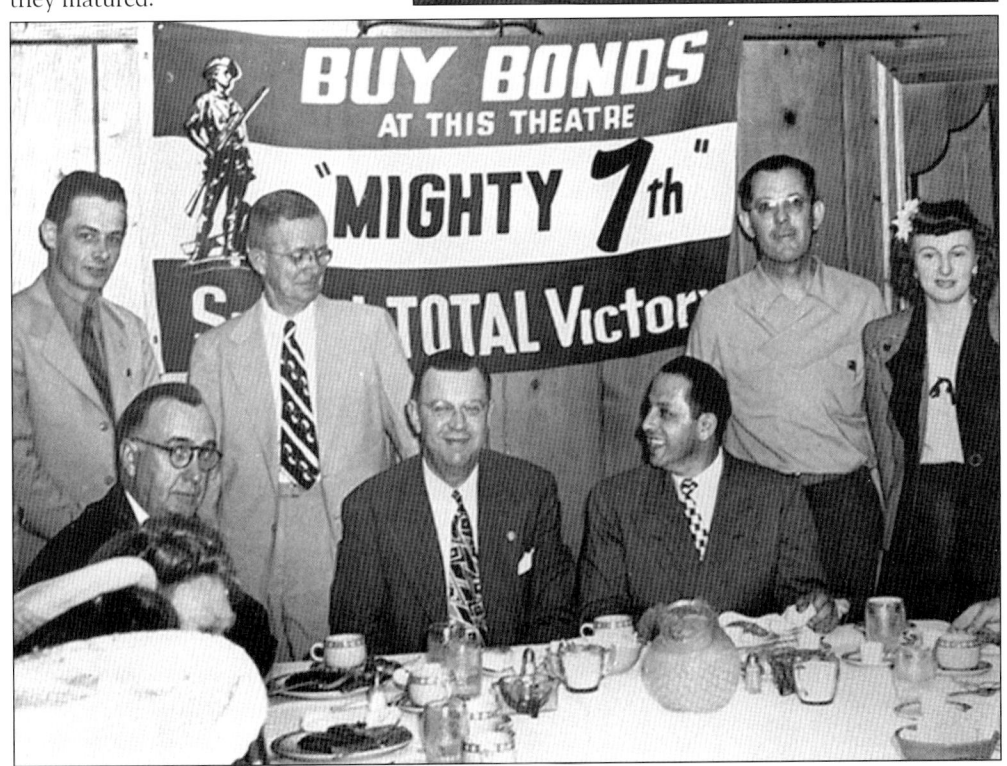

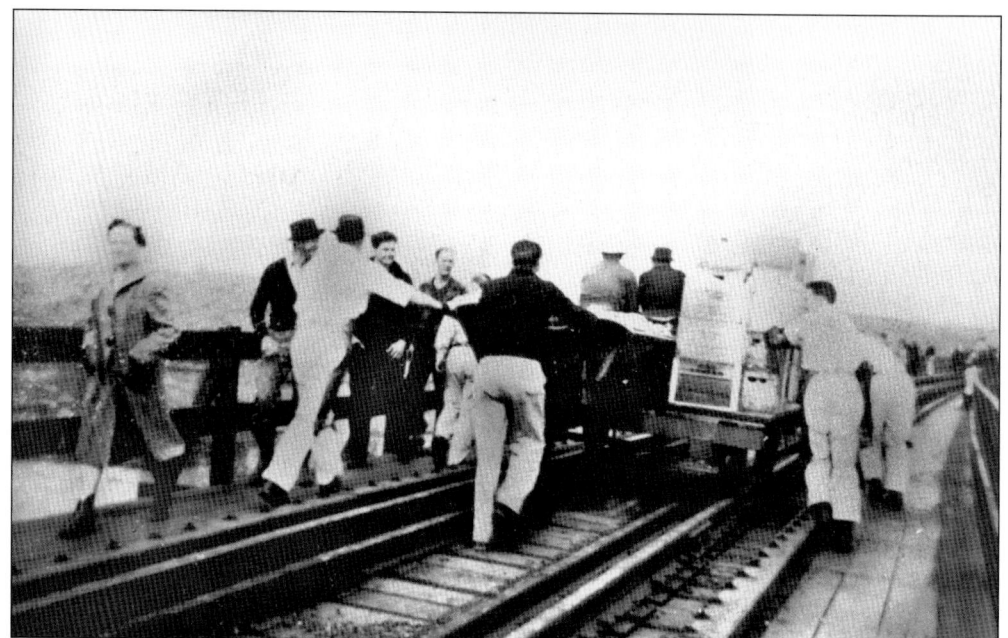

On February 28, 1940, Redding was isolated by a raging Sacramento River before Shasta Dam was completed. The three Redding bridges were unusable. Two of McColls' dairy trucks were stranded in Central Valley. Bill Bryant and a half a dozen employees loaded a railroad handcar with dairy products and pushed it across the trestle to meet with and reload the dairy trucks.

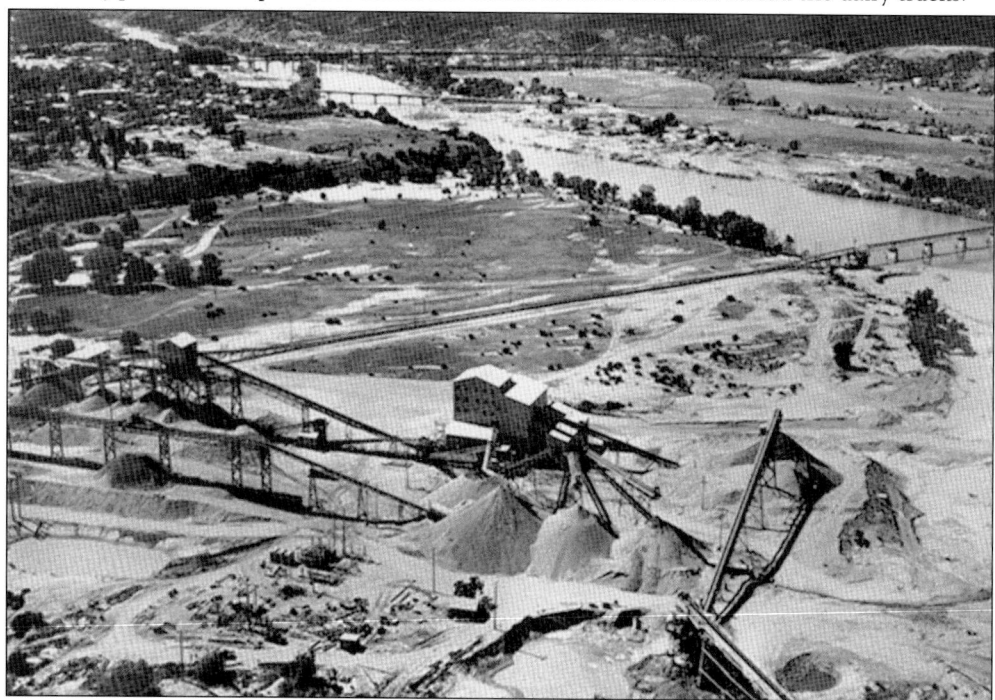

This c. 1940 aerial view shows the Shasta Dam gravel plant at Turtle Bay. The gravel crusher, now known as "the monolith," is the structure in the center. At the left is the beginning of the conveyer belt to the dam site.

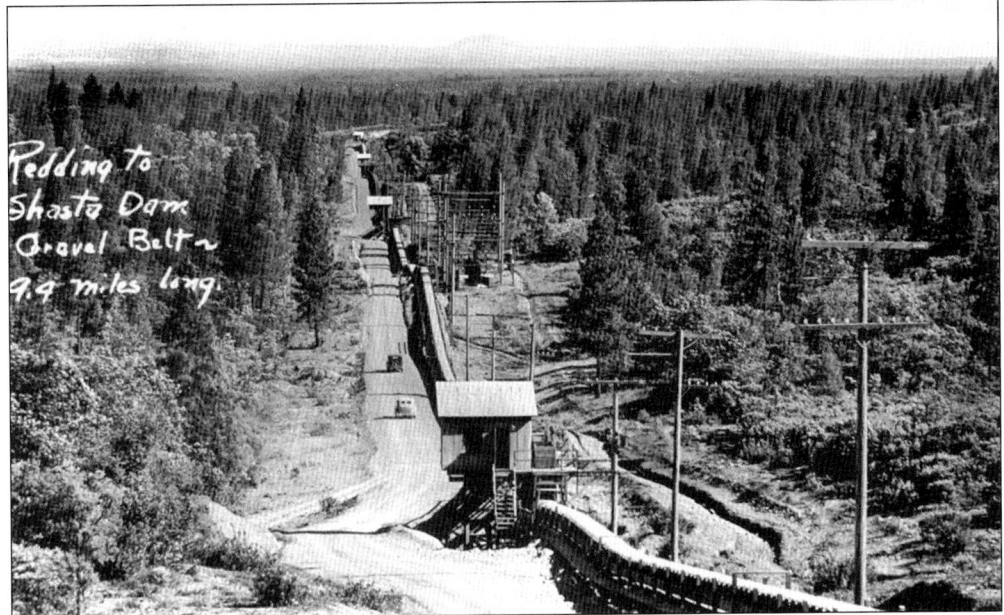

Today little remains of what was once the longest conveyor belt in the world, shown here in 1940. During Shasta Dam's construction, the yard-wide belt moved at a rate of about six miles per hour over a nine-and-one-half mile course. There were 26 separate sections to the belt, each powered by a 200-horsepower engine.

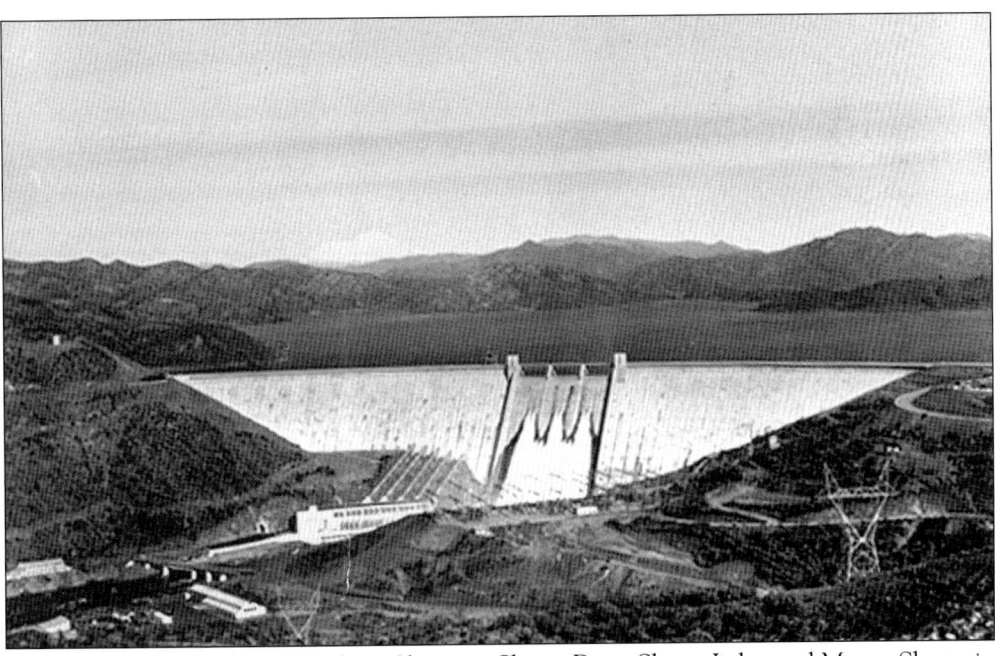

This undated photo shows the three Shastas—Shasta Dam, Shasta Lake, and Mount Shasta in the background. Shasta Dam was begun in 1938 and completed in 1944. It was built by Pacific Constructors, Inc. as the key structure in the Central Valley project. The dam was built at a cost of $100 million, employed 4,000 workers, is 602 feet high, and is the highest center spillway dam in the United States.

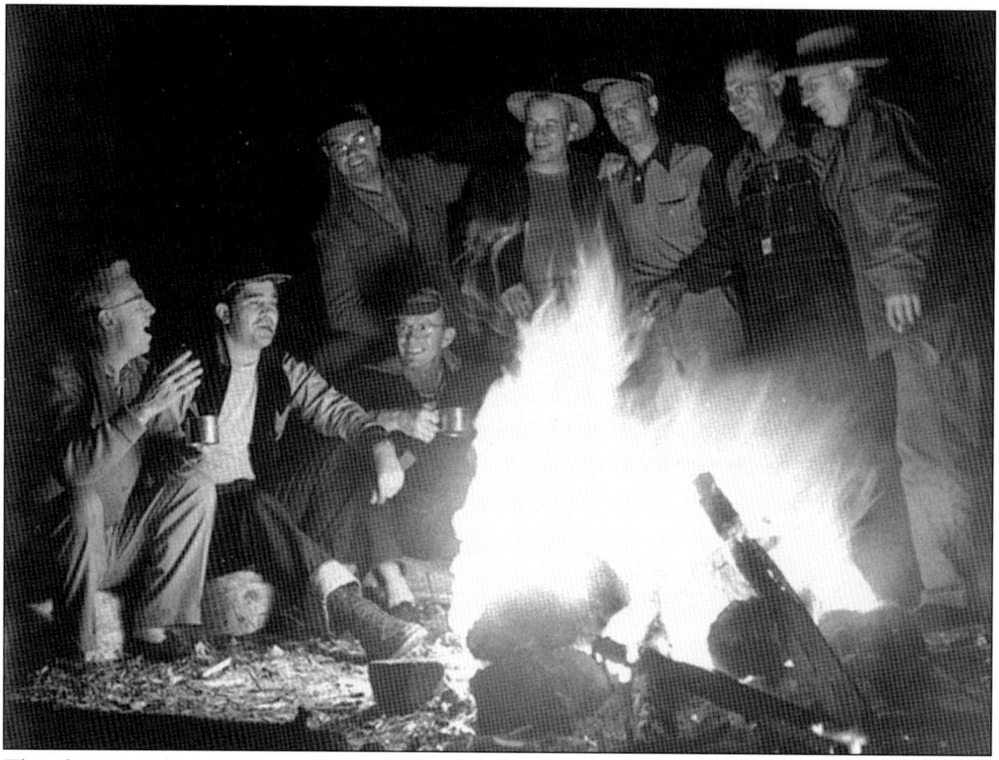

The first Kamloop meeting was held at Dekkas Creek in 1952. They were a far-flung organization of sportsmen dedicated to stocking game fish in Shasta and other lakes, streams, and tributaries of the Sacramento River. Shown here, from left to right, are Dick Hyland (*LA Times*), John Reginato (Wonderland Association), John Fitzpatrick (McColls' Dairy), Bill Carah (P.R. Dept. of Interior), Wayne Leitzel (ShasCade Industries), Hank Clineshmidt (Temple Lounge), John Diestlehorst (retired), and Larry Crosby (Crosby Enterprises).

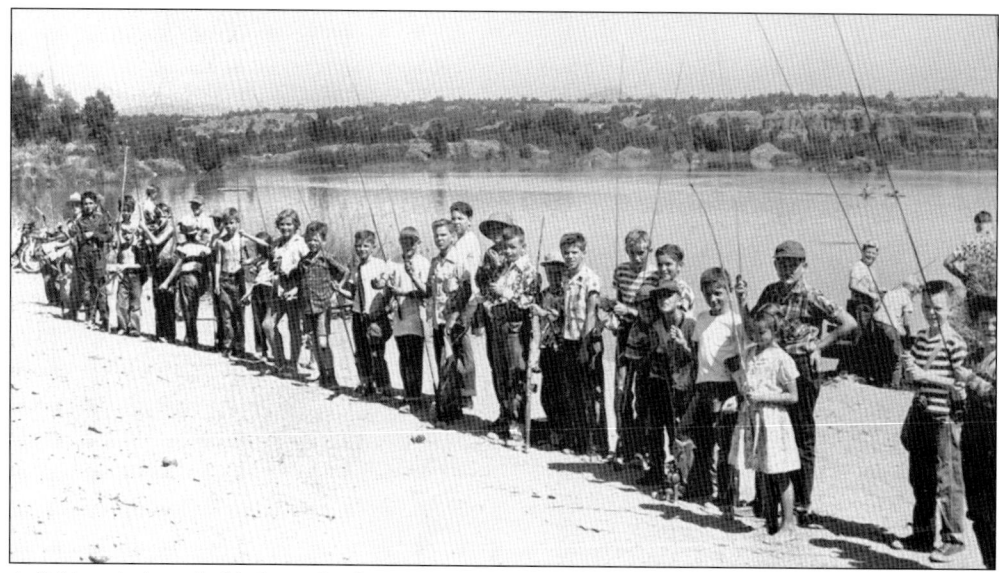

A fishing derby is held along the Sacramento River in the 1940s.

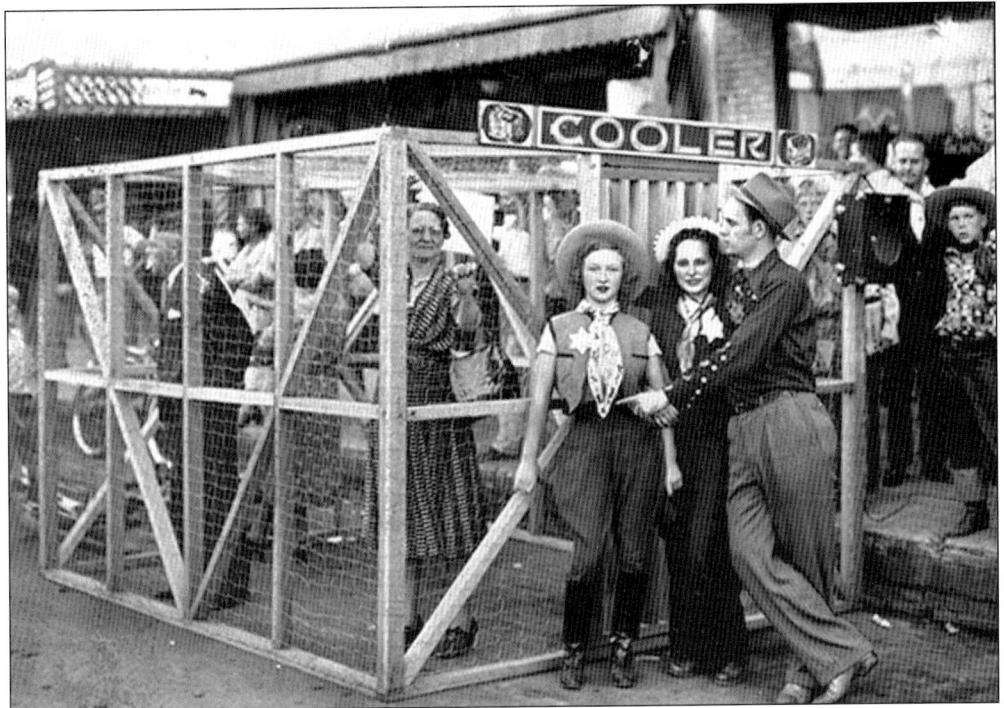

Rodeo week in 1945 included the Kangaroo Court hoosegow, where people are waiting for someone to bail them out.

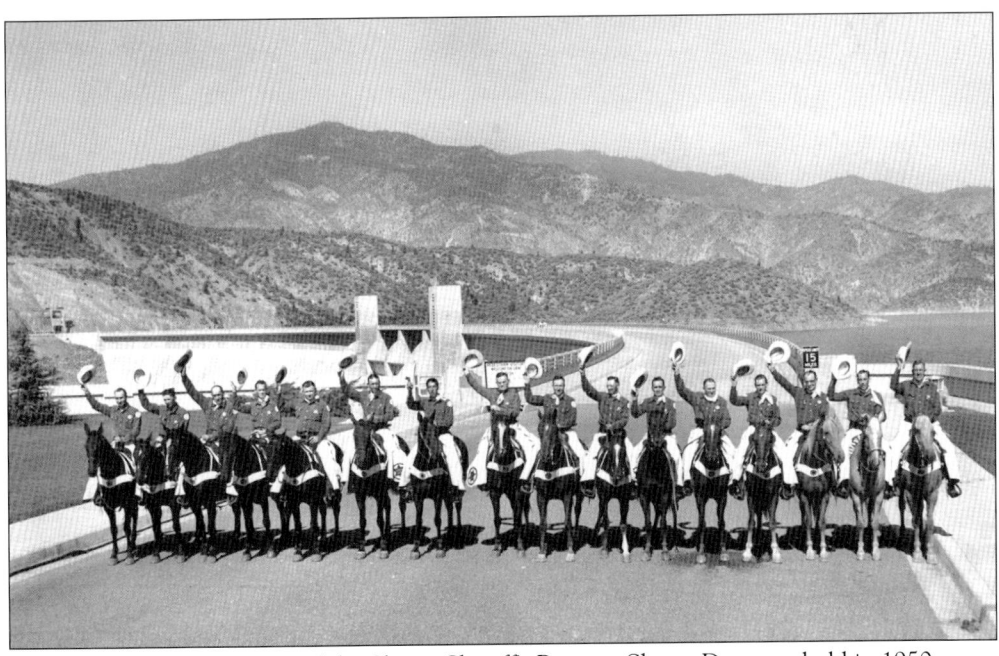

The centennial celebration of the Shasta Sheriff's Posse at Shasta Dam was held in 1950.

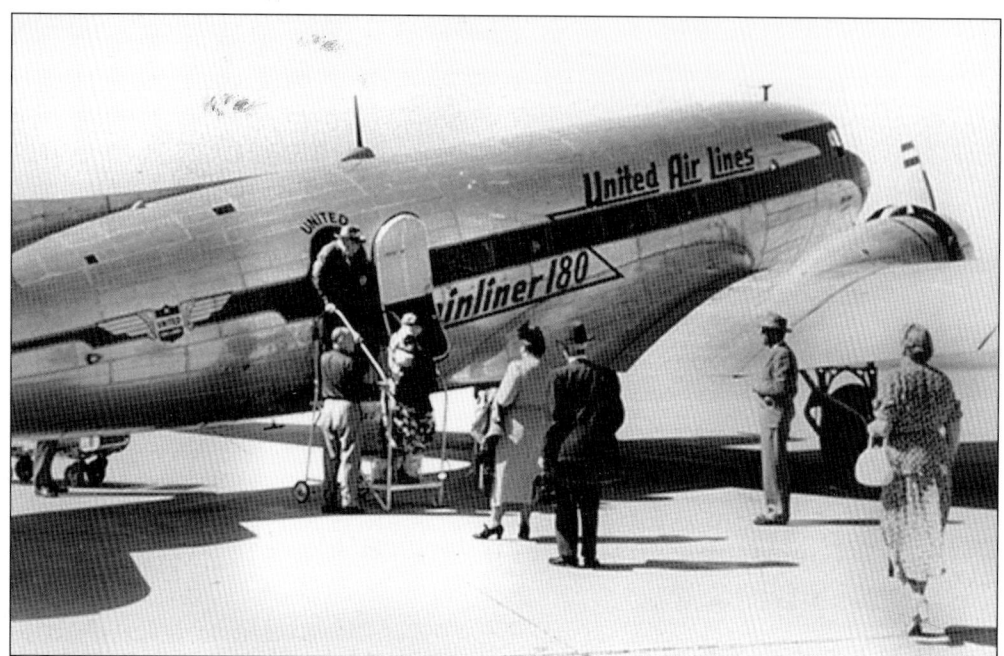

United Air Lines boards passengers at the Redding Municipal Airport in the 1940s. The airport was completed in May 1942 and was used that summer as a squadron base for P-39s and as an auxiliary field during the rest of the war. Redding acquired the airport in 1947, and commercial operations commenced with flights to and from San Francisco.

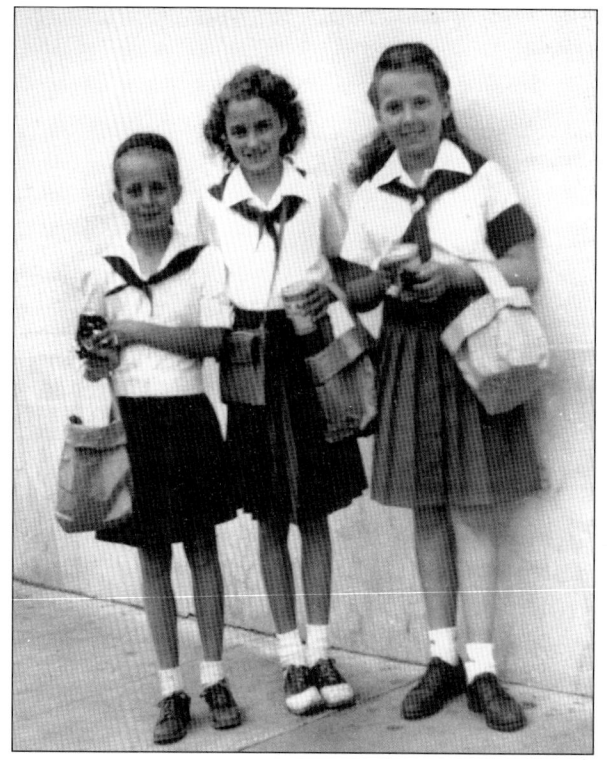

These three Campfire Girls selling poppies for the Veterans of Foreign Wars on the corner of Shasta and Market Streets in 1947 are, from left to right, Carlene Braathen, Betty Coyle, and Roberta Bertoldi.